To Man[...]

I hope [...]
this different journey!

Conti[...]

The Road To Mali

A journey from the world of motorcycle
politics to the deserts of Africa

Craig Carey-Clinch

Shuvvy Press

SHUVVY PRESS LTD
www.shuvvypress.com

First published by Shuvvy Press Ltd in June 2015
Copyright © Craig Carey-Clinch

Craig Carey-Clinch asserts the moral right to be identified as
the author of this work

A catalogue record for this book is available from
the British Library

ISBN 978-0-9564305-4-0

Edited by Nich Brown
Book design and typesetting by Jo MacDonald at JMDesign
Front cover concept by Paddy Tyson
Jacket design by Jo MacDonald
Typeset in Adobe Garamond Pro 11pt
Printed in Wales by Zenith Media Group

'Man in three hundred years has so far advanced from his first essay that now he builds glasses as long as a tent through which he counts thousands of unknown stars. Why are the Westerners always wanting all? Behind our few stars we can see God, who is not behind your millions.'

Auda Abu Tayi
Ard el Suwan, Arabia, 1917
The Seven Pillars of Wisdom TE Lawrence

For Barbara Alam, David French and Jane Milward

In memory of Simon Milward
1965-2005

Contents

Foreword   viii

Introduction   1

Part One – Forging Friendships   7

Part Two – Capturing the Overland Spirit   59

Part Three – Into Africa Again   121

Part Four – Northward   269

Epilogue   341

Foreword

By Sam Manicom

Every motorcyclist knows that crossroads are where adventures come to life and usually we are the ones calling the shots. Faced with a choice of which way to go, it's up to us to make a decision. Usually the route chosen on the road, or in life, allows us to explore our dreams and ambitions. But sometimes we find ourselves at a crossroads with no idea just how much life is going to change; events are beyond our control.

This is the story of how one inspirational man affects the life of others in unexpected and unforgettable ways. The impressive man is Simon Milward, and the author of this intriguing book is just one of the people whose lives were dramatically affected by his unique personality, courage and determination.

In 'The Road to Mali', Craig Carey-Clinch brings an important part of motorcycling history to life. I found myself irresistibly fascinated by this book of crossroads, adventures and respect. I've no doubt that this journey will surprise, challenge, amuse, inform and thoroughly entertain you. It's a true tale of the unexpected.

Introduction

This book is about a series of trips, events and circumstances that conspired to lead three friends to a lonely Malian road junction in the middle of a baking hot sub-Saharan baobab forest. But this is not a simple there-and-back-again narrative, of which many absorbing examples already exist. This book is about lives that are largely defined by a shared dedication to two-wheels and an engine.

I wasn't to know one cold morning in 1991, as I set out to ride my battered Triumph Bonneville a mere thirty miles to Swindon in Wiltshire, that this short trip would set in motion wheels that would keep turning, in one way or another, for nearly fifteen years.

Nor was I to know the profound influence one person would have upon me and those around me.

So this book is also about my late friend Simon Milward; political campaigner for motorcycling, traveller and humanitarian. He was many things to many people. He engendered respect for different reasons wherever he went, be it as an activist, an organiser of events, a motivator of people or a round-the-world motorcyclist.

Simon was a driven and complex character, hurtling headlong through life towards an unknown destination. Along the way, he grew in experience, stature and spirit. His last great journey, this time around the world, was undertaken with the same focussed passion as everything else in his life. It was to change him fundamentally and start something that became much bigger than him.

This book describes a series of journeys, which taken together comprise a truly life-changing motorcycle adventure. Some journeys were with Simon in person, others where only his spirit was there. It is a journey through some of the key moments in the 1990s motorcycle riders' rights movement (a phrase which describes political campaigning to stop or dilute legislation that affects the freedom to ride motorcycles) and its battle to preserve the freedom and spirit of motorcycling against unwanted laws and bureaucracy.

But most of all, this story is about the road. That place where the soul is cleansed and life takes on a new purpose and meaning. Where discoveries are made, some positive and life-changing, others more challenging – or indeed shocking.

The journey to Mali reached its climax in 2005. But for my wife Barbara and I the adventure continued afterwards, leading to other two-wheeled continental crossings and the friendship of some the kindest and most thoughtful people I have ever met.

Craig Carey-Clinch
Kerrier, West Cornwall
June 2015

The names of some individuals and organisations have been changed.

Brussels. December 1999

"What do you reckon?" asked Simon Milward.

David French and I viewed the neatly laid out display of items on the bench before us. Folded clothes, packs of food, tools, spares, maps, papers, books, a Psion computer, medical supplies, water bottles, camping gear and 101 other small things that Simon was convinced would be needed for the motorcycle ride he was soon to undertake.

Next to the bench sat the 'John T Overlander', a bulky and squat Rotax-powered motorcycle that had been specially designed and hand-built for Simon by John T; his great friend and half-brother. This unique machine incorporated all sorts of ideas and innovations designed to ensure the bike could withstand and adapt to all the demands Simon might need it to meet.

The bike had slowly come together over a year in John's workshop in Devon, England and by the time it was finished it was a hefty beast – even before it was loaded-up with enough spares and tools to run a small workshop. It was a tribute to Simon's riding ability that he managed to control the bike at all, and to his tenacity that he planned to ride it around the world.

Simon's round-the-world journey came about partly because of his developing motorcycle wanderlust, and partly because of his growing concern about wider injustices in the world.

Having been daily involved in the political microcosm of lobbying various governments and the European Union about motorcycle rider issues (known in biking circles as 'riders rights') since the late 1980s, Simon felt that it was time that he found out more about some these bigger issues. He told me that the tipping point in his mind – the point where he felt that he could no longer just stand by and do nothing – came after a motorcycle accident in Brussels during 1998.

While he lay in hospital musing about the immediate availability of the medical care that he enjoyed, he started to think about the less well-off in the world and how difficult or impossible it was for many people to get the kind of primary or emergency healthcare that we all take for granted in our comfortable westernised existence.

Upon leaving hospital he started planning what was meant to be an eighteen month sabbatical from the Federation of European Motorcyclists Associations (FEMA), where he had worked as General Secretary for some years.

The proposed ride was ambitious and designed to take in as many countries as possible. He defined two main aims: Firstly, to raise money for developing-world healthcare programmes with Medicines sans Frontieres and the charity Riders for Health being the main beneficiaries. Secondly, he wanted to explore his own personal faith by exploring the world's great religions to see if he could come to some conclusions about the nature of God and how this related to his own life.

He also wanted to take a look at how motorcycle riders in other countries represented themselves. What they thought of unjust legislation and indeed if they were in any way active in defence of their rights. But I somehow felt that this aspect of was more of a side issue, a way of explaining the trip to others who may not understand his true mission. After all, the deeply held motivation that he described to me was worlds away from his day-to-day life in Brussels.

Simon planned to take in around sixty countries. A reasonably robust pace was required if he was to travel around the world and visit the places and people that he hoped to in the time allotted.

Using the skills he had acquired during his years in riders rights, Simon built PR and sponsor support for his ride. His bike was built in Devon and when it was finished and he went there to collect it, he took great relish in testing his completed overlander in front of the media in the English South West, his old home. Doing jumps on rough ground, falling off and laughing – very much as he tended to do when showing off.

He was fairly well prepared for his trip, so there wasn't much to comment about in relation to his kit. Instead, we resorted to sarcasm.

"Dunno about the camp stove…" said Dave "…what if you find yourself somewhere where they don't sell matches or lighters? Better take an electric cooker."

"That pissy little computer won't last ten seconds" I said. "Why not pack 300 exercise books and ten packets of pens instead? A pigeon may be a good idea just to ensure that your despatches get home."

"You'd better make sure that you take enough fuel for the whole 57,000 mile trip" said Dave. "Some of these countries don't sell petrol you know."

Laughter rang out as we put the lights out, shut the door and headed for Flanagan's, our favoured Brussels downtown bar. It was a short time before the New Year, a new century about to dawn, as was a new chapter in Simon's life, and mine.

PART ONE:
Forging Friendships

Reflections on UK Motorcycle Riders' Rights
1991-1999

BATH, ENGLAND 1991

As always, I wondered if my battered old Meriden-manufactured Triumph Bonneville would make it. The journey was only a matter of thirty miles or so, but months of financial penury meant that all but absolutely essential servicing had gone by the wayside. This neglect was coupled with cracked and split gearbox casings from an earlier chain breakage. The result was that my trusty mount was bellowing balefully and belching oil into the damp February air while it struggled to maintain momentum along the lonely A-road.

Pulling into the car park at my destination in Swindon, I looked up at the blank façade of a modern business premises; representative of the type which inhabit a thousand 'business parks' as they are called nowadays. I wondered what the day would hold.

Marriage to my first wife in 1990 was followed by an ambitious attempt to relocate to the Western Isles of Scotland. Pipe dreams of employment and a gentler pace of life had disappeared in the harsh economic realities of the remote Scottish islands in winter. Unable to find proper paid work or accommodation, we returned to the English West Country with our tails between our legs. Penniless, homeless, embarrassed and with a child on the way.

A life spent dreaming about a mythical tomorrow instead of concentrating on the good things that lay in front of my eyes had landed us in a parlous situation. Fortunately, the assistance of friends and a job offer in a motorcycle shop in Bristol had set us back on track and after some pleasant months living in Bath, where our son Kieran was born, we settled a few miles east in the picturesque West Wiltshire village of Box.

Work in the motorcycle trade was tenuous at best during a time when a shrinking motorcycle market was cutting into the profits of manufacturers and traders alike. So I felt no great surprise a few months later when redundancy notices started winging their way from senior management. The dole beckoned. Reviewing my 26 years thus far, I figured that it was time to have a good think about what to do next.

A few years' RAF service in the engineering branch had been followed by various dead end jobs fixing exhausts and brakes in the garage trade. One position had been managerial but, all in all, it could be a grim way to earn a living, especially in winter. I'd then spent a couple of years driving vans, followed by time in the parts department of Fowlers Motorcycles, where genuinely useful management skills had been picked up while working for that outstanding business.

Motorcycle work as a despatch rider had followed; a year of adrenaline-filled warp-speed high jinxes on a Yamaha XS1100S. There were enough in the way of day-to-day close misses on the roads to make me regularly marvel at my continuing existence on this mortal coil. There was an accompanying lunatic lifestyle that at times was as adrenaline fuelled as the job itself. I remember high miles, high wages, but huge weekly running costs. A new rear tyre every three weeks was not unusual. Neither was mad alcohol fuelled craziness during 'down time'.

Deciding to get out of this lunatic world before it did for me, I spent a period flogging parts and building bikes in further motorcycle shops, then unemployment. Hardly a Curriculum Vitae to be proud of.

Then some idiot in Government proposed that motorcycles should be fitted with leg protectors.

Being a life-long motorcyclist, inspired in part by my father's 1950s experiences on his BSA and by the images of biking freedom and heritage which had impressed my young teenage life, I saw the whole leg protector issue as an infringement of my personal freedom of choice by a Government which unreasonably sought to protect me from myself. Something had to be done.

I re-joined the Motorcycle Action Group. MAG had been founded as a direct consequence of the 1973 law which made crash helmets compulsory for motorcyclists and the organisation was now campaigning on the leg protector issue. In my early biking days I remember being impressed with MAG and its 'fight for freedom'. It had appealed strongly to my libertarian sense and I had become a member in 1981 for what I remembered as being the princely sum of £2. I took part in my first MAG 'demo', in Bristol, at about the same time, on a BSA Bantam.

'A' levels and a short career with the RAF meant that MAG membership had not figured prominently in my life. But I remained happy that the organisation existed to defend my individual rights as a motorcyclist. But the leg protector issue was something different. If it was implemented it would have an immediate impact on the way that I would ride my bike and how it would look. The claimed benefits of such so-called 'protection' were also heavily in dispute, with industry research contending that the protectors could exacerbate injuries in a crash. Renewing my MAG membership after a long gap had been a natural thing to do.

What was less natural for me, given my life experience and skills, thus far, was the depth of involvement which would quickly follow. The local MAG group met in Bath and attracted a mixed but friendly bunch of local bikers, who strongly supported local activism on various biking issues – not just leg protectors. Writing to MPs, attending meetings and riding on demonstrations was heavily encouraged. So was the emergence of a personal skill set which I hadn't previously realised I'd owned.

Less than a year after joining the Bath group in 1990, I stood for the local representative's position. Having been duly elected, I very quickly found myself becoming embroiled in regional and national motorcycling politics. Fortunately, the Government eventually backed down on the leg protector issue, but many more issues needed tackling.

Unemployment meant time on my hands. Job hunting was not proving fruitful and I gradually came to the view that pursuing my new interests could open more personally fulfilling avenues – plus perhaps achieve things that could help others. I went back to college to study politics so that I could gain a better grounding for the new life that seemed to be opening before me.

So one February morning I found myself in the car park in Swindon, wondering what would come next. This was my first South West Regional meeting and it had been called by the regional representative Simon Milward.

At that point I was only just learning about how the national structure of MAG was put together. MAG activity was covered by a national team of reps and officers. Simon was one of this team, managing a huge regional area and unusually among his fellow regional reps, was paid a modest stipend to do so.

The meeting room was laid out like a lecture hall. As the group of local MAG reps settled into their places, Simon came striding purposefully in, acknowledging greetings. Revealing a slight lisp, he paused to talk to several people as he made his way across the room.

I was curious about Simon. As my regional rep, I'd already had some contact with him, but this was the first time that we'd met face to face. He had a reputation for dynamism and inspirational thinking that went beyond the requirements of his official position in MAG. Knowledgeable and insightful, his name had already been connected to several high profile campaigns.

To look at, he was diminutive and scruffily dressed in what could be called traditional biker gear; leather jacket, army boots, denim jeans, leather waistcoat and badges. Bespectacled, he peered through an unruly mop of hair and his bearded face wore a wide grin and a welcoming expression.

He guided us through the business of the day in a highly professional manner. I gained the feeling that I was engaged less in a regional meeting of an activists' organisation and more in a blue sky session of the Board of a major multinational. Simon encouraged a strategic view of the issues of the day, with targets, responsibilities and a coherent work programme.

I was impressed and wondered if I could live up to the expectations of our friendly, but sharp and inspirational regional rep ...

*

LUXEMBOURG, JUNE 1993

To my growing astonishment, my Triumph T140 Bonneville was refusing to die. Increasing responsibilities in MAG had led to temporary full time employment as Research Officer and high mileage riding to meetings all over the country. The poor old bike, with its broken gearbox casings, had an Exxon-Valdez like tendency to spray oil in all directions. But displaying the stoicism of times gone by in the country of its manufacture, it continued to soldier on. Colleagues in MAG were helping me shore the old girl up and Yorkshire MAG in particular had donated a new pair of tyres, to my lasting gratitude.

This latest journey was on Federation of European Motorcyclists (FEM) business.(FEM became FEMA – Federation of European Motorcyclists Associations in the mid 1990s). This organisation drew together diverse motorcycling groups with common aims from around Europe and lobbied in Brussels. MAG UK was a key founding member and Simon had become its General Secretary a few months after I had met him in 1991.

My destination was a meeting of the organisation in the forest near the Luxembourg border with Belgium. Along the way I took in scenic Ardennes back roads. This was one of those rides where the destination becomes less important as the delight of the journey itself unfolds and takes over the mind and imagination. The Bonnie rumbled along happily for once as I enjoyed the rolling and wooded countryside. Stopping in Bastogne, in the south of Belgium, I paid my respects to the 110th Airborne – the Screaming Eagles – who had held firm around the town during the Battle of The Bulge in December 1944.

Mindful of my oil-washed and inoperable rear brake, I took it easy along the winding forested roads, arriving at my destination, the oddly named 'Chateau Jim', early in the evening. The building was set deep in the forest and took the form of a large wooden Swiss style cabin with bunk rooms and a large communal area complete with bar – not so much a chateau, more of a hasty barn conversion. At best it was a youth hostel with a grand(ish) name.

The usual eclectic crowd of FEM delegates were there to greet me. All were representatives of their respective national riders' associations and familiar to each other. Friendships had been forged in the heat of motorcycle campaigning, debate and post-meeting parties. Valuable partnerships strengthened by shared passions. It was good to see everyone again.

Over a few bottles of the appropriately named 'Bier Simon', Milward outlined the plan for the coming days. There would be a Federation delegates' meeting followed by a motorcycle run to Luxembourg City; the idea being that we would ride across town to mount a protest against a European proposal to limit motorcycle power to 100bhp.

This was another barmy legislative idea. As with the leg protector proposal, it appealed to the inexpert in road safety terms, and politicians wanting to be seen to be 'doing something' about motorcycle safety. But no credible evidence could be found to link absolute power and speed to the likelihood of accidents taking place. Despite this, the generally anti-motorcycle European Commission were determined to go ahead and we were equally determined to stop them. Our meeting was designed to coincide with discussions about the issue at the European Council of Ministers building in Luxembourg's capital.

The Chateau was one of those affairs which had an open-sided upper storey under wide eaves. Drifting off sleep after an evening of pleasant socialising, to the unfettered sounds of rustling trees and the occasional noise of wildlife was a real pleasure.

Simon chaired the meeting the following morning, the event being held in the main room of the little wooden Chateau. A more formal business setting was created by the simple expediency of pushing a few tables and chairs into some semblance of order.

As matters were discussed, the door opened and a tallish woolly headed figure quietly slipped in. I looked over with interest; was this David French, the MAG Ireland delegate? I'd corresponded with Dave previously and had liked the 'cut of his jib' in the emails he'd sent to me. But I'd yet to meet him and was very much looking forward to a face to face chat.

The woolly-head was indeed Dave French. Following the meeting we cracked open a couple of drinks and soon found ourselves in the kind of deep discussion on a range of issues that leads to firm bonds of friendship later on.

The following day, Simon mustered about ten bikes for the ride to Luxembourg. This was to be a pleasant, though fast, ride through the hills and curving mountainous roads of the Luxembourg countryside. Lots of nice twisties and switchbacks, ending in a smooth ride into the city itself. Setting up camp in one of the city's parks was a lively affair. Simon pulled a battered looking tent from a bag which promptly fell to pieces as he tried to put it up. He'd packed it away wet on a previous occasion and it had rotted. Amidst gales of laughter he went from person to person trying to scrounge a place for the night in another tent. He eventually settled on the charity of a fellow MAG UK person, Frank Pearson, who had consumed a vast quantity of food that evening and was settling in for a long session of loud snores and other nasal mayhem.

A cool morning saw nearly 100 people gather at the Council of Ministers building in the European Community sector of the city. Bikers had come from all over Europe to make clear their feelings about the 100bhp power limit proposal and a sea of flags greeted governmental representatives as they entered the building for their meeting. Adjacent to the entrance, some wags had built coffins around two motorcycles to make a point about the proposed legislation leading to the death of powerful motorcycles.

After much waiting, a low roar came up from the crowd. Martin Bangemann, the European Commissioner responsible for the proposal had arrived by limousine at the entrance of the building. This character had made himself highly unpopular with his bombast and 'certainty' in support of the idea of power limits.

Wasting no time, Simon sprang forward to accost Bangemann with his arguments, taking the Commissioner's officials by surprise. This allowed Simon time to make his case, which was concise and to the point. Bangemann was wrong-footed by this and only able to declare in a loud voice "I know everything" before he hurried through the revolving doors. Simon followed him inside, emerging some minutes later to give press and TV interviews in English and advanced schoolboy French, criticising Bangemann's intransigence on the issue.

Another day and another demo perhaps, but this one had made real media impact and galvanised the campaign as we moved towards the showpiece of our lobbying and protest efforts; a forthcoming 'Euro Demo' in Paris.

Simon smiled and his eyes twinkled with pleasure behind his glasses. Another day, another good lobbying job done.

*

FRANCE, SEPTEMBER 1993

I thought I was about to die. In fact I had been anticipating my demise for about the previous two hours. I crouched low behind Milward's slight form as we stormed down the autoroute in the direction of La Rochelle. Driving rain combined with darkness to reduce visibility to just about zero.

Simon peered into the gloom, out of his visorless open face helmet and though rain-dimmed spectacles, wincing as the rain shot a million needles a second into his unprotected face. Our mount, a 900cc Cagiva Elefant, was held steady at about 100 miles per hour by Milward's firm grip. This was madness. Hurtling down a French motorway at night, two up through a downpour at such a crazy speed for the conditions, was the daftest thing I had ever let myself in for. Simon's reputation as a hard riding, risk taking, bike-busting nutcase was well known and I really should have known better than to get on the back of him for this trip, particularly given the state of the pair of us. We had only returned from an all-night drinking session about ten hours before.

We were on our way to an early planning meeting for the 1994 Euro demo. Simon had invited me along to help out and to support the position he intended to take on a number of matters. In a vain attempt to mentally detach myself from the immediate life-threatening environment I cast my mind back to what had led us to this point.

A few weeks before I had been elected Overseas Liaison Officer for MAG, replacing Frank Pearson who had decided to retire from front line activist politics. Simon seemed pleased that a like-minded person had been elected to the post and we both knew that the amount of time that we would be spending together on European issues and the Federation of European Motorcyclists would help to cement our growing friendship – a friendship which had been initially forged during his last days with MAG UK.

MAG had agreed to a proposal for me to spend some time abroad helping Simon with some work. Due to the loss-making management of the French-run 1988 Euro Demo, it was also suggested that Simon and I found out more about the organisation of the forthcoming 1994 Paris Euro Demo. I looked forward to the assignment with some pleasure and setting out from my Wiltshire home on the long-suffering Bonneville, I took a pleasant ride down to Paris. This was interrupted only by regular stops for gearbox oil, a clutch rebuild and a noisy night by the side of a French truck stop, sheltering on a small patch of grass in a leaking tent.

My initial destination was the flat of FFMC activist who I shall call Jean. He was a middle-aged gentleman with a colourful and fascinating past. Unfortunately, his acknowledged political acumen had been dulled by years of alcohol abuse. His apartment on the 15th Arrondissement, in the south west of Paris' centre, was near the venue for the French motorcycle industry show, that year's event coinciding with my visit. This was another good reason to visit Paris during what was a mild and sunny autumn.

Jean proved to be the perfect host and in his company, I spent a pleasant day at the 'Salon' as the bike show was referred to. I also met several of the Paris based riders' rights activists, including for the first time, Eric Thiollier, who would feature prominently in my professional life for the next few years. Simon arrived in Paris two days later. His presence as always, raising the dynamic temperature. He had a tough schedule of meetings with the FFMC in Paris and also planned to attend a major meeting of another group which was involved in organising the Euro Demo. This was to be in La Rochelle, nearly three hundred miles away. He asked me to accompany him on his various Parisian assignments. What followed was an inspirational but tiring round of meetings, as I kept pace with Simon's seemingly inexhaustible energy.

"So off to La Rochelle tomorrow Craig" he said as we left the FFMC offices for the final time. "My mate Dave Dunlop is in town today, he's asked us to go for a few beers, you up for that?"

I was, so after cramming some food down our throats, we jumped on the metro to meet Si's friend in the centre of town. What followed was a session of alcoholic excess which I have not since rivalled. Bar to bar, we crawled across Paris with an increasingly stumbling gait. In the early hours we finally ending up in a small café quaffing large cognacs and talking 'franglais' gibberish at each other – any thought about the forthcoming ride lost in a drunken haze.

At four pm the following afternoon, we woke in Jean's apartment. The shutters were down and it was completely dark inside leading us to oversleep in a monumental fashion.

"Bloody hell!" exclaimed Simon. "What time is it?" Groaning as he shot out of his doss-bag. We both felt as rough as old boots and were hard in the grip of monumental hangovers. To make matters worse, we needed to be in La Rochelle that evening.

Grabbing a fast coffee, we shuffled into our bike gear like a couple of old men and, firing up the Cagiva, exited Paris in a way which would have made Captain Kirk proud. The rain started to fall in sheets as we set course down the autoroute at a high warp factor.

Some hours later, apparent salvation was offered and I was stirred from my terror filled reverie by the Cagiva slowing down. "We turn off here" yelled Simon as we hurtled up the motorway slip road and onto a roundabout. The angle of lean on the drenched road made me clench my buttocks in renewed fear.

The national route we had taken was ridden at a slower pace, but now Simon had an opportunity to practice his Grand Prix racing skills. A heart stopping hour of almost knee-down riding ensued in the darkness, on soaking wet roads which shone in our headlight beam, before we finally reached the outskirts of La Rochelle. Despite the lateness of the hour, we were warmly welcomed with hot coffee. Warming up and calming down Si and I grinned at each other, the harsh wet, cold and fear forgotten as we celebrated a ride to end all rides.

*

THE FULDA GAP, GERMANY, OCTOBER 1993

How does a man so consumed by nervous energy keep going? Milward seemed to have almost inhuman reserves of life within him. From the hours we spent in the FEM offices, planning our next moves and trying to juggle barely adequate budgets; to long hours on the road on the way to another meeting full of motivation and inspiration from Simon's sharp mind. For him the pace never seemed to slacken.

At that point FEM was only a small operation in a professional sense and Simon more or less ran things by himself, with occasional part time help from MAG Belgium. Things would get better of course, particularly once the FEM expanded its membership base. But for several long years, the burden of responsibility for everything from lobbying and report writing, to ordering the stationary and doing the accounts fell mostly on Simon's shoulders.

The pressure to get by on so little, and with such a heavy workload, sometimes meant that corners were cut as Simon made compromises to make things happen. Not all of his decisions were well thought through and sometimes additional work and 'mopping up' was the result. But it was difficult to criticise the man; he was at the sharp end of our European work. Without the compromises he sometimes made, many important projects would never have got off the ground in the first place.

I would visit him in his office and find myself caught up in 101 little jobs which needed doing. We'd sit up late at night preparing reports, planning activity and looking at new ideas, only to be up early to get ready for a visit to the European Parliament, or one of the other European institutions.

His energy never seemed to wane and he would shrug concerned comments about his workload off, with a smile and a comment; "well someone's got to do it".

Hard work was broken by hard partying as an excuse to let his hair down. Many a night was spent in 'Flanagan's' a music bar in the centre of Brussels. Other times, he got his relaxation through long rides across Europe to attend meetings, or do something else related to FEM. A prevailing skin condition meant that his diet seemed to consist of little else but elaborately named dietary powders and coffee, supplemented by beer and 'roll-up' cigarettes. The occasional tin of food could be found in his kitchen, but not much else. Visits to his top storey office on the Rue General Henri were usually preceded by a trip to the supermarket.

Holidays were few, but taken in exotic locations, often reached by motorcycle. His doctor told him that sun was good for his skin, so he'd usually vanish for a fortnight or so in August for a bit of beach time in Italy, the south of France or further afield. It was also a chance for him to spend rare quality time with Christina, his girlfriend, who also worked with him in the office from time to time. Once he went swimming in the Dead Sea and returned from the trip brandishing a large glass jar of noxious looking black gloop.

"This is Dead Sea mud." he proclaimed to Dave French and I. "Magnificent stuff for the skin." he added, waving the opened jar of vile smelling muck in our faces. "Bugger." he exclaimed, losing his grip on the jar. A loud bang and all of us were splattered in the nauseous brew causing yells of anger and instant gagging. Dave went green and stumbled over to the widow for fresh air, retching as he went.

Hours later and still stinking to high heaven, we could do no more than laugh at Si's clumsiness over several bottles of Jupiler beer. It was either that or thump him.

One day, we were invited to address a meeting of the German organisation Khule Wampe. This crowd of left-wing bikers were more an anti-Nazi organisation than a riders rights group, but their leaders had passion and they strongly supported FEM's aims. I had arrived separately from Simon in the company of friends from the UK and Belgium. Fulda was reached at the end of a long day's travelling through light snow and heavy frost. Frozen, we had retired to our rooms to change and have an hour's rest before attending the semi-formal dinner which had been laid on in our honour. I didn't speak German, neither did my colleagues, but language wasn't an issue as we relaxed in the company of our hosts and tucked into a variety of different fish dishes. Conversations were held in English and we were made to feel welcome with several toasts and vast quantities of food.

The sound of a motorcycle outside and Simon stumped in looking grey, but still with his trademark smile. He was greeted with enthusiasm, but despite returning the greetings with lively conversation, he was clearly spent. As soon as was polite he vanished upstairs to a room we were sharing.

And that was that for him for much of the next two days. I attended various seminars about Khule Wampe's work, which were totally absorbing. Riders rights had an appeal to them because the principles of individual freedom which we espoused fitted neatly with their anti-Nazi work. The organisation was at that time also responsible for some of the preservation work which took place in the former Nazi concentration camps and described in depth the challenges they face, both practically in terms of preservation work – particularly at Auschwitz – and politically, in a climate of guilt about the past.

The old adage, 'going to Germany? Don't talk about the war', did not hold true here. My first visit to Germany was almost entirely spent talking about the war.

Simon didn't reappear all that first night and the next day. In the evening, we guests were due to give an address and I was starting to get worried about him. Looking in on him during the day revealed a bundle of blankets and quiet breathing. He didn't stir. I needn't have worried though. As I stood up to give my rather pathetic address Simon strode in looking bright and rested and grinning to all sides. A cheer went up from the room. After his speech, received with a standing ovation, he spoke briefly to a few of Khule Wampe's leaders before once again quietly vanishing. He didn't reappear until we were packing to leave the following day.

Many have said that Simon was obsessed with his work and had little else in him but riders rights. Maybe this was because he devoted so much of every waking hour to his work and this was all that people saw. Those of us who knew him well realised that he was more complex than that, even if he only rarely discussed deep rooted personal matters.

One time in Brussels he said in an unguarded moment "I can't do this forever you know. One day I'd like a wife and kids, just like anyone else." He looked distantly ahead as he rolled a cigarette and took a swig from a bottle of beer.

But even the most ardent activist sometimes has to switch off. Maybe he felt that in the company of the wonderful Khule Wampe and among friends, in the quiet countryside of the Fulda Gap, the former Cold War front line, he could just take some time to rest awhile.

*

PARIS, FRANCE, FEBRUARY 1994

Bright and crisp, the early morning sun shone across the Place de la Bastille. A tall, almost Romanesque, decorated column rose in the centre of the historic 'place', with traffic hurtling by in the chaotic manner in which Parisians excel. A few of us stood by our bikes in the shadow of the column blowing warmer air onto our frozen hands and taking sips of coffee from Styrofoam cups.

Jesus it was cold. A frozen ride to Paris on an ex-police BMW K100 that had been provided for me by MAG, which had allowed the long overdue retirement and repair of the Bonneville, had just about sucked every ounce of warmth out of me. Simon and I had arranged to meet at Jean's apartment. Resisting the dubious delights of the contents of our host's mouldy cheese-laden 'farting fridge', we had enjoyed an excellent grill and a bottle of wine at a restaurant around the corner.

We were in Paris to take part in one of the FFMC's regular motorcycle demo runs. These protest runs were a familiar feature of Parisian biker life, an extension of the French 'demo' spirit which is infinitely stronger than we see in the UK. Demos or marches about some issue or other are a regular sight in Paris; people power in action, active democracy, call it what you like. I've always appreciated the way that the French don't always take daft legislation just lying down. For Si and me, the main purpose of the demo was of secondary importance. What interested us was how the FFMC would organise the run, how well prepared it was and their competency in the all-important marshalling job that was required. It was only a few months until the Paris Euro Demo and we wanted to get a clear idea about the abilities of the organisation when it came to the anticipated thousands of bikers from all over Europe.

Sometime later the run got under way. About two or three hundred riders converged on the Bastille and with revving engines and blaring horns, the run moved off. Following us was a beaten up transit van with FFMC logos on the side and loudspeakers blaring political statements. I rode with Simon on the back of my bike. He'd caught the train to Paris, not fancying the cold ride from Brussels. The plan was that I'd give him a lift back to Brussels and after doing a bit of work head for Oostende and the ferry home.

Not being particularly involved with the political purpose of the event, I found myself enjoying the reasonably paced run through the city as a ride in its own right. Pleasant boulevards and tree lined shopping streets contrasted with the magnificence of the Place de La Concorde and the ride up to the Arc de Triomphe. The sun continued to shine and the quality of light remained exceptional, if somewhat blinding when travelling down east-bound streets.

Finally, we reached our destination, the Tour Eiffel, where among great two-wheeled confusion, the gathering throng of motorcycles were parked and their riders headed with one mind towards food takeaway vans for hot coffee and buns.

Milward was all for going up the tower itself. "Magnificent view from the top." he said.

A good plan, or so we thought. After a coffee we started up the stairs as the lift was out of order. The first level was reached and that was our lot; a sign declared 'closed for maintenance'. Still, the view from the first level, between the arching legs of the famous tower wasn't too bad, particularly towards the Ecole Millitaire. We were able to get some decent shots of the mass of bikes underneath us. A nice visual conjunction of traditional architecture and modern two wheeled transport, I absently thought as we both relaxed against the railing, lit a cigarette each and let the low warmth of the winter sun play on our faces. Just at that moment, Paris was the best place in the world to be.

The following morning the sun had been replaced by mist and gloomy murk. An icy and damp blanket of misery had settled over everything overnight and as we emerged from Jean's we could see a film of frozen condensation on the BMW. One or two people scurried-by, wrapped up tightly against the cold and glanced at the pair of us; both bundled-up in several layers of motorcycle gear. We received looks of obvious disdain at the idea of riding in such conditions. The weather forecast had rumoured snow and we were both keen to ride the four hours or so back to Brussels as quickly as we could. Leaving Paris, we settled into a fast pace along the autoroute, trying to put the biting cold out of our minds as the kilometres hurtled by. The day, though already dull, continued to get progressively mistier and a cold haze settled. This further reduced visibility and cast the roadside and the view beyond into a hazy shadow.

We stopped to slurp coffee, stamp our feet and puff on roll-ups before continuing through the gathering murk. As we passed Cambrai, the snow started to fall, a few flecks at first, which almost went unnoticed as they whizzed past our helmet visors, but soon large flakes were falling about us. A few kilometres later and we could see that it was starting to settle on the hard shoulder. A few more and tracks could be seen in the gathering slush on the fast lane.

Snow can be beautiful at the right moment, but on a French autoroute late on a frozen afternoon, this was the last thing we needed. I started to wonder if we shouldn't head off the highway at the next town and look for somewhere to stay for the night. But Simon urged me to continue and we pressed on as the motorway lost its outer lanes under a shroud of white. Cars which had been tearing past us a few miles earlier settled into the inside lane behind us.

We crossed the Belgian border as it got fully dark. The inside lane was still clear, though I wondered for how much longer. But the welcome lights of the Belgian motorway network encouraged us and with greater visibility came a slackening of the snow fall. Within a few miles the road was wide open again and not a drop of the white stuff in sight.

Later that evening we sat in Flanagan's and toasted our successful ride.

"Wondered if we'd make it?" I asked.

"Nah." said Simon "It was fine, just a little shower, you could have gone faster." We glanced at each other for a second and then Simon laughed, punched me in the arm and went to the bar.

*

FRANCE. JUNE 1994

I paused for a moment and looked up at the azure sky, squinting at the sharp brilliance of the hot mid-summer sunshine. A vintage fighter aircraft wheeled around the sky, its engine roaring in the turns, practising manoeuvres for an air show which had been organised for that weekend. Possibly a P51 Mustang I mused to myself. Further squinting failed to confirm this, but the exercise briefly diverted my mind from present troubles.

It was just after three pm and if anything the lines of motorcycles trying to get into the gate had become longer. I could no longer see the end of the queues which stretched along the dirt entrance lane to the Aerodrome De Cerny and away around a sharp bend. The air was filled with the deep rumble of hot bikes ticking over. There were sharp conversations in multiple languages, as those arriving attempted to negotiate entry tickets with the surly and unhelpful French marshals who were manning the gate.

'Jesus, what a bloody mess.' I thought as I sat down on a boulder. My back was hurting again, the reminder of an old RAF injury and a sure sign that I'd spent far too long on my feet that day.

A sense of helplessness stole over me as I began to appreciate the mammoth task ahead as the anticipated thousands of motorcyclists converged from all over Europe on that messy little half-abandoned airfield just south of Paris.

Relief came from a team of stalwarts that came from the Southampton contingent of riders from MAG. Passing me a can of beer, Pete, their Rep told me to get some rest and leave them to it. As I walked back towards the main arena, his crew were already putting in place a multi queuing system for arriving riders. They ignored the Gallic protestations of the French crew who had done a poor show of pretending to run the gate for the last few hours. Several of their number had sat in moody, beer-drinking huddles, ignoring the growing queues and deliberately not using their limited English when Anglo Saxon folk made enquiries. I remembered the well organised FFMC Paris demo of a few months before and wished that the same group had organised this aspect of the Euro Demo.

I wandered slowly up the path, trying to straighten out my protesting back, stopping only to appease an English guy on a Honda who yelled "Can't you bloody French organise anything?" Apologies followed as I was recognised as a fellow Englishman and we exchanged some mutual feelings about the chaos which marked the opening of the 1994 Paris Euro Demo.

*

The idea seemed good enough initially; organise a mass bikers demo to protest against French Government support for the country's 100BHP motorcycle engine power limit. The European Commission had grasped this idea as a way of reducing the number of motorcycle accidents each year and had proposed pan-European legislation. The limit had been proposed to match an existing French and German motorcycle power limit, which still allowed riders to use reasonably high performance sports bikes.

But we felt we couldn't ignore the evidence that a power limit was unlikely to make a difference to accident numbers, due to the fact that most accidents occurred at relatively low speeds, or at junctions or on bends. Our point was that laws should not be made on a bad premise. There was also the issue of freedom of choice. We had already lobbied at European level in Luxembourg; our job now was to target the government of a country which already had the 100bhp limit.

The often held public view that powerful motorcycles are intrinsically dangerous, is based on the false assumption that if a bike is fast and powerful it must be dangerous. But it's not that motorcycles, be they 10bhp or 200bhp, are dangerous in themselves, just as an axe is not dangerous in skilled hands. Motorcycle safety is often about how bikes are used and their interaction with other traffic, not how fast or slow they have the potential to be. Motorcyclists are also vulnerable to poor car driving standards and bad roads.

But motorcycle power outputs had become a mast for the largely anti-motorcycle road safety lobby to fly their flags from. Additionally, a large number of organisations and individuals in power were baying for further restrictions on motorcycling. This was because the issue had become a proxy for much deeper ideological antipathy to what motorcycling represented in an evolving political and social environment.

The transport policy debate was moving increasingly towards the notion that individual freedom of choice in transport should come second to the more collectivist idea of encouraging citizens to switch from cars to public transport, walking and cycling. The rationale being that motorised 'private powered transport' carried unacceptable environmental and social costs. Motorcycling, with its individualistic expressionism, implied rebellion, freedom from timetables and traffic congestion, and was a direct challenge to this emerging and rather repressive kind of thinking.

Because of this, there was a real concern that the Brussels burghers wouldn't stop at the 100bhp power limit and under the influence of 'progressive' transport policy 'experts' would ratchet the limit down from 100bhp, plus add other restrictions until motorcycling was sanitised, repressed and restricted.

The power limit issue was an opportunity to once again run a 'Euro Demo', the last having been successfully held in Brussels in 1992. Mass motorcycle demos were the most visible expression of 'rider power'; an excuse for bikers to let off steam about whatever issue was prominent at the time, get together in their hundreds (or thousands), ride together, have fun and make themselves visible to the public and politicians. Several had been held over the years, the largest prior to 1994 being the 1988 'Riders Rights Day' in London.

The 1992 Brussels demo marked the first time I had travelled abroad and the weekend of beer, biking and fun had made a huge impression on me. The ride through Brussels, past the European Commission, in the company of 10,000 other riders made me realise that 'rider power,' if used effectively, could lead to some very positive change for many ordinary people who were simply sick of bureaucratic interference.

The Paris event was billed as an FEM extravaganza, which guaranteed maximum participation by the twelve or so other European groups, but hosted by French riders groups.

The FFMC organised the demo ride itself, with another French riders' organisation tasked with putting together a camping rally and entertainment to accompany the demo. The FFMC's name loosely translated into the 'French Federation of Angry Bikers' and it consisted mainly of younger people, who typically seemed to ride sports bikes or else hybrid off-road bikes with sports bike wheels known as 'super motards'. FFMC had a very positive anti motorcycle theft initiative. Their attitude was slightly anarchic, with a tendency to get out on the streets and protest whenever the French Government ruffled their feathers – very much in the French socialist tradition. On a more business-orientated front they ran a highly successful magazine 'Moto', and were key partners in the 'Mutuel Des Motards', a successful insurance company which provided affordable motorcycle policies based on a deep understanding of how riders use their bikes. I found the mix of their left of centre campaigning character with a more market oriented entrepreneurial spirit to be a quite appealing marriage of philosophies.

Several months of event preparation and meetings had involved extended trips to France and Belgium to support Simon. We had both become concerned about the low level of attention that was being given to what seemed to be obvious business and budget matters in relation to the rally side of the planned event. Simon had attended to these areas whenever his regular lobbying duties in Brussels had allowed. But he was not often available to oversee some of the more crucial aspects of the business side of the planned demo.

My command of French had always been poor, but it was adequate enough to realise that two entirely conflicting philosophies were being applied to the organisation of firstly the demo and secondly the accompanying rally. The professionally organised FFMC were putting together a top quality demo operation in Paris, while the organisers of the rally revealed their philosophical leanings away from a rally which supported the demo towards a more ad-hoc bikers party with lots of bands and booze.

They showed little appreciation of the scale of the event that was being planned and came across as more interested in organising the piss up of the year than in supporting the demo ride itself; the raison d'être of the whole event. Simon and I were both alarmed by the entirely laissez-faire approach to organising the necessary on-site facilities for what could be several thousand people.

As a result, although the demo ride was organised with barely a murmur and to huge success and great acclaim, many decisions regarding the campsite infrastructure at Aerodrome de Cerny, particularly the need for essentials such as toilets and fencing, had to be taken at the last second and large costs were incurred.

We were fortunate in having a very competent promotions company managing the music, staging and bands. MA Productions resolved huge problems for us and most importantly, handled onsite cash management for us. This was an outfit which organised and promoted many a French tour for household names in the music industry. They provided the professionalism that the event really needed. Somehow though, the whole thing was pulled together and after a day of chaos as people arrived, the following morning's dawn chorus of roaring engines held promise of a motorcycle demonstration to end all demonstrations.

And so it was. The massed stream of 25,000 motorcycles appeared to cut Paris in two when described in the terms of an aerial observer on the day. Speeches were at the Vendome Palace, where Simon in his usual Anglo-French style got the crowd roaring. I also spoke, as did Dave French. The ride afterwards may have been hot and slow, but it was a triumphant progress through Parisian streets and along the Seine. The roadside lined with the cheering and the curious.

The 1994 Paris Euro Demo itself was judged to be a success in political terms and to be there on the day was to be a part of motorcycling history. But the months of recriminations and accusations that followed, for what ended as a financial loss-making event, sullied the marvellous achievement of aims and memories of tens of thousands of grinning and revelling bikers streaming through the 'rues' of Paris and away into the countryside. The whole episode affected Simon and I very deeply.

*

DUBLIN, IRELAND, JUNE 1995

I was shaken violently from my slumber. Liam Gallagher, the MAG Northern Ireland rep, thrust a coffee in my hands. I awoke to semi darkness, my place on the floor surrounded by people only half alive. My wakening brain came to the realisation that this was the day of the long awaited 'Bigger Than Borders' demo.

The demo had been planned as a joint effort between MAG UK and MAG Ireland. The objective was to highlight opposition to various anti-bike laws by holding a massed motorcycle ride between Belfast and Dublin, a significant event for the island of Ireland given the tortured political history of the country and province.

Event organisation was ambitious and involved bringing together two riders rights groups with similar philosophies, but different attitudes. Long meetings resulted in a working plan for the demo, with speeches both in Belfast and Dublin, and significantly, an exchange of national flags between the two groups when the demo crossed the border north to south.

I had spent several months in and out of Ireland, mainly in Dublin, assisting with the organising and also doing a great deal of work with Dave French.

We left Liam's place in Lurgan, County Armagh and rode at a manic pace to Shaw's Bridge, in the south of Belfast. As we neared the city, the sun shone through lowering clouds and atmospherically lit up the Black Hills to the West of Belfast.

We arrived at the campsite, where people were stirring in the early morning sunshine. There were hundreds of dew-stained tents and damp bikes were randomly scattered about; their owners there to support the demo. Tom, the Belfast MAG Rep greeted me. Organisers and marshals were rushing around, walkie-talkies crackling – 'where's the RUC?'; 'Do we have enough marshals?'; 'Is the road clear?' A mug of steaming coffee appeared as Tom vanished to take care of some issue or other.

Later, as the sun gained strength and warmth filled the air, the waiting throng of bikes stirred, filling the air with the sound of multiple engines starting and warming-up. Individually and in groups the mass of bikes moved up to the main gate to gather on the main road and wait for the police escort.

The Royal Ulster Constabulary arrived on their bikes, a convoy of flashing blue lights heralding their appearance. They formed up on the road and waited for the run marshals to signal the off.

Then with an increased roar of engines, gears were selected and bikes started to push forward. I nosed my way to the front of the run, my now repaired Bonnie snarled and spat from its open exhausts as I kept the revs above tick over, left hand slowly feeding the clutch.

Soon we were on our way. Several hundred bikes headed through the empty but picturesque streets of East Belfast. As speed built up, the disorganised mass of motorcycles started to form into in staggered twos, easing down the road in leisurely procession behind the two police bikes. Other RUC bikes and MAG marshals blocked junctions and took post at traffic lights as we followed our police front runners through red lights. The bemused faces of car occupants held at green lights were an amusing sight as we rode by.

Stormont Castle loomed ahead and the mass of bikes rode up the wide roads to the Parliament building. I parked my bike near the steps to the imposing building and looked behind. A long line of bikes were coming into the grounds, probably well over a thousand bikes by this time.

We gathered for speeches. The subject was the importance of riders rights to the future of motorcycling and condemnation of anti-motorcycle laws. Liam spoke with passion and the crowd of leather and Cordura-clad bikers responded with a roar. Dave French stirred the soul with his calls to action.

Afterwards, the motorcycles once again assembled. At first in ragged order, jostling for position, with the smell of exhausts, the sound of Japanese multis, the rumble of twin cylinder engines and the bark of singles filling the air. Then the run moved off, down the hill, out of Stormont and the road to Belfast beckoned. In no time, we seemed to be through Belfast centre, the RUC traffic control efficient and absolute. Belfast appeared almost a ghost town, with no traffic and only a few pedestrians to stand and stare as the long snake of motorcycles passed by.

Then we were heading out of town, riding the wide West Way road, past the Falls Road with its murals clear to see, past the mean high-rises of troubled West Belfast. More bike cops joined the demo, nothing is left to chance in Northern Ireland – not even a symbol of unity.

The motorway was practically empty. Those at the front were leading with pride in their eyes, MAG and RUC marshals ensured control and steady progress. Then we left the motorway behind and headed south on the A1 to Newry. By then the sun had gone and the rain had come. There was no time to stop and put on waterproofs. But no one cared; all were caught up in the passion of the moment. Newry approached and the run slowed. Anticipation of the border crossing grew.

Newry was busier. Saturday morning shoppers stopped to stare as the sound of massed bikes filled the air. Some riders revved their engines for effect, or created loud backfires with their engine kill switches.

Riders waved at ordinary folk and received friendly waves in return. The unexpected demo in the town giving something else to think about that was different from the day to day life of a post ceasefire province.

We rode up the hill, out of Newry and up to the border. The checkpoint approached and we by-passed the now silent and empty army and customs sheds. Then we were on the final Northern Ireland stretch. A UK Customs officer stood to attention in the middle of the road as bikes streamed past on both sides of him. Finally, we bypassed a vehicle search compound on a rough piece of new tarmac and were through the border. The Republic of Ireland – Eire – lay ahead of us.

Just past the border we stopped at a café selling sandwiches and coffee. The road was completely blocked by bikes as riders alighted and took their place in the queue for the free refreshments that were being handed out. A girl wearing an amused expression stood at the door of a bureau de change, which was advertising the latest exchange rate between Sterling and Punts.

Dave and Liam swapped notes with marshals on the radio before sending the word around that the police had counted 2,000 bikes through Newry.

A cop, a Gardaí, from the Irish Police – An Garda Síochána – arrived in a battered green Ford Sierra. Following him were two green Gardaí BMW motorcycles; all that could be spared by the police for the long ride to Dublin.

Liam, Dave and I talked to him, putting forward our photocall plan for MAG and MAG Ireland to exchange the Irish Tricolour with the Union Jack. He was tickled by the whole idea.

"No problem lads; but Jaysus, this'll be a first. Ye got any TV crews?"

We didn't; something that had pissed us off already. The newspapers and TV had expressed interest in our plan, but had sent no one to cover it. To us it seemed that they were more interested in talking peace than in reporting it. We were mystified. No one could recall another moment in recent history when flags had been exchanged like this. Perhaps editors were concerned about stirring up trouble with an image that would be provocative in some quarters...

So we went ahead with our symbolic act anyway. It was a stirring sight, a piece of history; a symbol of peace for a battered island – totally ignored by the media.

With a great deal of commotion and confusion, the run set off again. Now the only authority with us was the two motorcycle-mounted Gardaí leading the way to the capital at a steady, but brisk, pace. We ran through Dundalk, through Drogheda, down to Dublin. More bikes joined the demo all the time, the line of motorcycles stretching north behind us grew ever longer.

Massed groups of bikes joined the run at Whitehall by the edge of the city. The run, now numbering approximately 3,000, moved its way slowly into Dublin and down onto O'Connell Street. Traffic was total chaos, marshalling was less effective, rows started with car drivers, halted while trying to push into the stream of bikes.

Dave, Liam and I steamed ahead of the main mass of bikes and turned into O'Connell Street at breakneck speed. We roared down the historic street toward the River Liffey and parked our bikes on the central reservation of the wide road by the willowesque Anna Livia monument where we could easily find them later.

This time the press were waiting and it was my turn to take charge and going into 'spokesman' mode. I talked to as many journalists as possible and set-up interviews for key folk from our group and also for Simon, who had just arrived from Brussels via the ferry from Anglesey.

At the top of the street, the run waited; now headed by marchers carrying a broad banner which reached across the street proclaiming 'Stop Anti-Bike Laws!' Then at a signal, the marchers led the crammed mass of bikes slowly down towards us. The sound of thousands of loud exhaust systems filled the air, along with the haze of fumes from the packed mass of bikes.

Politically correct in environmental terms? No. Greener than the millions of cars which choke our city streets each and every day? Yes.

But that wasn't the point of this demo anyway. That day, we were calling for the undemocratic bureaucratic machine in Brussels to get off our backs and leave us alone to make our own choices about how we lead our lives.

The banner and the bikes rolled down the street and towards to the GPO building where speeches were due. TV cameras rolled, interviews were given, the excitement grew.

The street filled to bursting point and soon afterwards the sound of the mass of engines was silenced. Those of us who were due to speak climbed onto a flatbed trailer, pulled there by a lorry earlier in the day. Speeches started; an MEP, riders rights leaders, Milward inspirational as always. I also spoke. The core of all our messages: "Stop Anti Bike Laws!"

The hand of history reached out to us as some Irish members reminded us that the GPO was the key redoubt for Irish nationalists during the 1916 uprising against British rule.

Then it was over and a sense of relaxation stole over the proceedings. There were smiles all round, a feeling that the impossible had been achieved.

Slowly the bikes dispersed. Many headed back to Ulster, but the majority of us headed west out of the city anticipating a party to end all parties at a venue we'd organised in County Kildare.

Later, we sat outside the pub, several pints of Guinness already inside us. A medley of drunk folk and parked motorcycles mingled in the muddy car park. Some characters were already well on their way to oblivion. Simon grinned at Dave, Liam and I over his beer. We all congratulated each other and breathed a sigh of relief. Easy smiles and relaxed talk all round. One year ago such an Irish north/south event could not have happened. We felt like pioneers.

Riders rights? Did it matter? Who cared anyway? We couldn't answer that, but at that time we felt that the essence of motorcycling; the expression of freedom and emancipation that two wheels represented, was the essence of individual freedom liberty and democracy that should be available to all.

For us, 'riders rights' was a metaphor. We felt we were part of a movement for a better and freer future for all, a future that would realise the legacy of all those of different nations and in different ages, who had given everything in the fight for freedom and democracy.

Or were our dreams just naïve hubris?

FARO PORTUGAL NOVEMBER 1995

"I reckon two days." said Simon as the three of us piled into the Transit van that he and Bob Tomlins had hired. "If we get to Paris by lunchtime, we can pick up Eric and make the Spanish border by nightfall. We'll be in Faro by tomorrow night if we don't stop too much."

Bob pursed his lips. "Alright mate, but we don't want to go mad, I'm sure that it won't be the end of world if we're late."

We were on our way to a meeting of the FEM committee, a chance to get together with fellow riders rights activists from around Europe. Much had changed for me since the 1994 Paris Euro Demo. The fall-out from that alone had probably put years on me and for Simon it had also been a stressful time.

Although the demo had been a success, a combination of high expense and poor campsite infrastructure had left campers and traders alike complaining. Essential equipment that hadn't been ordered early enough was charged at last minute prices, so adding to financial woe.

We had been fortunate that the music and the infrastructure that went with it had been organised by MA Productions. They had taken a huge headache away from us with their cool competence. Crucially, they had held onto much of the cash until after the Demo.

The food and drink ticket system put in place by the campsite organisers had lent itself to widespread criticism. Some basic items like toilets were not provided in large enough numbers for the thousands of biking campers, resulting in a nightmare of overflowing portaloos.

The overall finances were a mess. The gate takings were lower than expected. Traders ran into issues when redeeming the cash equivalent for food and drink tickets. At one point concession holders threatened to riot. We began to seriously wonder if there would be enough to pay all the bills.

Late in the evening the MA team handed a large metal box of the remaining cash over to Simon and myself and told us that they felt it would be wise to get it off the site and banked as soon as possible.

Although it was late, Simon, Jean, Dave, Stef from Khule Wampe and I headed for Jean's apartment in Paris with the cash and put it somewhere safe.

We spent an uneasy night wondering what to do next. No one could sleep, sick with worry about money. To pass the time, Simon suggested that we count the cash again and try and tally it with the accounts. Piles of coins and notes in multitudes of currencies began to build on the dining room table, with all of us furiously at work sorting it all out and working out exchange rates in an attempt to reach a final Franc value. Simon punched figures into a calculator like his life depended on it, a sheen building on his worried looking face.

Some hours later, when figures had been checked and re-checked, Simon sat back with a sigh of relief.

"There's enough to pay the bills and about six grand left over" he said with obvious satisfaction. We all trailed off in relief to find our doss-bags and to get some sleep.

The following morning, our little troupe marched triumphantly into the offices of the rally organisers near the Boulevard de Clichy and dumped the large box and set of accounts on the desk in front.

"There!" exclaimed Simon to a startled looking character who had been sat quietly enjoying a coffee. "There's enough to pay the bills and there's even a bit of profit." The man looked at us with distain.

"But is there enough to pay these bills?" he asked, producing a pile of invoices and receipts for services and supplies which had not been mentioned in the various organisational meetings.

Simon went white. "How much?" he said quietly.

"These are for services from suppliers that we also use for other events." came the reply. "We made arrangements with these people which need to be honoured."

"But this was not expenditure that we knew about." replied Milward "And you still haven't said how much."

The pile of invoices added up to several thousands of Francs for various supplies, equipment and other rally-related items which had not before been logged as official expenditure.

The months of recrimination which followed left Simon and

I in fear for our jobs and concerned about possible litigation. Accusations were hurled, but eventually our actions in relation to the event were either supported, or given the benefit of the doubt by the main body of FEM's membership. This didn't stop the bad feeling in some quarters. FEM and MAG UK held their own enquiries into the affair.

The problem essentially revolved around the task of trying to organise a pan-European event, where several organising structures were separately organising key elements. This was coupled with the fact that there were several conflicting demands and philosophies from the different organisations in play which led to communications issues. There was an FEM element, which looked at headline political and PR aspects. Then there was the demo itself. Finally, there was local rally organisation where key figures, perhaps in some ways understandably, just got on with things in their usual manner without necessarily sharing all the detail with the wider 'group'. Despite many meetings it was ultimately clear that there had been an overall lack of communication on areas of non-headline expenditure and perhaps some element of 'we know best' on the part of the various parties involved. The result in business terms was catastrophic.

It was a bruising episode which left Simon a more thoughtful person, myself depressed and entertaining nagging doubts about my own part in the whole affair, despite assurances from colleagues and friends. All this was compounded for me by being personally identified with the serious difficulties and let downs that UK riders had experienced from a travel company who had offered a cross channel booking service, but had been overwhelmed by the demand.

A few months later, after a year of poor event income for MAG, my paid contract with MAG was not renewed. I was told that the reasons were purely financial, though I couldn't help wondering if the Euro Demo fiasco had played a part. Mentally exhausted, I also resigned as Overseas Liaison Officer, but retained a post as researcher and as a sort of special advisor on political matters. I remained on the MAG National Committee.

I took a job with the custom motorcycle magazine Back Street

Heroes as news editor and feature writer. I also worked on several other car and motorcycle magazines under the Myatt McFarlane publishing stable. This tangential move meant a fresh perspective on biking and a chance to start recovering from the damage done to my own confidence by the 1994 Euro Demo fiasco.

Outside of an entertaining professional life, working on a custom motorcycle magazine, opening new horizons and seeing another side of the motorcycle world, work with MAG still occupied much of my spare time. I found myself drawing closer to Dave French, who at that time was MAG Ireland's president.

The result was that whole weeks at a time were spent in Dublin, with me in danger of ending up more Irish than the Irish. Sometimes I'd go only reluctantly back to my Manchester office simply to file copy and catch up with my editor and work for a few days before returning to the Irish Sea ferry. Myatt McFarlane gave me surprising latitude given the nomadic existence I presented them with. But time in Ireland, coupled with following the UK rally scene and writing about political issues, resulted in some good copy for BSH. I was able to keep up with workload and deadlines.

I also worked on other magazines in the publishing 'stable', including a beer magazine. Some of the most interesting work was for an American car magazine. One major feature about importing American classics, led to a long road trip across the US Mid-West, researching articles for the magazine, looking for scrapyard cars to restore while investigating the practical and bureaucratic challenges of bringing them into the UK. The project was absorbing and I still treasure memories of those weeks spent exploring small-town America, living as a four-wheeled nomad in a V8 Oldsmobile, gathering material and meeting fascinating characters.

Back on this side of 'the pond', MAG Ireland matters consumed my time more and more. In Dave I found a meeting of the minds on a whole range of matters, both professional and personal. We would sit long into the night making plans and exploring ideas over numerous cups of coffee and sometimes something stronger.

There were rallies and ride outs, plus time spent exploring that marvellous country. Dave and I enjoyed good moments in many

Irish counties and sometimes of an evening we rode up into the Wicklow Mountains to escape the sprawl of Dublin. Dave had a good circle of friends and some like Rudi Monaghan and Ciara Nic-an-tShennaigh became special to me. I could feel myself mentally recovering. Sadly, both Rudi and Ciara tragically passed away in the early 2000s; Rudi after a long illness and Ciara after a terrible accident at home.

The culmination of my 'Irish Period' was the 1995 'Bigger than Borders' motorcycle run. In one fantastic day, I felt my confidence surging back in the white heat of the demo and the scores of revving engines, rousing speeches and passionate people. An event which was successful politically, organisationally and financially.

That November, Dave asked me to represent MAG Ireland at the FEM meeting in Portugal. MAG UK was accommodating and sent MAG's founder, another old friend, Ian Mutch to represent them. An opportunity to save travel costs found me sitting in the hired transit van, roaring down the autoroutes with Simon and Bob Tomlins. Bob, a former union man, worked for the FEM, managing its finances.

Wrestling chaotic Parisian traffic, we picked Eric Thiollier up from outside his flat, who grinning, hurled a kitbag full of beer into the back. We headed south, along the long autoroute towards the Spanish border. A combination of drivers and very few stops meant that we arrived in Spain at dusk and stopped for the night in the near-border port of St Sebastian Donostia, sometimes known in the UK as 'Berlin' in the movie The Battle of Britain. Sharing a single room, the four of us bundled inside like a pack of dogs fighting for a spare inch of floor to sleep on. An uncomfortable night lent us all a sallow eye as we hit the road the following morning.

With Bob driving, we headed across northern and central Spain, stopping only for food and fuel. Burgos flew by, as did Valladolid and with Simon driving we headed south at Salamanca.

Later that day we traversed the mountains north of Seville. Simon was driving as the road suddenly ran out to be replaced by gravel piste. Looking at the map, the red line of a major 'A' road was clearly marked, so we elected to push on. What followed was a terrifying two hours of being hurled around the back of the Transit as Simon, with head down determination and a fierce stare in his eyes did his best to break time and distance records on the gravel road. The van hurtled around blind corners, sometimes with steep cliffs on one side and precipitous drops into the depths the other.

We all were well aware of the fearsome reputation that Simon was gaining as a bike-wrecker. Now it seemed his carefree, but suicidal, style of riding was finding alarming new expression on four-wheels in his approach to unmade Spanish mountain roads.

I looked at Bob and Eric; both were white.

"Slow down mate." I called. No reply, just total concentration on the track ahead. The demons were in charge as far as Simon was concerned. It wasn't until we emerged, an eternity later, from a huge cloud of dust that we'd created, that he slowed down and agreed to let Bob take a shift on the blessedly welcome tarmac.

"Bloody good fun that." said Simon with a schoolboy look of innocent joy. Bob slowly shook his head.

That evening, we sat on the beach in Faro, relaxing on the sand and taking in the calm water and mild waves of a peaceful Atlantic Ocean. We watched the sun sink into the Ocean to the west. Large meals of shrimp and sardines sat in our bellies, along with a liberal offering of local wine. Mutch had joined us for this culinary extravaganza, which had helped to dull memories of heat, dust and being hurled around inside the Dagenham-manufactured tin box praying for our lives.

Mutch passed a brandy bottle to Simon. "You'll be the death of all of us one day Si" he said, having been regaled with our tale of four-wheeled terror over dinner. Milward took a swig and passed the bottle to me.

"Ah don't worry me mates, we're all gonna live forever I reckon." He smiled, leant back on the sand and snapped his fingers at me. "Pass the tobacco Craig."

BELGIUM, JULY 1997

Earlier in the evening folks who sat in the commuter trains which regularly rumbled by the place, had stared out of the windows into the middle distance, with an unfocussed and bored demeanour on their faces.

It was getting dark now and passengers on the trains that were still running, had more a look of incredulity about them as their gaze fixed on the scene that rolled by their windows.

MAG Belgium's Pond Party was a bit of an institution amongst those 'in the know'. Set in a small clearing in the woods, lush grass ran from tiny huts down to a small lake. Regular fishing stands marked the location of many a dreaming day with rod hovering hopefully over the lake. An isolated spot down a long country lane, the only intrusion was the regular train service, which did little to detract from a place which was the ideal venue for a good old fashioned piss-up.

I'd been in Belgium for a few days doing some work with Simon. Erwin from MAG Belgium had suggested a little jaunt into the countryside for a few beers with some mates. We'd packed some tents and headed from Brussels for a pleasant ride though a warm summer afternoon to the lakeside venue some miles from Antwerp.

A barbeque was already smoking away outside one of the huts and we were greeted with the fizz of opening beer bottles and a cheery welcome from the dozen or so people who had already arrived. A good selection of bikes was parked up and as the sun lowered in the sky I put my tent up and reflected on an enjoyable day and the pleasure of company with like-minded souls.

Simon had spent about a minute and a half erecting the latest of a long series of ruinously rotting and sagging tents. Bent poles held up a motley patchwork of decaying and ripped fabric. After bashing a few pegs in the ground, he studied the chaotic mess that he'd erected for a second. Then he shrugged his shoulders and headed back to the barbeque where a large stack of beer crates awaited.

The food and conversation was good and beer flowed. Also

flowing in liberal quantities was a healthy supply of Polish Spirit which some wag had brought along. Needless to say, it made a grand accompaniment to the regular bottles of Jupiler, which added a certain spirit to the carefree atmosphere. Boisterous party games were attempted by folk with wobbly limbs and amid howls of laughter. Entertaining for both us and the ever more boggle-eyed train passengers which surged by every half hour or so. Simon joined in the games with gusto, returning to the beer crates on regular occasions to ensure that his alcohol stream wasn't diluted with too much blood. For everyone the night was growing more drunken and surreal as the late evening turned to night and the stars came out.

With Simon, there was always a tipping point between happy-sloshed and being pissed out of his face. When the lake finally beckoned to his subconscious we all knew that Milward was definitely 'on one'.

"Look at me!" he proclaimed as he leapt fully clothed into the calm water. Disappearing from view for a few seconds, he reappeared happily splashing about. This was stock Milward stuff, water always beckoned when he'd had a 'few' and we knew what was coming next. Climbing out of the water, he set about removing every stitch of his clothing which was thrown in all directions. His spectacles had vanished, but being so drunk, it probably didn't make much difference anyway.

Without a care in the world he wandered over to the beer supply and helped himself, chatting to others about him, hand on hip without an ounce of self-consciousness. We set about taking the Mickey out of him with much laughter, to which he joined in with jokes and swipes about our own rapidly deteriorating condition. The Polish Spirit made another round and I felt myself starting to sway.

The females of our group were keeping to themselves. Sat around the campfire, they chatted and took amusement from the antics of their men-folk. Simon turned his attention to one of the few single girls, puffed his chest out and after walking over to her, launched into an extremely bad series of chat up lines using a combination of English, poor French and something completely unrecognisable. The women giggled as they eyed up and down the naked, drunken English apparition which was leering at them.

It seemed that even Simon had got to the point where support was needed to stay vertical, so reaching out a hand to lean against the back of one of the girls' chairs; he missed and promptly fell flat on his face. Everyone collapsed in gales of laughter.

Banging hangovers and green faces were the order of the following morning as we emerged bleary-eyed from our tents. Simon had made it as far as his tent, but had collapsed on top of it, dealing the final blow to an already ruined shelter. Someone had thrown a coat over his naked form.

While trying to drown my headache with a litre of coffee, Milward appeared looking like death warmed up and clad in only a pair of underpants.

"Gawd I feel dreadful and I can't find my specs."

"Try the lake." said Erwin unsympathetically.

A look of stunned comprehension appeared on Si's face.

"Bloody hell." he grumbled and wandered over to the lake's edge. Fair play to the guy though, he waded into the lake and after about ten minutes thrashing about in roughly the place he remembered being, he stood up and held a muddy pair of glasses up for all to see.

"Lucky bastard" muttered Erwin, trying to hide his astonishment behind the dour expression he usually maintained.

A few of us got the fire going again and arranged Simon's clothes so they would eventually dry. Si spread the contents of his soaked wallet around in a vain attempt to dry out his money, driving licence and passport.

"Good party." he said as he raised a mug of steaming coffee to his face. The old Milward sparkle reappeared in his eyes.

BONN, GERMANY, JUNE 1998

I hadn't seen Dave for a while and was looking forward to catching up with him in Germany. 'Yer man' had left Ireland a couple of years before and, after spending a few years working in

Amsterdam, was now doing a software engineering job in Stuttgart.

For myself, I had returned to MAG UK full time at the end of 1996, after the Myatt McFarlane magazine empire had taken a nose dive for reasons that weren't entirely the owner's fault. This time I had direct responsibility for all lobbying and campaigning at MAG and a move to Birmingham allowed me to be based at MAG's HQ. My marriage had come to an end as I had moved to Manchester and I was now living with Heather who I had met when we worked together on Back Street Heroes.

But it was slowly becoming apparent that I was reaching the end of my years as a full-time riders rights activist. The urge to move on was compounded by a strong need for new challenges and a change to my way of life.

Simon was still at what had become the FEMA after an amalgamation of the FEM with another European motorcycle group. Contact with him was not as regular as before. We'd both kept our heads down and got on with our respective jobs.

I'd worked on some successful Westminster based lobby projects, including a 1997 mass biker lobby of Parliament and a 'Bikers are Voters' campaign prior to the General Election that year. Simon had scored some good successes in the European legislation game. Things were also starting to change at FEMA, with much needed expansion made possible by the merger.

A week or so before the 1998 Bonn Euro Demo, there had been a knock on the door and the tall form of John O'Leary had entered with a flourish. John was an old friend from my Ireland days. He divided his time between his job at the GPO in Limerick, his motorcycle, MAG Ireland and the local bike club.

John's plan was to stay a few days with us before we headed to Germany via Brussels to meet Simon. He proceeded to camp out on the living room carpet and settled down to several days of chilling out while Heather and I got on with our everyday lives.

It was good to be on the road again and heading towards the continent, I remembered the 1994 fiasco and the much better organised 1996 Demo in Brussels. The Bonn event was being organised locally and I was thankful that this time I had no part to play in it, apart from being a mere punter.

Joining Heather, John and I was Guz Hirst, a Leicestershire man who had adopted Australia as his own. His diminutive figure a bundle of good humour, wrapped up in a hybrid English/Australian accent and bad jokes. It was good to have his bright personality and ancient Suzuki along for the ride.

Ian Mutch was collected from his house in the East End of London and Nich Brown, another MAG colleague and good friend joined us at the Channel Tunnel with his girlfriend Rae. Our group of six bikes roared off towards Brussels after the short train ride under the English Channel.

In the Belgian capital we found that the FEMA office was full of bustle as last minute preparations were made to the European public relations activity which would accompany the Bonn Demo. It was good to see everyone again, particularly Christina, who ran much of the administration and for a long time was Simon's girlfriend.

After a night's sleep in Simon's flat, we loaded the bikes and followed him back to the FEMA offices where we found Simon at his professional best; answering phones, replying to last minute emails, taking care of 101 little things and at the same time doing his best to be bright and entertaining to the people around him. Most were visitors, passing through on the way down to Bonn for the demo.

It was about mid-afternoon before he was ready to go. Although we had all planned to ride together, Simon felt that the fastest way down was the best way for him. He had several meetings planned for the evening which he didn't want to miss. There were a few final niggles that needed sorting before the demo the following day.

The rest of us took a more leisurely route southwards though the Ardennes and, after crossing into Germany, enjoyed a gentle run through the picturesque Moselle Valley; home of many fine German wines.

The road to the demo campsite lay above the valley in an old US Air Force station. Winding up a series of switchbacks, we climbed to an exposed plain as it started to get dark. A few miles further and the shapes of Cold War aircraft shelters emerged from the gathering gloom off the side of the road and behind a high barbed wire fence.

The curved nuclear aircraft shelters were a familiar sight

from my RAF days, but a checkpoint manned by huge bearded characters with motorcycle club back patches beside the main gate guardroom definitely was not.

After checking in we put our tents up in the shadow of one of the massive shelters before taking a walk around the site. The usual motorcycle rally attractions were easily found; bars, bands, beer, food, beer, bars, beer, more beer and drunken bikers.

We paused by a rotisserie where uncooked chickens on the top spit, dribbled lukewarm juices down onto the cooked fowl revolving on spits below. I figured that a meal should be chosen with care. John didn't seem to mind and tucked into half a burned bird. But by then he had already worked about eight cans of beer into himself and was beyond caring.

When we eventually found Simon, it was clear that he was distracted by forthcoming events and, in addition, was being constantly badgered by local organisers. We left him to it.

It was a pleasant if strange evening. John continued to get ever more inebriated, while Ian eccentrically muttered about not it not being appropriate to have a can of beer until 9.37pm. Nich and Rae were into the spirit of things, as was I – the rucksack full of cans on my back getting steadily lighter.

We passed from one group of campers to another; meeting friends, sharing laughs and swapping jokes. Dave French appeared with new girlfriend Anna in tow. It was good to see him again – it had been a while and we quickly fell into the usual manner that we adopted when we were together.

Anna was friendly and curious about the events around us. Dave had met her in Stuttgart and this was her first major bikers' rally.

The evening wound down in a blur of alcohol and laughter in the cool darkness, relieved by the occasional campfire and the torches of those wandering by.

The hangover verged on a serious dose of alcohol poisoning. I clambered groaning from my tent into the harsh morning light as memories of the aftermath of my night out with Simon in Paris a few years before came to mind. Everyone looked pretty awful apart from Ian who looked smug after his 2.3 cans of beer taken after 9.37pm. There was no sign of John.

While looking for a coffee, unsilenced engines started to burst into life as people began to get ready for the run into Bonn. I hurried back to the tent to get my gear on.

John's tent was unfastened so Ian stuck his head inside to wake the alcoholic Irishman, who was unconscious on top of his doss-bag. John appeared just as we about to ride off to join the run formation. He staggered about for a while, throwing kit in all directions before clambering into a jacket and sticking a helmet on his head. Mounting his bike, he managed to get it started and off the stand before falling straight off.

"Jaysus, I only got to bed about twenty minutes ago." he declared with a startled expression on his face.

"Do you think you should be coming on the run?" Ian asked with concern.

"Ah I'll be alright." replied John with a slightly cross-eyed grin.

He kept pretty quiet after that and our group of bikes set off to join the back of the run and wait for the 'off'.

Leaving the old air force base some time later, the run took off at high speed down a long straight and around a sweeping left-hand curve. I was having a hard time keeping up with the hangover that I had, but looking in my mirror, I saw John's bike career off the road with no attempt to negotiate the curve.

Bucking and sliding over the grass John seemed to come to his senses and, with the luck of the Irish, re-joined the road without falling off. He caught up with us, waving us on to join the rest of the run.

Arriving in Bonn an hour or so later, we traversed well-ordered streets expecting to be marshalled to a prominent city centre site where the speeches would take place. Instead, we found ourselves running alongside a river and out towards the edge of town, where we were eventually guided into what looked like a long abandoned construction site.

Parking the bikes, we looked around. Gravel paths led off in all directions around piles of rubble and shattered buildings covered in shrapnel scars. Clearly, the last visitors to this place had been the Royal Air Force, 53 years before.

"Some demo." muttered Mutch. "I foresee a day of great

historical significance and political influence – not."

When we found Simon, he was putting a brave face on things.

"Well, there were several thousand on the demo ride and it'll make the news tonight, plus all these bikers in Bonn; that must say something."

"Yeah, motorcyclists block traffic and make lots of noise and smell" said Ian. "Great impression."

"Hmmm …" replied Simon and strode off before he became the butt of more dismayed piss-taking.

Simon's eternal optimism did him proud as usual. Putting a brave face on things, he managed to persuade speakers from about ten countries to say a few words on stage to loud applause from the gathered throng. A TV crew or two had also turned up and by the time the speeches kicked off, there was a better atmosphere. Plus a general feel that there were plenty of worse places to hold demo than on a World War II bombsite miles from nowhere.

But perhaps things were moving on. Demos in central London were becoming rarer – we had been forced to resort to a very similar bombsite for the London Demo speeches that same year. Touring the remains of Luftwaffe, RAF and USAAF activity was fast becoming bit of a feature of riders rights life. We were starting to be forced out of sight and out of mind by the powers that be when we had something to protest about – what did that say about both our influence and abilities as a pressure group?

MAG's Chairman had refused to accept our marginalisation in the derelict East End of London and had led a massed ride to Buckingham Palace, but no such presence of mind was on display in Bonn.

A lot of old faces were moving on, tiring of the constant struggle with no change to the fundamentals of how the general public viewed motorcycling. Simon and many of the rest of us were soldiering on, but for how much longer?

We had enjoyed success and continued to score worthwhile political points against a 'bike-ist' political establishment. But the fire of protest seemed to be slowly dying, with 'rights' activists being replaced by the more cautious and technocratic end of the biking professional 'lobbyist' spectrum. Dealing with this new way of lobbying was consuming ever more of my time.

How much longer would the idealism that Simon represented survive?

*

BRUSSELS, DECEMBER 1999

It had been a while since I had seen Simon. In late 1998, I had finally left MAG to join the Motor Cycle Industry Association (MCI) as Director of Public Affairs. This was a logical career progression although some chose to view it as a betrayal of the riders rights 'movement'. I looked at my new position partly as a way of taking the more positive techniques and tactics of grass roots biker lobbying to a wider industry audience. Nich Brown saw things the same way and joined me at MCI.

I also felt (and still do) that there was much to be gained by having a positive partnership between riders and industry on the many public policy issues where common concerns and positions existed. Lobbies are won by unity. Discord is exploited by Government officials in particular, who look for any excuse to 'divide and conquer' in pursuit of their own objectives – with these sometimes at odds with even the wishes of elected Ministers. Someone once said that political parties may come and go, but the Government never changes – an accurate assessment of UK politics in my experience.

Throughout 1999, I was heavily absorbed in my new job at the MCI. I still sat on the MAG UK National Committee, but this was starting to create tensions, with the Chairman in particular. We had fallen out over a matter of tactics about an issue where we both agreed about the core principle. With hindsight, I think we were both correct. But to my dismay the tensions that were created in 1999 were to explode into open warfare a few years later.

Simon became a more distant figure during this year of change. A distrust which had, for some reason, seemed to exist towards the industry from certain elements within the riders groups had seemingly started to affect the way that he viewed me. Phone calls to Simon became stilted, as he was clearly less comfortable with talking to me.

This hurt. I do not know where this rider/industry distrust came from in the first place. Perhaps it was generated by individuals with an agenda of their own. There was certainly one individual, new to MAG's senior team, who for reasons only known to himself actively sought to drive wedges between myself and people I had worked successfully with for many years. His actions and duplicity were to later fuel the unpleasantness mentioned above.

It's true to say that industry and consumers will have different agendas from time to time. There will be different policies on consumer issues for example. But it's also fair to say that on the majority of transport policy related public policy issues, there's barely a fag-paper's thickness of difference in views between riders and industry. But the fact that some ridiculous rider group 'mythology' about the 'big bad' industry had started to affect my relationship with a personal friend annoyed me enormously.

One day I phoned Simon. After a few cautious pleasantries were exchanged I said "Simon, it's still Craig here on the end of the line you know. Just because I work for the industry doesn't suddenly change who I am underneath, or my feelings of friendship towards you."

This helped to clear the air and we gradually resumed our previous relationship, though we still didn't see a huge amount of each other – mainly because we moved in different parts of the biking world day to day.

I had come to trust Dave as I would a brother. We saw each other from time to time, but almost constant emailing and text messaging meant that our bond of friendship grew.

We both felt that we couldn't miss the opportunity of seeing Simon off on his epic round the world adventure. So we decided to descend on Brussels a day or two before he was due to leave and after he had already done all his official farewells.

The three of us headed into town and warmed up with a litre or two of beer at Flanagan's. We then troughed at a good restaurant, before heading to a night club. Drinks flowed, conversation was relaxed and exuberant. Plans were made, castles in the sky built, just as things always had been between us. Only this time, we were moving beyond the world of motorcycle politics. Instead, we discussed the cultures and people that lay ahead of Simon as he travelled. It was enormously refreshing.

Later that night we headed back to Simon's flat for a few nightcaps. Alcoholic 'goggles' had softened the rough edges of his 'Overlander' bike, which was now ready for the adventure ahead. We played around with the bike, discussed Simon's kit requirements at length and planned his run with him with fantastic optimism.

As I fell asleep on the uncomfortable sofa in Simon's flat for the last time, contented by the excellent night's fun and just a bit sad about my friend's departure.

Breakfast was slow and measured, taken at an Algerian café around the corner from Simon's place. We fell into one of those satisfying post-night-out conversations with coffee, which was probably partly fuelled by the alcohol which remained in our systems.

Simon was sure he would return fired up to do a few more years at the helm of riders rights. I wasn't so sure.

"Do you honestly think that you'll return the same person after a trip like the one you're about to do?" I asked. "Surely it's enough to change any man. You may feel differently about everything, see the world with new eyes and not want to return to something which may seem very stale after all your experiences."

Dave nodded and Simon looked at us both for a while thoughtfully.

"Well, you never know." he replied "But can you see me just doing some mundane job?"

It didn't seem likely and later on when I was ready to depart, I knew that I'd miss him badly. Bugger it, I already missed him.

"Just take care mate." I said.

We hugged.

A FRIEND AWAY, 2000–2005

There were of course many other journeys. Dave had undertaken a successful tour of the Balkans with Simon in the late 1990s, the pair of them visiting a heavily damaged post war Sarajevo. The three of us also made journeys in the United States, travelling in several US States as part of an involvement with the various motorcycle riders groups that exist there.

Simon, Dave and I took part in riders rights conventions in Pennsylvania, Minnesota and New Mexico. We visited New York, Chicago, Washington DC and Oklahoma City among other places. One American journey took Dave and me within a few hundred miles of achieving a coast to coast trip together. One motorcycle event in Florida allowed me to witness at close and privileged first-hand a launch of the Space Shuttle. The awesomeness of that ultimate expression of humankind's technical power left a memory that will be imprinted forever.

But many of these stateside sojourns became part of a wider and deeply political picture of events in the world of riders rights, far beyond the scope of this story. Perhaps it's a tale that will be told another time…

*

In January 2000, Simon left on his round the world odyssey.

Seeing him that final time in Brussels with Dave made me fully realise that this truly was the last we'd see of him for a while. I suppose that I had this view that he'd be off for a few months and come bouncing back as before. But viewing and tinkering with the Overlander and fiddling about with his kit, brought home to me how serious an undertaking his journey was.

I started to feel that this particular turning point for Simon was an irrevocable one. I strongly doubted that he'd return either as the same person, or to once again take up riders rights work.

Simon's round the world odyssey deserves a book in itself. Sometimes, as I browse through the volumes of his diaries, notes and pictures, I wonder if it will ever be possible to completely do justice to his personal and spiritual achievement.

The descriptions of people and places, the path of his spiritual journey, the successes and the failures of his ambitions alongside scribbled notes hinting at adventure. Underpinning it all his enthusiasm for the endeavour and the pure joy of a life settled and peaceful as the road ahead unwound.

Upon leaving Brussels, Simon headed south. Some adjustments were made to the trip from the start. A decision not to tour Iberia led him to take the boat to Tunis, where he attempted and failed to enter Libya, where he had intended to ride onwards to Egypt. So returning to Europe, he headed east, travelled through Turkey and then south to the Holy Land.

All his sponsors and friends received email updates. Always starting with a brief press notice and always full of enthusiasm about what he'd seen and done.

From Israel, he went to Egypt and received an offer of marriage, an event which would thereafter feature in the fund raising presentations that he made as he travelled – along with a photograph of the nearly lucky lady.

The Middle East beckoned and from there Pakistan, where Malaria caught up with him. He'd stopped taking the anti-malarial drug Lariam sometime before, due to the mental and physical effects that this dangerous neurotoxin can have on people and which were indeed affecting him.

Time in a sanatorium 'taking the cure' as he put it, allowed thought and reflection. Mainly on spiritual matters it seems. After some weeks he set out once again. This time on the road to India. While touring there, he had the good fortune to meet the Dalai Lama and talk to him about his ride and charitable fund raising work.

South East Asia beckoned and then through Singapore, Indonesia and onto Australia. Here he conducted radio and TV interviews about his journey and in the midst of the Olympic Games unsuccessfully attempted to raise cash for his charities. First world countries can sometimes be the toughest nuts to crack it seems.

Then he went to the island of Flores in Indonesia and everything changed.

Willy Balawala was an aid worker with whom Simon found that he had an enormous amount in common. They sat and discussed healthcare on the beautiful but impoverished islands that comprise Flores and the Nuasa Tengarra district of West Timor. To both Simon and Willy, it seemed clear that the work pioneered by Riders for Health (RfH) in parts of Africa could work extremely effectively on Flores.

'Riders' had developed a system which had motorcycles at its core. Machines were provided to healthcare workers to enable them to reach remote rural areas of developing countries, sometimes to places which had never before had the services of a healthcare professional.

Using motorcycles for aid work is nothing new. The big aid agencies spend millions providing motorcycles and other vehicles to projects in developing countries. But wastage is huge. Bikes are often merely handed over to local projects and very often no systems are put in place to manage them. The result is that they often last no more than a year or so. Something basic breaks and the bike is binned. Sometimes four-wheeled vehicles that are only a few years old end up being used as chicken sheds because the infrastructure is not in place to service and repair them.

So RfH developed a systematic approach to operation, servicing and maintenance of their vehicles which starts with training the rider to look after their machine every day. This system of Transport Resource Management (TRM) ensures that vehicles are properly managed to deliver reliable service over a reasonable life expectation. Thousands of lives have been saved simply because TRM means that health workers can rely on properly maintained motorcycles and other vehicles for their work. Quality of life is improved for many thousands more.

Simon set about trying to interest Riders for Health in the idea of setting up a project on Flores.

Given the nature of their operation, Riders were not at that point in a position to drop everything and help in Flores. But they were keen to support Simon and Willy as far as ensuring that Willy received basic training in the Riders system of TRM logistics.

So Willy flew to the Riders academy in Zimbabwe for his training and Simon concentrated in raising funds for the motorcycles that would be needed for the emerging Flores project.

The tenor of his round the world mission had changed. He focused on fundraising for the Flores project from this point onwards and set his mind to working out how an international network of TRM projects could be established.

Japan was his port of call a few months later and while enjoying touring the country itself, he was able to set up a meeting with some of the main Japanese motorcycle manufacturers. A nice pile of cash was the result, plus a deal with Yamaha which allowed the delivery of several 115cc motorcycles to Flores. 'Health for All' – HfA – as the Flores project became known was finally up and running.

China did not seem at all keen to host the intrepid round the world rider, so upon entering eastern Russia, Simon turned his wheels towards the Road of Bones, a tough stretch of bad road and rutted tracks which winds its way through hundreds of miles of forested tundra towards the city of Magadan.

Days of fording rivers, hard riding, falling off and drying out a drowned bike were to follow. This is one of the toughest roads in the world and is only traversable through focus, determination and hard work. I've heard it said that his ride on the Road of Bones was to partly inspire Ewan McGregor and Charley Boorman to travel the same route during their acclaimed and widely publicised 'Long Way Round' expedition.

This stretch of the run marked another release for Simon. It helped him to clarify his views on spirituality and made him realise that he wanted to return to the fold of Christianity. He also decided that the run would last for as long as it lasted. A return to his old life in Europe no longer held much significance or appeal for him.

His experiences on the road and the work he had put into setting up HfA in Flores, brought him to the realisation that a new social ambition was beckoning, one more worthy than simply going back to the world of motorcycle riders rights.

Upon reaching Magadan, he communicated his final resignation to FEMA in a long email which outlined his enthusiasm and hopes for global healthcare logistics. Then he flew to Alaska, with the Overlander following in a crate.

Simon touched the minds and hearts of many individuals as he evangelised both about Motorcycle Outreach and also his rebirth into Christianity. One of the first things he did on entering the US was to have himself baptised. His journey round the world had firmly become, for him, a journey to Christ.

America consumed well over a year of his time. He toured extensively, raising funds through his presentations and gaining the support of many individuals and motorcycling clubs and organisations. Indeed, most of the money he was to gather was raised in the United States.

Talking to old friends at the American Motorcyclists Association led to support for setting up a new legal entity for fundraising. 'Motorcycle Outreach' was incorporated under American law as a charitable corporation.

He also made two trips back to the UK for family reasons. Very few people knew about these quiet visits, but in addition to allowing those closest to him to have some time with him, they also allowed extensions to his three month US tourist visas.

But his travels around the Land of the Free had to come to an end at some point. Having finally outstayed his welcome in the USA, Simon headed south and across the Mexico border.

The journey continued to be focussed almost entirely on the aims of Motorcycle Outreach; to raise money for Flores and also to introduce the TRM system elsewhere. South America revealed countries and communities which were crying out for a basic system of healthcare delivery. Contacts were made, projects discussed, business plans developed, particularly in Argentina and Chile. Some like Pilotos Solidarios, a project in Argentina, was to operate for some years.

His arrival in Tierra Del Fuego at the end of 2003 became a celebration. He enjoyed himself with a large number of overland riders who had congregated from all over the world to take part in the unique 'overlander' New Year celebrations. An impromptu session of off-road bike racing ensued in the forest of this remote southern region and a memorable party left sore heads. A fitting end to the Americas as Simon prepared for the jump to South Africa.

Simon kept in touch with me in a sporadic way throughout his journey, always though personal emails. I kept him up to date with developments back in the UK and told him about changes to my life: my move to London; my new relationship in 2002 with Barbara Alam and then our engagement; work with the industry and so on.

Simon's work for Flores and his enthusiasm for Motorcycle Outreach had also affected me. I offered to help if I could when he finally reached the UK and the end of his run. He sent me several documents and a business plan for comment.

He also offered me kind and thoughtful advice on more personal matters, or on things which were bothering me. Strange to be trusting a guy on a motorcycle half way around the world with some of one's deeper thoughts. But Simon had a manner and a clarity of vision and purpose which made such emails appropriate. His emails always brought a measure of peace and tranquillity.

In Africa, Simon headed up the eastern side of the continent. He seemed to be more relaxed and, although still focused on his mission, he took the time to enjoy himself as a more conventional tourist. Diving in Zanzibar and a climb of Kilimanjaro featured in a schedule of motorcycle touring. This brought envy and desire to the readers of his still regular email updates and press releases.

On reaching Zimbabwe, Simon visited the Riders for Health Academy and as Barry Coleman at Riders put it, "finally realised what motorcycle transport resource management was really all about and how it worked". The visit was positive and sparked another series of emails and exchanges with both HfA on Flores and with those of us on his email list. He found further heart in what he was doing and pressed on more determined than ever to make his Motorcycle Outreach idea work.

Tougher times were ahead, with the crossing of several danger zones in Central Africa. Risky moments and non-existent roads across mountains and through jungles became standard and sometimes terrifying fare.

But after making it through to Nigeria, local conditions started to improve. Threats receded and heading northwards he entered Burkina Faso. He started to think about the impending end of his long journey around the world – his spiritual rebirth and how to bring his ambitions for Motorcycle Outreach to life.

He continued west and entered Mali.

PART TWO:
Capturing the Overland Spirit

Morocco, July 2000

The autoroute ride was evolving into a computer game. I glanced idly at my arms. They seemed to belong to someone else. A feeling of disembodiment flowed through me as I returned my gaze to the blacktop stretching to the horizon. It occurred to me that a quick flick of my elbows to see if they really were part of my arms could be in order. I glanced at the speedometer and saw that I was still holding the high speed that I'd settled down to an hour earlier.

The road continued to flash past under my wheels. 'Bordeaux 90km' read the quickly glimpsed road sign. I looked at my arms again. No, they belong to someone else, surely... another road sign flew past as the feeling of relaxed disembodiment settled into my mind, hypnotised by the road.

A quick head shake and reality returned. 'Jeez; gotta stop.' I thought with alarm. I slowed down as the sign for an 'Aire' appeared in the distance. Pulling in, I stopped the engine, tore off my helmet and threw myself onto the grass for a few seconds shut-eye.

Simon's departure had left a surprisingly large void in my life. There was an element of jealousy, but also a 'flat' feeling about my own life and the rather mundane course it was taking. Of course I had a good job which I enjoyed and I had already seen and done many things that some would argue that one could only dream about. But the void was still there. I needed to find something to fill it.

Dave had also been enthused by Simon's trip and wanted to

extend his own overlanding boundaries. We discussed by email all kinds of different ideas for short and long-term journeys, including a madcap three month around the world trip. Ideas were discussed, rejected, reborn and rejected again, but gradually the common view emerged that a short trip to North Africa would be a good way to dip our toes into more 'serious' overlanding.

Morocco seemed like a good place to start. A fair few people had already ridden a motorcycle there, but it was still far enough off the beaten track at that time for it to be an interesting and fulfilling personal challenge. Everything we read about the place enthused us; gorgeous scenery, passable roads. A safe and pleasant place to visit – and within easy distance of Europe for a two to three week overland holiday.

Dave, who now lived in Stuttgart, planned to ride down to Ceuta in Spanish Morocco with Anna, where it was agreed that Heather and I would join them. The pair of them also wanted to include some round-Europe touring.

My main issue was what to ride. All I had in the 'stable' was the old Bonneville and the by now fairly tired K100 BMW. It had been presented to me when I left MAG in what the chairman had jokingly called a 'plastic handshake'. Good as it was, it had turned into a bit of an untidy 'nail' and had very high mileage. An identical bike that had been in Simon's keeping had a broken gearbox, though this was probably as much down to Simon's 'enthusiastic' riding style than anything else.

After some calls to industry contacts, Triumph stepped in, offering to lend me a Sprint ST, a large capacity sports touring triple cylinder. The Sprint looked capable of eating more miles in one day than we were planning to ride in two weeks. I was extremely grateful for the loan as it made the trip possible for Heather and me.

The bike came with plastic panniers, which were a boon, but motorcycling self-sufficiency requires more than just a pair of weekend-away panniers. More robust luggage was clearly called for, but we settled instead for extra saddlebags, bound to the bike with a nest of bungies. The whole arrangement was topped off by a tank bag. Hardly professional overland gear, but it did the job.

The itinerary allowed two and a half clear days to cross Europe and meet Dave at Ceuta. A harsh, fast and challenging ride, involving long hours in the saddle would maximise the number of days available to tour Morocco. I was happy that the bike would make it, but wondered if I, or indeed Heather, would cope with such a hectic pace. I tried not to think about the long miles that awaited us in France and Spain.

Travel to France was via ferry to Cherbourg. A fitful night's sleep in uncomfortable chairs was punctuated by the snoring and groaning of fellow passengers as we all tried to kid ourselves that the unforgiving ferry seats were in any way going to allow deep and refreshing slumber.

Tired and dishevelled, we disembarked very early the following morning. Low cloud hung over everything and all I wanted was to find some coffee – hardly an auspicious start.

Risking the game plan, it seemed a waste not to take a detour via the Normandy Invasion beaches. We rode past famous sites from 1944, marvelled at the dummy parachutist on the steeple in St Mere Eglise and photographed the remains of the famous 'Mulberry Harbour' littered around in the off shore surf. We also paused for a long hour at the United States Cemetery at Omaha Beach where each perfectly aligned grave stone marked the short life of a man who gave his life so that ours could be free. I wondered what they would make of what the modern world had done with their legacy.

Then we turned the Triumph southwards and focussed on the journey ahead.

*

NOTES FROM A CONTINENTAL DASH

The road calls and we fly. The wheels turn ever-faster offering the promise of unfolding scenery and new experiences. Towns and villages pass by, with the occasional stop for coffee or a bite to eat, taking fluids and shade under soaring trees. Then the road beckons and we're off again. The countryside gets softer, then harsher and dramatic, then softer again as whole regions flash behind us...

Later that day the autoroute is reached and, feeling that it finally has the chance to have its head, the Triumph eagerly picks up speed away from the Peage plaza, 100 horses of energy howling from three cylinders of finely engineered motion.

Finally we tire, speed becomes a computer game and fear creeps into the monotony. A short break evolves into much needed sleep. The westering sun casts lengthening shadows as once again the Triumph is unleashed to do its thing, as only it knows how to.

From Bordeaux, it's a long run through a flat and deeply forested area. We're running late and dusk is creeping forth. Tired and forcing ourselves on, my head is buzzing and I feel psychotic with fatigue. Strange concepts and ideas fill my head; reality has to be grasped before my mind makes me play stupid tricks with the bike.

Forest gives way to habitation, Biarritz and St Jean de Luz offer accommodation and rest so we turn off the highway, forty kilometres short of our target for the day but satisfied and needing beer food and sleep.

The next morning is cool with dark and brooding clouds offering the prospect of heavy rain.

We leave as the first heavy drops tumble from the sky. Entering Spain in a torrential downpour, we hide in the first service station to grab coffee and a bite.

"Nothing for it." I say; "Just gotta get on with it and see what happens; we need to be near Malaga by tonight".

My partner groans and wraps her scarf carefully around herself, trying to stuff damp fabric in any gaps in the neck of her jacket.

The road climbs through the Pyrenees, rain replaced by thick fog as the low clouds are breached. Still we climb as the Triumph urges itself towards the high mountain passes and the promise of better weather.

A climatic barrier is breached and, as we slow down for a break at the Miranda de Ebro service station, clouds swiftly vanish and the sun shines forth.

Burgos passes to starboard as the auto pista turns south to Madrid. The road flashes by under our wheels, time is spent counting kilometre posts as we urge ourselves ever onwards. Heat starts to build, as does the traffic as we approach the capital.

The motorway merges with several others as we take a fast dual carriageway through the capital. Homicidal drivers are kept at bay in our determination to escape to the south – our target, the Cordoba Autopista. Finding the correct route, we stop for fuel and contemplate the acres of shanties that lie alongside the road. Reminding us that even modern European countries have their sharp contrasts between rich and ultra-poor.

The heat is intense and uncomfortable. I start to realise that I'm wearing entirely the wrong gear. Black full-face helmet and black padded all-purpose motorcycle suit. With no alternatives, there's no choice. The Triumph continues to roar south.

My head is pounding, the road shimmers ahead, and I feel disembodied and anxious again. Time to get water and shade at a cool spot by a service station. Light traffic flashes by, car occupants insulated in air-conditioned luxury. Passengers glance absent-mindedly in our direction as their drivers take them to their destinations at breakneck speed.

Castilla La Mancha reaches out on a flat plain in all directions and acres of olive trees hang their branches limply in the heat. The headache is gone and the afternoon feels pleasant. Another cigarette to take advantage of more stolen moments to chill out and remove the road from my head.

Then we're off again. Mile after churning mile passes by and the flat land gives way to a dramatic mountainscape. The road traverses steep passes and twisting bends as the prairie-like terrain gives way to hilly peaks and deep valleys. Now it is cooler and we turn west for Cordoba, riding towards the sun, blinded by a penetrating glare, which hides the road ahead.

As we ride, we pray for twists and turns to take that burning orb away from our eyes. Only a few deviations give relief as the road continues westward.

Little by little, the glare gives way to the gentler sun of late afternoon. The numbered kilometre posts count down as Cordoba approaches.

We're behind schedule. We stop and consult the map. We're

not going to make it to anywhere near Malaga today and we're due to meet Dave in Ceuta by noon tomorrow. Heather spots a regional route that snakes southwards from Cordoba towards Malaga. Seems like a good option to us both, tired as we are. Regional routes mean a better chance to find a small town with a nice hotel or roadhouse.

The sun drops behind the hills as we start to enjoy the change of pace, winding our way along a single carriageway road after many hours of motorway thrashing. The cooling air adds to a sense of fulfilment and enjoyment.

With the light fading from the sky, Montemayor becomes our stopping point. Vineyards and olive groves surround this little agricultural community. A wisteria-draped hotel provides rest for the night. Huge black ants march across our luggage as we unload the bike. Food is enjoyed in rustic surroundings.

Four am. It's just getting light and there's a chance to grab our itinerary back. We head out on a cool and lonely road as workers head for the fields for their morning's labour.

A spectacular and enjoyable run through the morning air, the winding road taking us southwards through a rolling landscape and around small olive tree covered brown hills. A mountain range gradually appears ahead, the peaks gaining definition in the growing light as we get nearer.

We join the autopista again and head through the mountains and down towards Malaga. A stop for coffee, and to consult the map.

"Keep going like this and we'll make it just fine." I say.

The road falls from the mountains and traffic increases, as does the heat. Breaking out of the lower hills to join the Autopista de Costa De Sol heading west for Gibraltar, we stop only for fuel on a baking garage forecourt and then to buy a ferry ticket to Ceuta.

Marbella, Estepona. The tourist 'buck' is being sought by hungry developers and builders as huge building sites raise utilitarian concrete block resorts amid a chaos of traffic and fumes.

Fat bodies on beaches, crammed into resort hotels with zero atmosphere, offering nothing of the real Spain. Drunk parents and screaming kids; gangs of youths stuffing McDonalds and cheap lager, seeking the heat of Spain with the familiar comforts of England.

We pass swiftly on.

The Rock of Gibraltar is spied along the coast as we head towards Algeciras and the ferry. The road brings us into the ramshackle town, which serves the huge sea cargo and ferry port. We turn into the port without stopping and almost immediately, the European journey is over as we are directed into the waiting lines of cars for the catamaran crossing. It's noon. We've made it!

An hour later the stern of a catamaran sends shooting columns of water rearwards as its Rolls Royce gas turbines power us across the Straits of Gibraltar. Europe falls behind and we turn our heads eagerly towards Africa as the Spanish enclave of Ceuta emerges, becoming clearer in our view. The mighty Rif Mountains tower in the distance.

The catamaran slows as it manoeuvres into Ceuta port. We can already see Dave and Anna standing by Dave's Yamaha TDM850, waving as our transport nudges its way to the dockside. Then we're off, greeting our friends and riding the few hundred yards to the Hotel Africa.

"Only an hour late." grins Dave.

I slap him on the back. "An hour late at the end of a ride of more than 1,000 miles – me arse!" I say, "So where's the bar then?"

*

AFRICA VIRGINS

We explored the town. Ceuta has a lovely colonial atmosphere once away from the tangle of roads that lead from the port to the border with Morocco. Fortifications and moats lent a medieval atmosphere, only slightly disturbed by young people racing their jet skis along the moats. Old cathedral buildings jostled for space with modern shops and offices and local folk promenaded in the gentle heat of the afternoon sun.

Lunch on a promontory overlooking the Mediterranean was followed by beers in a Caribbean style beach bar. A further walk around town in the dusk was livened by groups of people conversing on park benches. Young lads with mopeds preened themselves as they chatted to groups of attractively dressed girls. Ceuta has a laid back independent style, which is engaging and leads to a view that there are plenty of worse places to live.

The following morning we braced ourselves for the new experience of Africa proper. Loading our bikes, my bird's nest of bungees contrasting with the neat metal luggage boxes on Dave's Yamaha, we joined a steadily moving queue of traffic to the border complex. This soon loomed ahead as we rode a few short miles round a small coast road, which headed towards mountains in the interior of the country.

A melee of vehicles and people slowed our progress as we neared customs; but Spanish border officials ignored us as we headed out into the short no-man's land towards the Moroccan border. Soon, large numbers of men in a colourful mixture of western and Arabic dress tried to gain our attention, waving sheets of paper at us. We soon discovered that the pieces of paper were an essential form that needed to be completed in order to process our bikes through the Moroccan formalities.

Not knowing that we could pick up the forms at the border itself, we took four of them from a gesticulating Arab in a long flowing black robe, the djellaba, who immediately assumed that he was now our 'guide' for the border crossing.

We stopped in a queue of traffic at the border. A confusing crowd of people and vehicles were milling around several tiny windows set in a long white building. Our guide explained that we had to work our way from window to window, with officials at each processing a different part of the Moroccan border formalities. It was clear that this would take some time.

Dave worked his way through a dense crowd of people and thrust our passports through the tiny window. He glanced in and saw a group of men in bits of uniform sitting around a table.

The one nearest the window was inspecting each passport in minute detail before passing it to his colleague next to him, who repeated the same laborious operation. A third man did exactly the same thing, if anything taking even more time to leaf through each page and analyse every entry. They all clearly enjoyed the power that they had. Finally, a fourth official took each passport and in one-finger hesitant style, laboriously entered details into an ancient computer before passing passports to a fifth guy, who after undertaking yet another long-winded inspection of the much scrutinised passport, stamped an entry visa and the unique ID number that every visitor to Morocco receives. This number lasts the lifetime of the passport.

If passports were sentient, ours would have been paranoid and gibbering by now.

Dave noted the towering pile of passports awaiting inspection and came back to us.

"This'll take some time." he said. "Let's sort out vehicle formalities."

This was done at the second small window. After negotiating another tightly packed crowd at the window, I handed over our vehicle documents, driving licences and the completed white forms. A small dark furrowed face, looking not unlike Yoda from Star Wars, glanced quickly through the bits of paper and said "You have no insurance, you get insurance and then come back."

I pointed to the insurance Green Cards.

"No." he said. "Morocco insurance needed."

This was confirmed by our 'guide' who'd been lurking about, hustling persistently. Finally, he made himself useful by taking me over to another small building, where two well-dressed Moroccans quoted a reasonable fee for two weeks insurance for both bikes. This paid, I headed back to the second window, where Yoda took our papers with a grunt and disappeared into the gloom of his office. Probably to scan them using 'The Force' or something, I mused.

We hung around among the stressed crowds of noisy people, waiting in the growing heat for something to happen. Both girls were sitting in the shade, keeping an eye on the bikes and looking bored. I smoked a cigarette while Dave consulted his guidebook, ate a chocolate bar and looked unfazed by the whole thing.

It was an new experience. The strange atmosphere of an unfamiliar border; sharing our time with the patient, the resigned and the angry, all railing against the unnecessary bureaucracy, delay and hassle from pumped-up officials at this busy major international border. Hustlers wandered around adding to the colour, confusion and stress. A strong smell of unwashed bodies hung in the air.

It was also slightly unsettling to hand over all our paperwork and passports without an indication of when we'd get them back. I had a weird feeling of nakedness. Our 'guide' grinned at us, revealing one or two broken and blackened teeth. "Only a few minutes," or "Half an hour perhaps" he commented from time to time.

Unhelpful and slightly annoying, when he seemed to have about as much clue as we did about how long things would take.

The number of people at the windows stayed fairly constant. Some got through quicker than others. Tourists, it seems, were the lowest of the low and had to wait while others took priority. We'd not been asked for, and were not, offering bribes but, after a while, we suspected that fast progress could only be assured by a few sweaty notes pressed into furtive palms.

An hour passed before we finally we heard "Meester Clench, Meester Frinch". Dave collected the passports, while I finally lost my patience and went to find out what was going on with our vehicle documents.

Having forced my way to through the competing press of people to the small window, it took some minutes to get the attention of Yoda. The wizened Jedi simply smiled, rummaged about on a desk covered in papers and handed a large pile of paper though the hole to me. He demanded the equivalent of about £20 per bike to pay for 'formalities'.

"You go now." he said with a grin. "Welcome to Maroc".

"And may the force be with you." I muttered under my breath.

I looked at what we've been given with interest. All our papers were there, including the all-important letter of transit that Triumph had provided to indicate that I had permission to ride a motorcycle registered in the factory's name rather than in mine.

In addition, there were other official looking documents in French and Arabic, covered in impressive looking stamps and what looked like two UK vehicle tax discs in Arabic. Closer examination revealed that our bikes had been temporarily imported and allotted registration numbers. We were told that we could ride with our regular number plates, but the 'tax disc' had to be displayed somewhere prominent.

We climbed aboard the bikes after tipping our 'guide'. Yep, the guy scored somewhere between five and eight on the hustle factor scale, but it couldn't be denied that he'd made life a little easier for us. The girls were stiff from sitting for so long and asked to stop again as soon as we were through. We headed towards the high barred gate where freedom beckoned from the other side. Two customs officials glanced at our luggage and opened the gate, waving us through with deadpan faces.

We headed out into Morocco feeling pleased that we'd negotiated a potentially difficult hurdle, but slightly annoyed at the two or three hours it had taken to do it.

There was a large open space of concrete beyond with another gate at the other side. We slowly rode past two untidy looking cops, who had almost comatose expressions on their faces and then we were free. Out into a chaotic scene of multitudinous beaten-up Mercedes taxis, clouds of dust and crowds of shabbily dressed people shouting and waving at us as we passed.

Women dressed in multiple layers of clothing sold food and water from dirty blankets on the ground, while dozens of semi smashed mopeds milled about with broken exhausts and belching clouds of blue and black smoke. The stench of unwashed humanity and dirty clothes was unbelievable and we were smacked in the face with unexpected culture shock in the shape of such desperate looking and filthy humanity.

Dozens of ancient yellow Mercedes taxis were parked in lines, awaiting customers. Dented, with broken lights and decorative drapes hanging in the interior, these old cars looked well past their sell-by date.

We rode carefully down the dusty road, mindful of debris and fearing a puncture and quickly found ourselves passing through a small town. Street traders were selling all manner of shabby and decaying goods from the front of rows of half built, or half-demolished, buildings. The dusty pavement merged with the broken road as we negotiated mules and carts, piles of rubbish and aimlessly wandering people.

Folks looked dull and dirty; torn shirts and hanging djellaba were the universal modes of dress. The stink of rubbish heaps combined with the smell of overripe fruit and stale bonfires. Buildings had broken doors, no windows and loose rubble piled against them.

The culture shock continued to assail. I knew that things could be bad in Morocco, but this bad? Would we have a week of hell, or did the country have more to offer?

Breaking free of the hellish town, we rode out into the more pleasing scenery of lush pasture and small fields. Small hut like dwellings replaced the broken down depression of our first Moroccan experience.

Mopeds dogged our wheels as we rode. Crazily ridden bikes, always two-up, kept up with us on the rutted and potholed road, the riders yelling at us to stop as they struggled to keep up. Some were waving trees of cannabis plants at us, others were shouting "Hey! Hey!" It was both unwelcome and intimidating. I hunched down in my saddle wanting them to go away and leave me alone.

Dave pulled into a modern looking service station. With relief, we saw the horde of moped riders continue up the road.

"Bloody hell." I said to Dave. "That was awful, let's hope it's not all like this."

Dave pursed his lips. "Arr. Hectic enough all right. Should get better now though."

The girls looked shell-shocked, but said they were OK.

We fuelled up, amazed at the dramatic plummet in prices, and drank water. Maps were consulted and we decided to head directly south through the Rif Mountains. They loomed in the distance, offering cool and pleasant riding.

The road was badly maintained, but fine to ride at a moderate cruising speed. We headed towards Tetouan, where the road branched west and south. It was a chance to chase away the shock of our unpleasant first experience of Morocco and for me to get back into my stride.

The countryside was captivating. Cultivated fields spread into the nearby foothills of the mountains. Traffic was light, though old Renault cars were regularly seen, badly driven and poorly maintained. I started to enjoy myself.

Tetouan approached. A city of white buildings and mosques followed the folds of the foothills. Pleasant to view from a distance, but appearing impoverished and dowdy as we approached. The outskirts of town were marked by tenement blocks inhabited by people who kicked around in the dusty paths which surrounded their dwellings. Our road seemed to be the only one with tarmac in the area. Dirt, disease, poverty and the absence of jobs hung in the air like a shadow. Not as bad as the first settlement we had seen, but still a sobering sight on Europe's doorstep.

The road passed around the eastern edge of town. Traffic filled the streets and we saw several of the smoke-belching semi-broken and heavily overloaded trucks that plied their trade right across the country, with tassels in their windows and colourful designs painted on their front and sides. Sometimes they had an old CD disc wired to the front grill.

The smell of open sewers filled the air as we passed through the suburbs. The busy highway filled with people and a fascinating kaleidoscope of poor, but often colourful, shops sold all manner of items at the roadside. Once again, people mingled with traffic and we slowed down to walking pace. A goat ran across my path.

We could now see further into the city, where grand but faded colonial buildings were glimpsed and the dome of a large decorated mosque loomed over the townscape, its huge dome reflecting the sun. This was more like it.

Breaking free of Tetouan, we headed down a minor road, which took us towards the mountains and the Berber town of Chefchaouen. We took a left turn at a junction where an unkempt, but intelligent looking, young traffic cop waved at us.

As the road started to rise, we passed more affluent plots of housing surrounded by walls and orchards of apple trees and the occasional olive tree – grown more for horticultural decoration than for their fruit it seemed.

Cool forests absorbed our attention as the peaks rose higher and the road climbed the sides of plunging valleys offering breath-taking views. As we traversed tight diesel soaked bends, the 'gas-oil'-dissolved tarmac added to the pleasant riding challenge. We stopped for a time where the road overlooked a long tree-filled chasm with miniature dwellings flanking a river far below. A truly lovely spot.

We dismounted and stretched lazily. It had been a long morning and after the stress of the Ceuta/Sebta border experience, some chill-out time was welcome. Dave took photographs while I sat on a bank and drank some water. Our partners also looked more relaxed and we enjoyed each other's company for a time.

The road climbed higher and the hot air became fresher and sharper. Chefchaouen was our planned destination for a late lunch. The town had been given a good write-up in the guidebook.

Bumping over ruts and avoiding potholes, we rode into town leaving a trail of dust behind us. There didn't seem to be an obvious place to stop, so we settled for a parking space on a large tree lined dirt roundabout. It didn't take long to be spied by local hustlers, who zeroed in on us as we removed our lids.

"You want to eat? I know restaurant, need souvenirs? I know everything, I help …" and so on; the soon to be familiar opening mantra of the Moroccan hustler.

Doing our best to ignore pitches from these characters and other inquisitive enquiries, we dived into a maze of alleys that climbed towards the densely packed central 'Medina' area of town. We had no idea of the geometry or geography of this place, but marvelled instead at blue painted medieval houses, with small open windows offering glimpses of cool dark interiors.

We kept an eye out for somewhere to eat and having been diverted into a restaurant with low tables, cushions and an 'Arabian Nights' flavour, we settled instead on a pavement café. Bread, water, tea and tagines were quickly brought.

It seemed a shame to move on. The town had a nice atmosphere, was reasonably cool and the guidebook laid out an image of great history. There seemed to be buckets of architectural and social delight in this ancient Berber stronghold.

However, the itinerary beckoned. Finding our bikes again, we headed south through the mountains.

PROMENADING IN OUEZZANE

An hour later and the Rif were behind us as we descended to a fertile and cultivated plain. The undulating and potholed road ran ahead through a rolling landscape. Our destination was Ouezzane, a market town between Chefchaouan and Meknes. According to the book, an evening could be spent relaxing at one of the few guesthouses on offer. (It has since grown in size to become a very large town).

We arrived late in the afternoon and were immediately surrounded by much more persistent hustling than we'd experienced so far. The girls looked intimidated and stood silently by the bikes. However, the attention of the waving, jabbering throng was clearly focussed on Dave and me. This was our first experience of the way that women were treated in Morocco. Females were largely ignored by most men, often rudely so.

We had discussed the hustler issue before arriving in Morocco. Both Dave and Anna favoured not paying anyone for anything in the way of 'guide' services – their theory being that such payments and bribes for other services merely perpetuated certain aspects of poverty and developing-world oppression. Laudable views certainly, but as we were now discovering, nowhere near the reality of dealing with situations on the ground.

The group of hustlers were simply not going to give up, so after a brief discussion, Dave and I settled on a likely looking chap and asked him to find us a hotel. Anna pursed her lips disapprovingly but, as if by magic, the crowd of young male parasites vanished once it was clear that we'd finally engaged a 'guide'.

The hotel looked uninspiring from the outside. Merely a large ancient wooden door in a dirty rendered wall. But as we entered the tardis-like 'Pension' (as it more accurately was), we could see it expanded far to the rear. Further investigation led to the discovery of a number of clean cool rooms.

The foyer looked a likely spot to park the bikes. The ancient and toothless proprietor had no objections after our security concerns were explained to him by Anna, the most competent French speaker in our group.

Dave tried to ride his bike in but was thwarted by the high door ledge. I didn't bother having a go; if his TDM850 couldn't make it in, I was certain that the Sprint stood no chance.

A conversation with our guide resulted in another young chap appearing, along with an offer to watch the bikes for us. We weren't experienced enough to know if he could be trusted but, choices being what they were; we parked the bikes on the large town square, festooned them with locks and left them under the grinning and watchful eye of our newly appointed guard.

Ouezzane was not a mainstream tourist spot. No dispensation was given to Western frailties and there was little choice but to become familiar with local Arab tastes. Our evening meal was taken at a small street barbeque, the seemingly ubiquitous lamb kebab 'brochette' cooked to order and presented in fresh and tasty bread. Lovely.

We hung around a café for a while, amusing ourselves by seeing who could stomach the acquired taste of the strong, sweet mint tea – a common African beverage. Dave and Anna stuck at it staunchly, expressing over-emphasised satisfaction with every slurp (in fairness to them both, they eventually did acquire a taste for the stuff). Heather also expressed satisfaction. Although I felt that the strong sour tea probably made a pleasant change from time to time, I figured that one cup a day was more than enough.

While the others ordered more tea, I tried a café latte and discovered that Moroccan-prepared coffee in tall glasses is possibly the best in the world.

Later that evening, we promenaded with the locals. After nightfall, half the town seemed to emerge to wander the square and converse. Groups of women stood, chatting and laughing among themselves. Those who were veiled or dressed in sober Muslim garb mingled with other women who were dressed in surprisingly liberal, if modest, western style and sported fashionable hairstyles. I wondered what the more conservative of the menfolk made of this. Sometimes two women wandered along talking and holding hands, one veiled the other a picture of western casual style that could be seen on any European high street.

Men also wandered together, or held court in small groups.

Most were cloaked in djellabas, some with large pointed hoods. It seemed normal for men to hold hands as they walked, conversed and smoked.

It was a friendly relaxed atmosphere. Children ran around and played under the eye of their socialising elders. Teenage boys flitted in and out on battered bicycles with laughter and the occasional shout.

We felt quite relaxed ourselves. Buying some bottles of Coke, we sat on a low wall surrounding the square and whiled away the time talking. We weren't being hustled now – perhaps there was an embargo at this time of the evening.

Some of the young men who had surrounded us earlier, spied us and came over to ask us more about ourselves. They seemed much more relaxed than they were earlier in the day. We were glad to oblige and soon had a group of people gathered around us asking about what we were doing in their town, telling us about their 'Brother in London' and so on, practising their English.

"Language is our escape." one said. "With languages we can help people, we can get job".

One or two knew three or four languages. Language, it seemed, was a passport to the outside world.

Later we wandered through the small Kasbah. Strolling up the path between old buildings, we looked at the few small stalls that were still open at the late hour. Most stallholders had packed up for the night and disappeared behind closed panelled doors. Anna pondered some jewellery and I looked inside the small opening behind the stall. It was lit by a single dim light bulb and there was nothing but a bedroll, a bottle of water, a small silver kettle, some glasses and a few personal possessions. The marketers clearly lived where they worked. Unsurprising, given that daily sales probably barely sustained existence.

The following morning I awoke full of energy and took a walk around the sunlit town drinking in the fresh air of the early hour. The sharp light of the early morning cast long shadows. A few people were already up and about and I stood watching some scaffolders building a precarious platform up the side of a house with long slim logs and yards of rope.

Bundles of rags in various quiet corners of the main square stirred to reveal prone figures that appeared to have nowhere else to sleep. A group of about four women were going from person to homeless person with jars of water and fresh bread, perhaps a form of local welfare to ensure that the most desperately poor at least see one friendly face each day. The sense of community in this small town was strong indeed.

I joined Dave and the girls who were sitting outside on the hotel's rooftop veranda having ordered breakfast. Breads, oranges and coffee arrived – all very civilised. We gazed over the square as it came to life as the sun rose higher into the sky.

Less civilised were the ablutions. The dirty shower trickled lukewarm water and the 'hole in the ground' toilet cubicles had dried excrement smeared on the walls from those who had chosen to clean their left hands on the walls rather than use the bucket of water which is often left for this purpose.

Our motorcycle guardian was as good as his word and cheerfully greeted us as we hauled our luggage out to untouched motorcycles. A few dirham coins and he strode away whistling happily.

*

VOLUBILIS AND VOLATILITY

We set off through the rolling landscape and rode along tree lined undulating roads. Passing donkey carts and the odd tractor, the traffic was generally light, but the cars and trucks that were encountered were driven recklessly along the narrow main road. We stopped for a quick brew and a snack of bread and tinned sardines, using Dave's aluminium boxes as a table. It was pleasantly cool under the trees and, every so often, a farm worker ambled by with a soft greeting.

The landscape flattened out for a while and we continued to head south. Huge prairie like fields now dominated as more organised agriculture took over. Trees became a rare sight and as the miles passed more mountainous terrain rose in the distance.

Our plan was to visit the Roman ruins at Volubilis, a UNESCO world heritage site, and then head onwards towards Meknes. But our dawdling riding style meant that it was well after noon before we saw the ruins. They were impressive indeed. What seemed to be a large ruined town, with numerous columns and arches, appeared around a bend ahead of us. We approached along a rolling sun kissed plain, now partially filled with Olive trees.

A sign indicated that the Hotel Volubilis was keen to have our custom and a quick conversation ensued.

"These ruins need to be appreciated properly." said Dave.

"That means a rushed ride quite late in the day to Meknes." added Heather.

"OK, then let's check this hotel out, spend a good amount of time at the ruins and relax for the rest of the day." I suggested.

The hotel looked promising, but as we rode up the drive it quickly became apparent that it wasn't going to be cheap. There was some vexed debate, particularly from Dave and Anna before we decided to check in. Not cheap, bloody expensive actually, but the views from our rooms across Volubilis and the rolling countryside beyond were to die for.

Leaving our gear we trudged down a track to a slender and striking Roman arch though which we saw the layout of the ruins themselves.

The main buildings in Volubilis date from the second and third centuries and are among the best-preserved ruins in Africa. One would probably need to go to Leptis Magna in Libya to see a better town complex. A broad avenue led us past townhouses and public buildings, the layout of each very clear to see. Many walls still stood to head height or above and columns of different designs pointed well-preserved fingers into the summer sky.

We learned that the city was inhabited until as recently as the 18th century when it was plundered for material to build Moulay Ismail's palaces in Meknes. Enough remained though to give a good impression of life in a Roman town.

We wandered entranced through the ruins site and stopped for some water and a quick snack by a well preserved 'forum' style building in the centre of the Roman town. A Stork flew by making small noises. We followed it with our eyes until it landed on top of a tall column, which was crowned with a mess of matted twigs.

Dave took photographs and I wandered away from the others to explore some former dwellings where only low walls had survived.

Within these I discovered breath-taking gems; complete floor mosaics, open to the elements and unfenced. Invaluable artefacts that anyone could wander across, or sit down upon to eat snacks, drink, or pass the time of day. The others joined me and gazed at the beautiful and well-preserved designs in silence.

The occasional guide wandered through the ruins. They didn't hustle us at all and for a few pennies were glad to explain some of the history of the place to Dave and Anna. I also noticed the odd person, with a goat or two, who lazily followed their charges as they sniffed around the ruins.

Another Stork winged by, this time with a loud croak.

We wandered back to the hotel as the sun started to set. Heather and Anna repaired to the rooms to spend some time relaxing, so Dave and I headed for the bar and the first beer since we entered the country.

"Odd." said Dave. "This is the first time that I've felt relaxed for days and it ain't just the beer."

I knew what he meant. The trip was embedding good memories into my consciousness, but the overall atmosphere between us four was a little strained at times. The relaxed and mind-melded approach that Dave and I usually adopted on trips was strangely absent.

Travelling with our partners took something of our usual banter away as personal responsibilities became more pressing, but in addition I was starting feel pressurised and slightly on edge about some of the views of that Anna held. She tended to have some sort of 'pity the poor oppressed' opinion about most things in Morocco. I respected her general position, but was starting to tire of the implied anti-Western invective that sometimes crept in. There was also the issue of Heather's enjoyment of the trip because of this. She wasn't saying much, but had mentioned her concern about Anna's views when out of earshot of the others.

Dave wasn't saying a lot and I was, as usual, talking too much to mask the tension that I felt.

My hopes of a happy travelling foursome were fast disappearing. It wasn't that we were starting to fall out in a big fashion, but these twenty minutes or so of quietly tension-free time with Dave contrasted starkly with the overall atmosphere that was starting to develop on the trip.

The girls joined us and we sat down to dinner in a large empty restaurant lined with silk hangings. No one else seemed to be at the hotel, so we relaxed in the opulent surroundings while trying to make sense of the menu.

It was difficult, as always, to banish my paranoid caution about most of the menu on offer and I settled for grilled mutton chops and various garnishes. Dave and Heather chose the same, while Anna picked something vegetarian.

Explaining our choices to the extremely angular-faced waiter was a challenge, given our absence of French and his seeming very dark mood. He glared at me with thinly veiled contempt as I strangled the French language and pointed vaguely at the menu. Anna mercifully came to the rescue with her better command of the colonial tongue.

Having taken our order, he wandered off with a superior air, casting a look of serial killer hatred back over his shoulder at me.

"You wanna watch him mate." grinned Dave "He'll be in your room with a long curved knife later, you wait and see."

I suppressed a smirk, Heather glared at Dave and Anna added a few words about rich Westerners turning Moroccans into an oppressed serving class. Heather sighed.

Dave and I glanced at each other and buried our heads in our beer.

Although the flesh was barely cooked, it wasn't a bad meal. We took several slow nightcaps on the balcony which overlooked the ruins. These were haunting in the moonlight. And then to bed for satisfied sleep and peculiar dreams of Bacchanalian Roman parties. We didn't get a midnight visit from our Berber waiter, who was much more cheerful the following day and told us something about his work at the hotel – another wrong first impression banished.

Sunrise swept across our luxurious room from the balcony and the early morning view of Volubilis and the rolling fertile plain beyond made me gasp. Low sunlight shone across the undulating plain, casting soft shadows and a golden light, which contrasted with the soft blue tints of the hazy hills beyond. The ruins stood out in starkly lit relief. It was an early morning vision that filled my soul with peace, beauty, and the urge to go no further, but instead become absorbed in the sheer loveliness of it all for a few days.

Dave had again walked the ruins during first light and felt the same.

But our motorcycles awaited and, with regret, we turned our wheels southwards once again.

Not for long though. Seeking some coffee at the less than exorbitant rate charged by Hotel Volubilis, we took the turn off to Moulay Idris a few short miles later. The ancient town's white buildings hugged the slopes of the curving and ever steeper foothills that rose from the plain.

Moulay Idris, a historic and spiritual town, was closed until recent years to westerners. Even in the year 2000, it wasn't easily possible for Westerners to stay there overnight. They say that it's an alternative place to do the Haj – the spiritual pilgrimage of the Muslim faith – the more usual destination being Mecca.

We rode into a town where time had stood still. White buildings climbed the hillsides away from the mosque and medina. A large square surrounded by arched walls, where traders plied their wares, provided a focal point.

Djellaba frocked men and veiled women went about their daily business in large and busy numbers as we slowly rode to the centre of town, feeling like unwelcome crusaders on our steel and plastic horses.

The usual hustlers seemed absent, but people were friendly and as we pulled up to a pavement café, the owner waved and motioned us to sit at the plastic tables outside his little restaurant.

Sitting down we drank in the medieval atmosphere of the white painted higgledy-piggledy buildings that radiated away and upwards from the centre of town. A donkey harnessed to a cart, which seemed to be little more than a car axle with a plank of wood on top, greeted us with a loud 'ee-orr'. The view back down towards the plain was outstanding in the mid-morning sun, which for once wasn't glaring in our faces.

Three mint teas and a coffee for me and we conversed in a relaxed fashion. Dave and I pored over the map and consulted the guidebook while the girls occupied themselves with conversation about the world going by on the street.

More tea and coffee. I paid the man, leaving a few dirhams on the table as a tip.

"You know that your tips keep these people in poverty." said Anna, fixing me with a glare that had instantaneously replaced her placid gaze of a moment before.

I bit.

"Really, so how does that work?" I asked caustically, though already knowing Anna's answer.

"Tips provide an excuse for employers to pay low wages and as tips can't possibly make up a decent wage, the poorest get poorer."

I pondered this for a second. The argument wasn't put in the best way, but Anna had a point. The same thing occurs in the Western world, often to the detriment of poorly paid workers. The problem was that all these theories about exploitation and equality and other comments from Anna, implying that we rich exploiters from the West should wash our racial guilt in the waters of empathic denial of personal comforts, were starting to get on my nerves."

"Yeah?" I replied. "Well you try telling that chap over there that you're not going to give him a tip because if we do, he will have been exploited by us mean nasty imperialists from Northern Europe. I'm sure that he'll be incredibly grateful that we've left him out of pocket after drinking coffee and tea that cost us the equivalent of about five UK Pence.

"The problem with you Anna" I fumed "is that you're all trendy liberal theories and ideals, but you fail to appreciate what the real deal is for these people. However unfair the low wage practices are in these parts, tokenistic idealism from us isn't gonna change a thing. People here will just think that we're a mean bunch of arseholes if we refuse to give tips. They'll be the ones that are out of pocket on this day, in the here and now of the real world."

Mistake. A row ensued between Anna and me with Dave looking embarrassed and Heather startled. It wasn't that Anna was wrong, but after a few days of her philosophising, I'd had enough.

The dispute finally fizzled out in a truce. Although we disagreed over the day-to-day practice of tipping in developing countries, we were both in agreement about the fundamental problems that affected these places.

I tend towards the view that one doesn't have to live, breathe, eat and sleep like the locals in order to appreciate their problems and form reasoned opinions. Anna and to a lesser extent Dave, took a more rustic view of travel.

I expect that all of us were right in our own way.

The row didn't prove fatal, but it certainly changed the nature of the relationships within our group. It seemed clear that meaningful conversation about complex social issues and our feelings about these were to be avoided at all costs and I felt that I was treading on eggshells with Anna for the rest of the time that we were together.

Having emerged from this exhausting episode we paid for our drinks, left a (small) tip and clambered aboard our steeds for the continuing journey.

Leaving Moulay Idris, we headed out on the main road towards Meknes. A route that curved around the base of hills that fringed the broad plain, passed olive groves and continued through ever more rocky terrain. The weather grew warmer as we rode the last few miles to the Imperial City, where we intended to spend the afternoon looking at the reputedly huge medina that graced the old town.

*

CHICKEN SHARPENING

The terrain became uneven as we approached the city, with smallholdings occupying various bits of rough partitioned land. These steadily became more densely packed, merging into ad hoc suburbs. The road into town went steeply uphill around some bends and through an area of smart townhouses. Then we suddenly found ourselves among the fast driven chaos of urban traffic and wondered where to go next.

We stopped in a busy square with a main road running through it, to see if any of our maps would help. They didn't.

"Let's ask in that petrol station." suggested Frenchie, motioning to the other side of the square.

As Dave asked for directions in a surprisingly modern looking Elf station, I became conscious of a building feeling of personal distress. Weakness and anxiety was spilling over me and I felt knackered and disorientated. I got myself out of the sun and sat under a sheltered wall wondering what was going on.

"Good news." said Dave. "There's a hotel just over there." He waved towards the blindingly obvious hotel sign. "How did we miss that one?" I asked. "Can you go over and check it out Dave? For some reason I feel like crap."

As Dave wandered off, Heather came over looking concerned.

"You OK?" she said anxiously. "Not too sure…" I replied weakly. "…feel pretty rough, you got some water?"

She handed over a nearly full bottle that had been warmed to the temperature of passably hot tea in the fierce sun.

"How much water have you drunk today?" she asked.

"Probably not enough." I replied and took several long swallows of the disgusting tasting hot water. Sidi-Ali, a popular mineral water in the area, didn't taste too bad cold, but taken hot, it was sour and made me shudder as I forced it down my throat.

Dave reappeared. "Good news, it's cheap and clean, plus there's a locked area for the bikes."

I stumbled weakly to my feet wondering why this feeling of nauseous lassitude had taken me over. With some effort, I got on the bike and rode the 100 yards or so to the hotel.

The lobby was air-conditioned and as I walked in, the cool blast seemed to have about the same effect as water on a wilting flower. I almost immediately felt bright and alert, though still a little weak.

We checked into our modest rooms, sparsely furnished, but comfortable. Ours had a television at head height, just the kind of thing to bump into at the dead of night.

We went back to the lobby to consider our moves for the afternoon. Long cool glasses of mineral water in the air-conditioned area restored me to full health, though still with the underlying sense of internal tension that I had felt since entering the country.

"I reckon that you had a light touch of heat exhaustion." said Heather "Better take it easy in the direct sun and drink plenty."

Good advice that later on in the journey I deeply regretted not following to the letter.

We took a walk over to the Medina, one of the most renowned in the Kingdom. It was a fair step from the hotel along the side of a busy main road. We noticed that Meknes seemed to comprise two distinct central areas; an older traditional Moroccan city, with a modern administrative district of concrete block buildings added later on its eastern side.

The road we were following joined the two halves of the city across a dry riverbed or 'Oued' as they are known in these parts.

The old city lay behind a huge and ancient wall of tremendous width and as we walked through impressive gates, the noise of road traffic outside diminished, allowing conversation to return to normal levels.

Following a narrower road, which curved inside the old wall, we walked along a street lined with various shops. Their owners vied for our attention as we strolled past each one. All were very grubby, but vibrant, colourful and interesting, selling all manner of useful goods and knick-knacks.

Dave and Anna fancied something to drink, so we stopped in a likely looking juice bar where we took refreshment while chatting to the rotund and cheerful owner. Mohammed scraped a living selling mainly orange juice and bars of chocolate to locals and tourists alike.

Mohammed's English was good and he seemed happy to sit with us and talk, given that trade wasn't exactly bustling that afternoon. He was also happy to raid my pack of cigarettes on a regular basis.

Travellers are advised to avoid two subjects when talking to locals in strange countries, particularly Muslim ones: religion and politics. Mohammed seemed to want to discuss both in some depth. He revealed that he used to be a journalist and teacher, but after a series of crackdowns on press freedom by the Government of the old King, Hassan II, he had decided that life would be much safer if he went into dealing in citrus fruits rather than writing comment columns. He had fallen foul of the administration on more than one occasion and felt that his luck would have soon run out if he'd stayed with his newspaper. "No one wants to spend time in a Moroccan prison" he said.

"Freedoms here are poor, no opportunities to criticise – a dangerous game. Mind you," he went on "we have new King now, Mohammed VI. He talks a better word than his father. Will he be better? Time will tell. I think selling juice is a safer game – at least for now."

He shrugged his shoulders and turned again to fill up his juicer with oranges. Another round of drinks; this time on the house.

We left his bar with regret and in a thoughtful frame of mind. Mohammed had been a good host and had given us much to think about. The Morocco we were experiencing was a country of beauty and friendly people. Filthy dirty at times, but in a strange way compelling. But that was our 'outsiders' experience. Who knows what lay underneath, what tensions, culture and politics dictated the direction of people's lives – sometimes against their will?

We turned through a tall arched gateway, which led through another hugely thick wall and found ourselves transported back through time as we entered the main part of the Medina.

Here narrow lanes were lined with small shops and stalls of all kinds. The acquisitive could purchase everything from wooden boxes, to silver teapots, spices, paintings, shoes and carpets, a plethora of interesting products, sights, sounds and smells. Shopkeepers motioned us to enter and view their wares and, if we weren't careful, it was easy to be 'snared'.

Hustlers swarmed around like packs of angry wasps. "You come this way."; "Come to my shop."; "English! My brother is in London, do you know him?"; "I have bargain, much bargain."; "I can show you Medina and best prices, my brother has best shop." and so on, and on and on.

This continual irritation was in serious danger of spoiling our visit and we only managed to make progress by demonstrating a fixed determination to keep moving on.

For all this hassle, the Medina was enchanting. Narrow lanes led between high walls and ancient tall buildings, keeping the worst effects of the sun at bay. As the lanes meandered, more discoveries were made and I began to regret not bringing an articulated lorry to stock up on low priced, quality goods.

Aside from the hustlers, the crowds of people going about their business were huge. Lots of children also ran about, shouting or running errands for a few small bits of cash. From time to time, we'd see groups of them filling up battered mineral water bottles from public fountains.

Walls rose high on each side of the narrow lanes through the Medina. Sometimes the sun glared through to the ground, but often its harsh light was diffused by drapes that were hung high across the lanes. The contrast of light and dark, with the crowds of exotically dressed folk wandering through the dusty air was almost biblical.

Then we emerged from the other side of the Medina into a large square, which seemed to double as a bus station, the local Gare de Routier and a place for community gathering and conversation. Groups of people sat in lines on low walls that almost seemed to have been constructed for the purpose of sitting and conversing.

Anna spotted a large building to one side with high curved gables and several arched entrances. According to her guidebook this was the meat and produce market. We strolled over and entered through a low door, to find ourselves once again struggling through crowds.

The produce market was simply amazing. All kinds of fruit, vegetables, dried produce, spices and herbs were laid out with intricate care at each of the hundreds of stalls. Neatly stacked olives in perfect shape and geometry were on display. Cones of precious spices were another photogenic attraction and sacks of spices lay open with scoops ready for the customer to dip in and fill a bag. Everything was incredibly cheap, particularly the spices; which in the UK at that time would set us back the GDP of a small African country for a few grams.

Neat and orderly rows of carrots and other vegetables added to a kaleidoscope of colour and fresh smells.

Dave and Anna saw an opportunity to stock up on spices. So, as they entered discussions and bartered with stall holders, Heather and I wandered down the sloping stone floor towards the meat market.

We were expecting hanging carcases and bloody remains, but this place was something else. Sheep's heads were set in rows at one stall and all had the tops of their skulls removed to display the grey matter inside. Bloodied butchers were hard at work carving up beasts at the front of their stalls while bellowing and mooing from behind the scenes gave notice of yet another bout of slaughtering. The smell was simply horrendous, sweet and sickly, with the faint waft of decay from time to time. Blood flowed across the floor. We both started to feel a little green.

The last straw was the row of chicken stalls at the far end of the market. Each had cages packed full of protesting poultry and at the front of stalls, what appeared to be an enormous pencil sharpener.

Curiosity about these strange devices was quickly set aside with revulsion when we observed an old woman, standing hunched in a long black and veiled outfit, completing the purchase of a hapless looking skinny bird. The wiry stallholder nodded to the woman as they completed their deal and without emotion scooped the bird up by the legs and thrust it squawking head first into the 'pencil sharpener'. Immediately a terrible grinding and ripping noise started and the squawking was cut short in a shower of bloody feathers. Blood started to run out of the base of the machine as we continued to stare with fixated horror.

A few seconds later and the chicken was removed; plucked and almost ready for the oven, headless and featherless. All that was needed was some gutting and stuffing.

Heather went white and I must have looked the same as we stumbled away from this fascinatingly dreadful scene. The pair of us repaired to the fruit market where the sights and smells were less likely to turn our soft Westerners stomachs.

"I'm never gonna eat chicken again." said Heather weakly.

Having found our companions, we took a long walk down some

side streets away from the main markets and soon found ourselves on a street full of motorcycle repair businesses. This was an excellent antidote to chicken sharpening and we marvelled at this industrious street of small workshops labouring away to keep hundreds of mopeds and step-thrus farting and whizzing around Meknes' streets. Every shop was busy, with quick repairs undertaken with the customer standing by, through to major rebuild jobs. Ancient parts were carefully cleaned, renovated and used again. No waste here.

New spare parts were rare and a careful rebuild of engines, with the ingenious repair of broken parts, was the order of things. Mechanics worked on the street, or in dark dingy shops, covered in a layer of oil and grease that looked as though it was a permanent addition to their bodies.

There was lots of cheery gesticulating and conversation as we asked them about their work. Heath Robinson had nothing on these guys. With the number of people arriving with a two-wheeled problem to fix at the various workshops, it was clear that business was brisk. I loved the place.

Walking can be a tiring business and when this is combined with the need to keep hustlers at bay, we eventually started to flag. We agreed that it would be a good idea to seek refreshment. The four of us soon found ourselves in a typical pavement café. We sat on an upstairs floor with a balcony that looked over rows of people with pots of mint tea. They were sat in chairs arranged so that the clientele could look out to the bustling street scene while they took refreshment, conversed and smoked.

"Ah, they do food." said Dave. "Chicken Tagine all round then?"

Heather gave 'yer man' an evil look. "Lamb Tagine for me I think."

Soon all four of us were tucking into a quite exceptional meal, with fresh bread washed down with Coke. The sauce was excellent as were the vegetables but as a sign of the poor status of the establishment, the meat was not much more than a greasy knuckle in the middle of the dish, with a few shreds of flesh and fat. What was there served to provide flavour to the rest of the dish, which was otherwise excellent.

Another stroll through the Medina as dusk settled saw Dave seriously contemplating some pointed Berber slippers and me thinking about getting some sleep. But it was quite late when we slowly walked back to our hotel, pausing only to buy some bottles of water for the morning.

*

BERBERS BELLY

Poor quality loud speakers on numerous mosque minarets woke me with their religious wailing. This was a sound that was fast becoming familiar and strangely welcome to me.

Struggling to life, I knew that something was wrong and a visit to the latrine soon confirmed that I'd been gripped by a dose of Berbers Belly. Well, I've got Imodium if it doesn't clear up, I thought to myself as I struggled into my riding gear and went in search of breakfast.

The others were downstairs already tucking into fresh bread rolls and coffee. I took my place and downing some coffee unfurled my map.

"The countryside opens out a bit from here." I said, "but both the Middle Atlas and High Atlas mountains lie beyond. We could make Er-Rachidia if we push it out a bit – the town is just inside the Sahara as well."

"Stopping at Zaida for lunch could be a good plan." said Dave, concurring with my suggestion.

Soon we were on our way, bikes loaded and heading out through the fresh early morning light. This gave the city a far different feel, a sharper feel than the soft dusk of the previous evening.

The heat was quickly building; again, I cursed my inappropriate riding gear. I was glad that we had stocked up on water, but wondered how long it would last. Perhaps even at that early stage of the day, my brain wasn't focussing properly – clean bottled water could be bought from just about anywhere.

Our aim was simply to cover miles and, taking the road south, we passed through El-Hajeb where we were waved on at a police checkpoint. We marvelled at the half-constructed appearance of many houses which otherwise seemed densely inhabited. I learned later that a newly completed building attracted certain taxes, so it was common to leave the upper storey in a rough incomplete state – even though the rest of the dwelling was perfectly OK to inhabit.

Continuing south, we came to the picturesque town of Azrou, set in a pleasing location in the foothills of the Middle Atlas. A mixture of interesting shops and cafes crowded onto the major east/west/North/South road intersection in the centre of town.

Our route climbed out of town through a cool cedar forest and curved around rocky outcrops where Barbary apes could be spied looking out over the rocks at us. Glimpses of these engaging beasts could also be seen in the trees when we stopped for a moment. They were much skinnier than their well-fed counterparts on Gibraltar.

As the road climbed higher, we emerged from the trees and marvelled at the panorama opening up for us as the diesel-drenched road took us ever deeper into the Middle Atlas Mountains. Ranges of soft peaks marched into the distance and the road curved and swooped around high outcrops and into hot dips and valleys. Colours alternated between deep reds and soft yellow as the sun baked this high and ancient country, resembling as it did the backdrop to a biblical epic, or a scene from 'Lawrence'.

We didn't see many people, but the road was busy and care was required when negotiating curves in case a car or truck came careering around the corner on the wrong side of the road, a fairly common occurrence. Getting past diesel-spewing lorries took some care and attention as well. I often had to drift along on front of a lorry for some time, waiting for Dave to take his chance to overtake as well.

Near the centre of the beautiful Middle Atlas, we stopped at a roadside stall. A young Moroccan was looking after a large display of minerals and semi-precious stones, many of which were in a raw and uncut state. All were laid out untidily on his stall and the friendly owner was glad to explain the properties and origins of each stone.

For me though, a different experience was starting to play out.

Not long after stopping, I knew that the growing turmoil from within me was about to explode into open warfare. I grabbed a toilet roll that we had liberated from the hotel and dived behind some bushes.

Misery engulfed me. I could also feel the dreadful weakness and anxiety of the day before stealing over me once again. I slowly drank water and joined the others at the rock stall.

"Hey, this stuff is really cheap." said Heather. "I've bought a few nice ones for us." She showed me some strikingly beautiful minerals, which in my state of mind I wasn't fully able to appreciate properly.

"I'll pack them onto the bike." I said and looked around for somewhere to sit down.

The back of the stall was in the shade and a gentle cooling breeze stole over me as I lay down for a while. At one edge a 'hut' of sticks and cloth revealed where the rock man lived, tending his stall and making just a few dirham from passing trade. A poor existence set among some of the most dramatic views on the planet. The young stallholder came and sat beside me. He stared out at the incredible view without saying anything.

"Come on mate." said Dave. "Time to get going, only a few 'K's to Zaida and some lunch."

I popped an Imodium and got to my feet. "Excellent." I said, trying to bolster my own spirits, though not convincing myself.

The road now curved much more sharply and riding required a degree of concentration that denied full enjoyment of the rocky outcrops and trees of the Middle Atlas. Heather was free to enjoy the view and would occasionally exclaim when she saw a particularly dramatic scene.

The ride was enjoyable, but was now heading downhill towards a wide plain that separated the Middle and High Atlas. As we headed lower, the heat became stronger. Apart from a few quick stops for a drink, we pushed on through the flatter landscape and straighter road until Zaida appeared in the heat haze ahead.

The little market town appeared to double as a truck stop and dodging the badly driven battered and colourful lorries involved a few hair raising moments. The centre of town was full of roaring and manoeuvring vehicles. Drivers leaned out of windows to shout at each other and everything else. Smoke poured from exhausts, tempers frayed, dust rose in huge choking clouds to mix with the fumes and make us cough.

Weaving in and out of the vehicular chaos on the broken roads of the town, we parked outside one of a line of butchers-cum-roadside cafes. Dave ordered some brochette and I went to look for a toilet, settling down on the edge of a stinking pit behind one of the buildings to spend ten minutes groaning in discomfort.

The other three had taken a table and ordered some food. I eased myself into a chair and took a swig from a bottle of cold Coke. The canvas awning that we were sitting under gave a good view of the comings and goings on the street outside and enabled us to keep an eye on the bikes.

We shared space with two slaughtered and skinned sheep. One hung swinging slightly in the breeze just behind our table while swarms of flies buzzed about. The 'counter', if you could call it that, sported a large chopping board and several knives which bore the evidence of repeated sharpened over many years. The tableau was completed by the detritus of recent butchery, which was liberally scattered about for the flies to feast upon. A sheep's head lolled drunkenly on one side with its tongue stuck out of one side of its lifeless mouth.

"Grand spot." I muttered sarcastically to Dave. "You wanna poison us once and for all?"

"Stop moaning." he retorted. "If the meat I've ordered isn't cooked properly, we can always get it burned some more."

I sat back miserably. The 'dose' I'd picked up was getting worse and the Imodium I had taken was clearly not working. Frankly, the last thing I needed now was a filthy germ filled lunch in the stinking, noisy and fume filled cauldron of the sun that Zaida seemed to be.

Food arrived via a rotund Moroccan who had rather more hair that we had come to expect. With a flourish, he deposited the plates of cooked meat and bread on the table. It smelt gorgeous and was clearly cooked right through. The others tucked in with zeal, but I couldn't manage more than a few mouthfuls before feeling slightly sick. "Bugger" I thought and picked slowly at a flat loaf of the ubiquitous and delicious fresh bread that seemed to appear out of nowhere, each and every morning, everywhere in Morocco.

We left Zaida in a cloud of dust and the searing heat of the unforgiving sun. We rode a few miles of straight road as ahead of us the mighty High Atlas started to emerge from the haze. We stopped for a brief moment under some trees which spread their welcoming boughs across the road, offering a few minutes of much needed shade.

Dave fiddled with his bike and Anna went to stroke a donkey that stood quietly, partially covered with a blanket. Its head was drooped and it appeared to be suffering from both heat and mistreatment.

I viewed the scene uncomfortably. The poor treatment of animals was an aspect of Morocco, which was immediately apparent almost as soon as we'd entered the country. Skinny dogs and ill-treated cats ran free on the streets of every town and village, covered in sores, and sometimes limping.

The sight of animal cruelty or mistreatment always make my blood boil, but in a country which seemed to make an institution of this, what could one do? I had noted with pleasure, an article which celebrated a long established donkey and mule sanctuary that was somewhere in Morocco. But one sanctuary, the purpose of which was probably not well supported, or even understood by many in Moroccan society, was hardly going to change general attitudes to the beasts of burden. 'Domesticated' animals hardly seemed to exist here.

We left the poor beast to its lonely and miserable reverie and headed onwards again.

The road turned to the left to run alongside the foothills of the increasingly breath-taking range of mountains. Hues of gold and brown marked the rolling escarpments of the High Atlas as they rose in dramatic fashion from the lighter coloured scrubland floor of the valley. Small villages and the occasional patch of greenery huddled at the base of this endless range of behemoths, offering a welcome contrast to the eye and further emphasising the change from flat barrenness to the rising drama of soaring peaks.

The heat was becoming a serious issue for me. My black riding suit and black full-face helmet felt like mediaeval instruments of torture as the temperature built up inside. I began to feel not just anxious, but desperate. Every once in a while we'd stop for a drink and I tried to force down the vile Sidi-Ali against the protests of a body which was crying out for moisture, but at the same time wanting to reject what I was putting in. The sun relentlessly beat down and I started to feel like I wasn't really there any more, a sort of detached and vacant observer of events.

The ride helped take my mind from my deteriorating condition. After several miles of travel, passing ancient mud villages, with the occasional green tree and mosque, the road finally cut in towards the mountains and started to rise away from the plain.

Long sweeping curves and switchbacks marked our progress upwards. Gradually we climbed away from the flatter lands below and a view of light brown emptiness shrouded in heat haze opened up in the distance to our left.

We started to notice small piles or rocks, with a Coke bottle placed on top, every few yards. Stopping once to attempt rehydration, a young boy of about ten years old appeared from behind a rock nearby and eyed us up curiously.

"H'oca H'ola?" He asked. A "Non." from us made him try harder.

"Is there no escape from the hustlers?" I asked. "Dave laughed. "Not likely, I've heard that sometimes even in the deep desert, there'll always be a character behind a rock, or grain of sand, waiting to have yer."

Dave's levity bolstered me once again and after forcing more Sidi-Ali down and again sliding my sweating head into my full-face torture instrument, we continued our climb. (I gave up wearing full-face helmets after this trip).

Now, normally the rule is that the higher you climb, the cooler it gets. Not today. It must have been about two pm and the hottest part of the day in the hottest month of the year. Climbing into the High Atlas seemed to result in even higher temperatures for some reason. I yearned for escape from the beating sun and blazing heat

Such a shame that I allowed my thoughts to become consumed

by my own miserable feelings and worries about the heat – heat that I simply wasn't consuming enough water to counter. The scenery was stunning and I was in danger of missing all of it. The road was good, the mountains fantastic, the Triumph running like a dream and all I could think about was how ill I felt.

The High Atlas gave the impression of being not so much a single mountain range, but a collection of many ranges. Our climb finished in a high pass, which opened into a straight run through a rocky plain to another high pass and another plain. There were several of these and, in each of the flatter areas, we would see the occasional farm or small village. Occasionally a medieval fort could be spied far off.

Boys herded sheep or camels, with these sometimes sheltering against the shaded banks of dried Oueds. The sunlight created strong contrasts between the east facing cliffs and the areas of rock, which were exposed to the sun's glare, bringing a certain majesty to the imposing mountains.

Sometimes, in the distance, we would spot Berber encampments – their large black tents filling me with curiosity about these enigmatic folk.

Passing though Kerran-dou, we stopped briefly for a police checkpoint. Lazy and sweating cops idly checked our papers while I found a sheltered spot for yet another urgent call of nature.

Crazy thoughts filled my head as we set off once again; of cold rooms and cool drinks, of being anywhere but here. Crazy and desperate. I had to continue, but for how much longer? The road dipped down into another valley. We were through the main part of the Atlas now and glimpses ahead showed more mud settlements and a beautiful and truly ancient mosque rising from the centre of a small town. Mountains that were majestic a few miles back now seemed merely tall.

Then we saw a tunnel ahead and checking the map on my tank bag, I recognised the place as the 'Legionnaires Tunnel' – roughly blasted by the French in 1930 to open a route to the south and into the Sahara. Reaching the entrance, I stopped my bike in a small lay-by, threw off my jacket and stood in the shade trembling with exhaustion, sickness, dizziness and anxiety.

A cool breeze came from the tunnel and I revelled in the chill that blew against my body.

Goodness knows what the others thought of my strange frame of mind this day. Heather was quietly concerned and had reminded me to drink on several occasions while we travelled. Anna said nothing and Dave was as inscrutable as ever, trying to focus on enjoying his trip.

The tunnel was a good spot though and I enjoyed the cooler air while Dave scrambled down some rocks to get some photos of the river Ziz running far below. Some sheep were grazing alongside the water and starting to think a little more clearly, I mused on my lack of a decent lens to capture the idyllic scene below.

Across the river, the land was folded into amazing shapes of exposed sedimentary rock, with the individual folds casting small shadows which accentuated their profile.

I wandered into the tunnel deciding to walk the 200 yards or so through to see the view from the other side. Soon I observed two figures detach themselves from the tunnel wall and start walking towards me.

I figured that caution was wise and slowly wandered back to the bikes followed by the characters who, walking faster, would reach the tunnel entrance at about the same time as me. The others had spotted my followers, who as they drew nearer were recognisable as soldiers. Greetings were exchanged when they reached the bikes.

They didn't speak any English and it took a while for Anna to figure out that there was an army post on the other side of the tunnel, that it was a miserable and boring posting and that we were not allowed to stay in this spot any longer. After some friendly exchanges all round, they left us gathering our gear and preparing to depart.

We climbed aboard the bikes and headed slowly through the tunnel, passing the two soldiers. At the tunnel's exit, we acknowledged the waves from a few others who were sat on broken chairs outside a decrepit looking small barrack style building at the tunnel's exit.

We headed down a valley that led from the tunnel and the heat once again settled upon us like an oppressive blanket.

The road passed by numerous small settlements dotted along the riverbank and another grand mud mosque. Many of the low mud and corrugated iron habitations sported huge satellite dishes and air conditioning plants.

With the swift return of my terrible heat-exhausted symptoms, the idea of settling in a primitive hut, blasted by cool air and refreshed with sweet mint tea seemed extremely appealing.

Looking at the map, I could see that only a twisting run past a huge lake remained between us and our destination for the day. I pressed on, leading the way as usual, with head pounding, dry mouth and a vague feeling of disorientation and sickness.

The area of settlements petered out as the terrain became once again very rocky and stony. Then around another curve of the mountains and a huge vista of sand, rocks and shimmering sun opened up. We could see miles ahead into the bright yellow desert until sand merged with sky in a blinding glare. We had reached the edge of the Sahara, or more specifically the Hamada du Guir and Hamada du Draa areas of that vast desert.

A long straight road opened up. With a sense of elation at having reached the Desert, coupled with a feeling that enough was enough, I opened the throttle of the Sprint and roared down the road. The Triumph triple breathed freely for the first time in days.

Dave didn't try to keep up, and instead continued to amble along with Anna as Heather and I sped into the distance.

The bike surged forward like an unleashed horse, as the roadside sped around the lake. I was feeling just about all in, but this was an enjoyable blast so I kept the throttle open for several miles until in the distance the road curved around to the left for a last long straight ride into Er Rachidia.

After a few miles, we slowed down and pulled into a fuel station not far from the outside of town. Switching off the engine, we climbed off the bike and I headed into the shop looking for a cold drink.

The owner looked at us and nodded in a friendly way as though he had been expecting us all along. We sat at the table. Cold refreshing drinks arrived from a fridge as we waited for the others.

Soon all of us were sat with a second round of cold drinks discussing what to do next.

"I'm all in." I said. "Need rest… any ideas about where to stay?"

"We'll head for the town centre and cast about until we find something…" suggested Dave. "Does this petrol station have any petrol?" he said, motioning about him.

It didn't, so once again we set off, this time with Dave leading.

The town quickly rose from the desert floor, like a set from a Mad Max movie. Er Rachidia was clearly frontier territory; land use constraints weren't an issue and buildings were dotted about in random fashion. We found petrol at a station awash with spilt diesel and staffed by excitedly shouting black African attendants.

For me, the whole thing was gaining an air of unreality. I had reached the end of what I could offer that day. Sick, weak and anxious, I wanted a bed and rest.

A wide main street ran alongside an army garrison in the town. Some side streets led off and while I sat slumped on the bike on the verge of the main road, with my head on the fuel tank, Dave sped off to look for somewhere to stay.

Returning, he grinned and said that he'd found just the place. I summoned energy for a final effort – a 200-yard ride down a broken and rutted side road, full of run down shops and curious faces. We arrived at the steps of a tall guesthouse which was fronted by a Maison-du-The.

Dave and Heather checked in while I stood swaying with our luggage in the lobby. It was quietly taken from me by my companions and I slowly followed them up the stairs to our rooms. Heather and I slumped, faces down on the bed. We were both silent. My head was pounding and singing, I felt sick and disorientated. My body seemed to radiate heat and a glimpse in a mirror revealed that I was bright red. Things became vague for quite some time.

Heather roused me from my unpleasant reverie.

"I don't feel so good either, just been to the toilet. Do you reckon it was the tagine yesterday?"

The previous day seemed a world away and I struggled to collect my thoughts.

"Dunno… the other two are OK, maybe it was the uncooked lamb at Volubilis."

Silence fell again for a time, soon to be replaced by a loud wailing of a hysterical Imam played through a worn out stereo system at a shop next door.

After what seemed to be about 38 years, Dave appeared.

"I've found a secure place for the bikes." He said. "You both look dead rough. If it's any consolation, I've got the runs summat chronic as well. I'll be up in a bit, so we can figure out where to eat."

I groaned inwardly at the prospect of food and sank again into a head-pounding, half-conscious, existence. Then something occurred to me.

I reached over to the other side of a comatose Heather and picked up our guidebook. I remembered that there was a section on maladies and other medical issues and wondered if it would give any clue as to what the hell was wrong with me. Until now, all I knew was that I felt awful and being unfamiliar with African travel, was badly frightened by the prospect of being ill in the Sahara, far away from the medical comforts of Europe.

I leafed through the pages for few minutes and suddenly found myself reading all about, well, me. All the symptoms were there apart from the explosive and alarmingly frequent diarrhoea. Medium level heat exhaustion.

A wave of relief tinged with concern washed over me. Reading further it became apparent that another hour or so out in the sun and I would have been very seriously ill. As it was, I still felt dreadful, but now knew what to do about it.

When Dave reappeared, I asked him to fetch some salt and fresh water, plus salty biscuits. "Can't face dinner either. Just need a few things and plenty of rest I reckon."

"OK pal!" he replied brightly and set off with his peculiar shopping list.

I forced down what water that I could and encouraged Heather to drink. She seemed to be suffering the same sort of symptoms, though these had set in after we'd stopped.

Musing on this I did a metal tally of my own water intake

that day and realised that I had drunk less than three litres all day and had disappeared behind rocks with the shits on average about every 45 minutes. All this in up to forty-degree heat in the shade. Riding in the open sunshine meant that the actual heat inside my suit would have been much higher. The whole miserable experience augmented by my heavy black riding gear and full face helmet. No wonder I felt terrible. Pretty much desiccated actually. It occurred to me that I'd had a lucky escape from my own stupidity.

Dave concurred with my thoughts when he reappeared. "You don't drink enough water in this heat." he said. "Little and often, but keep drinking."

"I also got you these." he said and handed over two tubes of Pringles and a small bag of salt. He also had six litres of Sidi-Ali. "Drink all of this by morning or else." He said. "Oh and by the way, I found a doctor and took some advice. He was pretty helpful. Just get some rest; you should be OK in the morning. The quack had a pretty rough surgery though. Got the impression of worn out scalpels and bent needles, Dirty place.

"I've also checked out how to get you out if you get any worse. A lorry will take you both and your bike to Ceuta for about 500 dirham if necessary. Bloody cheap. Anyway, Anna and I are going to have some dinner."

He left us to our dinner of salt, water and Pringles.

It took some mental effort to force this unusual meal down us both, but we managed it and felt almost immediately better. The bathroom still beckoned with monotonous regularity, but the worst effects of dehydration seemed to have passed.

We slumbered fitfully, with vivid thoughts and images passing through our heads. It was still hot and the still air of the hotel room remained stifling long after the sun had gone down. Feeling better was a relative term; the effects of the day's accumulated heat lingered. Although we had rehydrated, we were both far from well.

The sonorous wailing of next door's pre-recorded Mullah filled the room in a never ceasing bellow from the poor stereo. It was clearly some sort of cassette recording because every hour or so, the whole sequence of adulations to Allah started again from the beginning. I began to feel like an expert in Muslim ceremony.

Dave reappeared after what seemed to be another 67 hours.

"Anna's gone to bed, I'm still shitting, but dinner was good, if somewhat sandy. A bit of breeze out there now."

He paused.

"Actually, my chicken meal reappeared, undigested, out of me arse about thirty minutes after I ate it." He looked vaguely troubled.

"Breeze?" I replied. "It's stifling in here. Oh, before you get some kip, can you do me a final favour mate; can you buy that racket that is coming from the shop next door, I can't stand it anymore."

Dave smiled and vanished. A few minutes later, the noise stopped and he reappeared, slinging a cassette on the bed.

"Some souvenir." he said. "I'm for bed."

Blessed silence for a few minutes and then to my horror a different wailer started howling from the stereo next door. I buried my head in a blanket.

That night passed in a fitful half-sleep full of hallucinations and crazy thoughts as my mind ran away from me. I still felt seriously hot to the extent that each time I went to the toilet I would also stand under the tepid and dribbling shower for a while. At one point, I found myself slumped in the corner of the shower with the cooling water easing away the heat from my glowing limbs. The painful radiation of heat would start once again when I returned to my bed.

Heather slept the sleep of the dead while I tossed and turned – my mind full of utter craziness as I passed the time between bed, shower and toilet.

I kept up the water intake and at some point during the early hours, my 'fever' broke and I started sweating and shaking, but in a manner that felt refreshing. My mind became clear. But I still felt weak and ill, still needing the close proximity of a toilet bowl, still far too hot …

SOLO BIKE TRAVELS

At five am, I was sat at the window smoking a cigarette, finally feeling calm and enjoying watching the light grow outside. Heather awoke looking utterly drained.

"I'm not sure that I'm much better." she said "But I don't feel any worse."

I felt much better but badly scarred by the events of the previous day and fearful of another foray into the Saharan heat. Rationality suggested that a good, regular hydration routine, some salts and regular stops would mean a heat managed day. But there was still diarrhoea to contend with and there was still no sign of this slackening.

Frankly, I was too nervous to go on until I felt much better.

I communicated these fears to Dave at breakfast. He looked at me slightly uncomprehendingly as I suggested hanging around for a day or so until Heather and I felt a bit better.

"I'll help sort ye out." he said "but we ain't hanging around, Anna and I want to be in Ouarzazate by tonight."

This was a blow. For me, the last thing I'd do in the world would be to abandon a mate in the desert of a strange country. I felt crushed, though it was only later that I suspected that Anna may have put Dave in a position that was impossible for him. My disagreement with her in Moulay Idris still lingered and I knew that she didn't enjoy my company.

Heather was not at all happy about this turn of events either. She suggested that we go on, but I knew that without a day's recuperation this would be madness. Possibly resulting in a repeat of yesterday's pathetic performance.

Nothing much was said, but bad feeling lay below the surface all around.

Dave to his credit went out and found a decent hotel with air conditioning just across a small bridge about 300 yards away. He booked us in figuring that air conditioning was probably of value beyond price for us both.

He'd judged this well and we decamped to the Hotel Rissani. This was a place which catered for wealthy visitors and where the contrast between rich and poor once again became apparent. We saw clean rooms, an alcohol bar and fat bathers beside a shaded swimming pool.

Dave fussed about quite a bit as we settled in. It was obvious that he was feeling uncomfortable about the whole situation and asked me a couple of times if we would rethink travelling that day. But I knew that unless I took some time to rest and stay cool, another day in the direct heat would finish me off once and for all as far as this trip was concerned.

So we bade a sad and frustrated farewell to our travelling partners, who later that morning set off southwards towards the sun, in a cloud of dust and the diminishing sound of a twin cylinder engine. Feeling miserable, Heather and I retired to our room and sat in front of the air conditioning unit, whose cold blast felt like the ultimate refreshment.

That day we hid in our room, stayed cool, drank fluids and ate sparingly. English TV channels and mobile phone coverage lent an air of unreality to our stop in the desert. Our sojourn in the hotel became a strange interlude in our travels, stranded in relative luxury as we were.

But by evening I yearned to get moving again. The day's enforced rest had done the job. Feeling more my old self, I determined that one day off the saddle was enough. We also both felt that that after food poisoning, heat stroke and desert stress, we needed to see the sea and get back to a cooler region.

Looking at the map, it seemed that a determined ride could see us back in the fertile coastal area of the country in one long day. We resolved to leave before first light so that we could get some miles under our wheels before the heat grew.

Late in the afternoon, after some cold Cokes by the pool, I wandered out to check over the bike. An old man emerged from under a palm tree.

"I watch your bike, this is my job in the hotel." he said with a broad grin.

"You have my thanks." I replied "We go early tomorrow."

"Is OK, I will be here." the parking guard answered and settled down under his tree again. His dark clothing gave the impression that he was merging with the trunk, as he shaded himself from the still intense afternoon sun.

That night a distant rumbling sound, almost like artillery fire, filtered through to our room. Clouds had gathered over the distant Atlas Mountains as darkness had settled over Er-Rachidia. It seemed that we could be in for an unexpectedly wet ride as we headed west.

"If we'd come here a day or two later, we'd probably had not got ourselves messed up by the heat." remarked Heather.

We both awoke feeling more refreshed than we had for days. It was four am, dark and hot. Packing took a short minute and after a hurried coffee, rustled up for us by a bleary eyed porter who had been sleeping in a chair, we packed the bike and got ready to go. Energetic help lifting our luggage was provided by the old parking guard. Overnight he'd spread a blanket by the Triumph, so that he could be as good as his word regarding sleeping with the bike. Sterling service which earned him genuine gratitude and some dirhams for his trouble.

I glanced at the thermometer by the hotel reception. 28 degrees and this was four am. I mused for a second at the naivety of our planning for a ride to the Sahara in July. The wrong riding gear, not enough hydration and not enough general daily personal care – given that the itinerary allowed for no real time off if things went wrong.

It had been a valuable lesson in how not to do things.

Dave had planned better, but even he'd been caught out by a dose of Berbers Belly. I'd learned much already from this trip and thanked my personal God that we'd had a lucky escape from the potentially serious situation that had threatened to engulf us only thirty hours before.

We set off into the pre-dawn light and headed out of town, retracing our journey back into the Atlas. The dark streets were empty as we turned west and the rose tinted glow of the approaching sun appeared in my mirrors.

In the distance, along the empty and arrow-straight road, the mountains rose ahead of us and gave promise of dramatic dawn light upon the rocks.

I felt great. The ride was already taking on an exciting air. With the absence of heat induced stress, I wondered why I hadn't suggested early morning starts before we had reached the desert.

As the road climbed, the light started to grow and the temperature slowly fell, a different experience from previous mornings. It was an exhilarating ride, though I kept to a respectable speed so that we could enjoy the emerging views of mountainous crags and the sharpening contrasts of colour as light started to define more features on the landscape.

Through the Legionnaires Tunnel again and we found ourselves in an area that had been thrashed by rain storms the previous night. It suddenly became very cold and although the mind-sharpening chill was welcome, we stopped to add a layer of clothes and to take a drink.

An open topped, flat-bed lorry roared past, its ancient long nose covered in Arabic script. It was blowing its horn and was packed to the gunnels with shouting and waving people. Workers on their way to Er-Rachidia for whatever menial task they had secured that day. As they did so, the rising sun touched high peaks which marched into the distance and a warm pink light oozed across our view to bathe the terrain in a magnificent fresh light, breathtakingly beautiful and soulfully uplifting.

By eight am, we were once again on the northern escarpment of the High Atlas, looking down on the flat plain that lay between the High and Middle Atlas. The ground below slowly disappeared into a haze from which hints of the Middle Atlas emerged almost ghost like. With the descending road flattening and straightening out, we risked a spurt of speed to get us across an area that we knew would become a searing blast furnace of heat by about 11am.

A quick coffee in Midelt, plus some toiletry relief from the still lingering lurgie and we set off once again. We soon found ourselves enjoying twisties that gained altitude and the reappearance of pine trees and long shadows as we climbed the more gentle inclines towards the Middle Atlas. Smoothly rounded and eroded rocks lined the road, with all kinds of plant life taking advantage of cracks to spread their roots and gain a foothold in this arid area.

Weaving around the mountain roads with lighter hearts we

found enjoyed the ride much more than we had done on the way down. Sometimes it was slow going as lorries blocked our path, belching smoke and splattering us and the bike with unburned diesel. Other times a clear road ahead offered biking possibilities that could not easily be found in much of Europe.

We stopped at the mineral and stone seller's place once again. This time feeling fitter, we were able to appreciate the view with a better eye. The stall was shut and our friend was nowhere to be seen.

Leaving the Middle Atlas behind with no small measure of regret, we passed once again through Azrou, stopping only for a short refreshment break. Then north through the flatter agricultural area which lies around Meknes.

Our plan was to get somewhere near Rabat, with the ultimate aim of dipping our toes in the Atlantic to wash away the desert dust. Looking at the map, it seemed that we would have a pleasant if long ride along the N6 through Khemisset and out towards the Capital. But on the way south from Meknes I had noted a motorway intersection, though this was not marked on the map. I had dismissed it as merely a motorway project under construction, plus at that point in the journey I had no real interest in riding on this type of road.

Today though, our objective was to cover as many miles as we could. As we neared Meknes, I saw huge blue signs pointing the way to Rabat at the intersection. We took the indicated road.

The ramp led us quickly onto a European-style autoroute; wide, open, empty and brand new. I opened the throttle and the Triumph responded. The countryside flashed by and Meknes was soon behind us.

We stopped for fuel and a coffee. It was noon and a thermometer in the station registered 39 degrees in the shade, meaning an open road exposure in the mid to high forties, only tempered by a wind cooling factor. But unlike previous days, apart from feeling a bit hot, we were both OK. I didn't even feel much need to take my jacket off. Proper hydration and acclimatisation were having their positive effects.

Taking the motorway could be viewed as a bit of cheat, but this was enjoyable fast riding. The countryside west of Meknes unrolled before us, huge folds of land and undulating terrain, sometimes covered in olives, sometimes vineyards, often barren open 'downs'. Absolutely lovely.

We saw little traffic and what we did see were cars that were fairly new or current models. In a sense, the motorway was part of the new Morocco, but westernised modernity had also brought its own inequality. The lack of traffic was essentially due to the motorway toll, which when converted from Dirham to Sterling, was pricey even by French standards. This was a rich man's road, with prices far beyond the means of average incomes.

Denial of this smooth and efficient artery to the less affluent of Moroccan society had done little to stop the now familiar Moroccan diversity from European highway norms and we regularly passed lines of washing pinned onto the central reservation wire rope safety fencing. Sometimes we passed lines of people walking on the hard shoulder. Occasionally, someone could be seen lazily crossing the motorway on foot. On two occasions livestock were being driven down the hard shoulder and slow lane. I slowed down, these unusual hazards may have been quirkily enjoyable, but a major prang now would be the last thing we needed.

I was soon glad I did. Looking into the distance I could see a line of cars pulled up under a bridge. Getting nearer, I could see that about eight cars had chosen to shelter from the heat of the day under the shadow of the bridge, lining up to steal the shade and blocking the entire road in the process. Someone was even cooking some Brochette on a small charcoal stove in the middle lane.

This seemed almost insanely risky behaviour, though we both laughed at the peculiar sight. Picking our way between the cars amid friendly greetings all around, we set off once again.

Another feature of this ever more interesting experience, were the number of abandoned car wrecks. It seemed that it was policy to leave badly damaged cars as a deterrent, warning people of the consequences of dangerous driving. These macabre relics were perched off the edge of the hard shoulder, reminding the unwary of the horror of a high speed crash.

Once we were past Khemisset, the peculiarities of the

motorway seemed to become fewer and we noted small convoys of Gendarme BMW police motorcycles being ridden at high speed up and down the road. Once, one of them peeled off from his group as they hurtled by at warp speed, slowed, came alongside us, looked us up and down, waved and roared off into the distance once again. The local cops seemed to enjoy their own private and largely empty race track it seemed.

Within another hour and Rabat was getting close. Coming out of the wonderful rolling landscape and long views, we came into an area of dense woodland and more frequent intersections. We paid a huge toll at a very orderly, European style Peage plaza and noted an immediate increase in traffic levels. The quality of many cars returned to the usual battered smoke-belching and ruinous condition.

A further glance into the forest and we could see that it was a massive Cork plantation. Trees had their bark peeled to about head height, with huge stacks of the stuff piled up and waiting for collection for market. Occasionally workers were busy 'peeling' a tree. The sunlight contrasted with long shade under the trees. It would have been nice to stop for some pictures. But the ocean beckoned – we knew that we would be in Rabat before three pm, after ten and a half hours of probably the best riding we had ever experienced.

Crossing the intersection of the motorway that runs from Tangier in the north to Casablanca further south, what was now a very busy dual carriageway curved its way down towards the city itself, through small tree-clad hills, where estates of white houses nestled. Cars were everywhere, some driven mildly, others wildly. White gloved Gendarmes started to appear at traffic intersections blowing whistles and generally trying to look important. Pedestrians waited in bus queues as countryside gave way to a suburban and then an urban backdrop.

Rabat is not a huge city. It has been described as quiet and colonial, with a French air about it. To me it didn't quite match that sympathetic description. Roads bustled with chaotically driven cars, buses and trucks, which fought their way along wide boulevards, piling up into traffic jams at the narrower intersections.

But generally, vehicles seemed to be in better condition and there was a generally more 'ordered' feel about the place.

Shopping streets offered a greater variety of goods and products than we had seen elsewhere and these were interspersed with residential areas. Housing was often of good quality, with well-built villas and walled gardens. It seemed that we had entered the city via a more upmarket area.

We turned off the main highway near the centre of town, looking for a hotel and found ourselves riding up a very quiet road. There were immaculate mown grass verges, regularly spaced identical palm trees, high walled properties and white uniformed guards by every entrance. We figured that we were either somewhere near the Royal Palace, or in the diplomatic quarter. So turning off towards the west, we plunged again into the chaotic streets and traffic fumes of central Rabat.

It was some effort dealing with navigation, while avoiding instant death in the form of a crazily driven car. Dust, heat and smell mingled with the cacophony of traffic and pedestrians as we sweated under the beating sun trying to find a way through the jams.

We turned a corner and suddenly found ourselves on a long seafront promenade, with a line of large white buildings marching into the distance along the shore. The wide blue ocean spread before us – a welcome sight for the weary traveller.

We stopped in a car park and walked a few yards onto the beach. In moments our riding boots were off and we laughed with joy as we waded into the cool refreshing sea, not caring that the crashing waves were soaking us to waist height, a heavy swell threatening to suck our feet out from under us after each wave had spent its force. The feeling of the sea after so much dry barrenness was the perfect antidote to our tired and overheated souls.

We sat for some time on the shore, drinking water and enjoying a smoke. The beach was quite busy, with men and children in the sea. Women demurely strolled the water's edge, clad head to toe in light robes. Several teenage lads wandered by, with jet black skin and bleached long hair, carrying either battered surf boards, or packing case lids, carefully fashioned for wave catching.

"Arabic Point Break." muttered Heather with a half-smile, making us both grin at the contrast between these local surfers and the Keanu Reeves Hollywood surfing blockbuster.

After a time we dragged ourselves away from the cooler sea shore and set off once again to look for accommodation. The cheap hotels that we found seemed to be full and in trepidation of our wallets, we started to ask at places that were a little more upmarket. One place, near a busy intersection looked likely and I went inside to check for an available room.

The receptionist, a small wizened chap in a fez, seemed happy to give us a room for the night, but there was no secure parking for the bike. There was no way that I was going to leave the Triumph on the street. So feeling a little frustrated, hot and thirsty, I saw the hotel bar and figured that it was time to have a drink and consider our options.

Heather came in, also looking fairly jaded, so we ordered two beers and sat down for a breather.

One of the guests, a westerner, came over for a chat. Dressed in a cool white canvas suit and the kind of trainers we used to call 'daps' a school, he introduced himself as Hank, an American who worked for Reuters.

"Worst damn posting I ever had." he said after sitting down with his drink. "I spend most of my time sending reports back to head office about nothing at all exciting and the rest keeping the A-rabs happy; bloody nosey lot."

I figured that Hank must have watched 'The Year of Living Dangerously' too many times as he affected the air of an American journalist in a war zone.

It turned out that he'd been in the country for five years and his job seemed to comprise sifting items from the local media and sending anything interesting out on 'the wire'. An occasional interview with a Government official represented the high points in his life as an 'outpost' journalist. He didn't leave the city if he could help it and waxed lyrical about some of the night clubs in town. Hank lived in Rabat, but didn't 'see' the country. Just another stop-over on a stalled career it seemed.

We mentioned our current predicament.

"Try the garage over the way, they'll park you up for the night for a small fee, tell them I sent you."

This cheered me up and after Hank offered to pay for our drinks, life seemed quite mellow again. Hank drawled a farewell and went back to join his djellaba-clad local friends at the bar.

I walked over to the garage. Large hanger style double doors led down a ramp into a huge underground workshop. Half a dozen shifty looking characters in filthy overalls leaned against some benches smoking vile-smelling cigarettes. Several old cars were scattered about, most covered in a thick layer of dust.

A short conversation and I was out of there. Yes, they could garage the bike, but only if we left all our vehicle papers and 200 dirham. Hank? "Non monsieur, we do not know him."

Great. So feeling like two refugees, we resumed the hunt for a hotel.

Salvation was the Hotel Balima on Avenue Mohammed V, right across the road from the Parliament building. An imposing place, it proved to be reasonably priced and our room was comfortable and had loads of character. Being at the top of the ten storey building, it had a balcony which gave a good view over the rooftops and satellite dishes of the mostly white painted buildings of the capital.

The Triumph was not garaged, but under the watchful 24 hour eyes of a hotel porter. Satisfied and freshened up, we went to the bar for a drink.

Settling into the luxurious sofas of the air conditioned bar, I mused about our fortunes of the previous few days. I tried to contrast where we were now with the sand and dust of the desert only the day before. It all seemed a little unreal and I gave up trying to sort out my tangle of thoughts. I put the whole experience down to what Dave was to later describe as travelling 'inversions' – where you'll be expecting one scenario and end up with another entirely different experience.

We ordered beers and took stock of our surroundings. Drinks were served by quiet and neatly dressed waiters who worked from a small bar which was almost hidden behind a wickerwork screen at the back of the sumptuously furnished room. I later heard that most alcohol bars in Morocco were similarly discretely located due to Muslim attitudes to intoxicating drink.

Lounging about, or sprawled on the comfortable chairs, was an interesting variety of people. They ranged from suited businessman to more rustic looking types, some with the pronounced Berber look and piercing eyes. All were drinking alcoholic drinks and sat in various poses which suggested a desire to maintain privacy.

Several smart looking girls in western style dress also sat around. Their demeanour was rather different. They sipped soft drinks and chain smoked as they glanced about them, trying to catch the eye of male guests.

After observing these girls for some minutes, it became clear that they were touting for custom of the carnal kind. It also became apparent that they were being 'managed' by at least two of the men who were in the lounge. From time to time, the girls would glance in the direction of one of these two individuals, who seemed like ordinary guests, apart from their sharper gaze and shiftier look.

The bar was clearly a place for picking up prostitutes. After a while, one of the seemingly disinterested fellows near us, finished his drink, peeled himself off his sofa and after a quick conversation with one of the girls, walked out. She followed close behind, adjusting her short skirt as she walked. She gave a backwards look at one of the pimps, who nodded at her as she left the room.

Soon tiring of this sleazy tableau, we felt it was time to take a walk down to the medina and see what else Rabat had to offer.

The wide Avenue of Mohammed V led towards the sea. Lined with public buildings and stalls selling newspapers, magazines, books, drinks, food and clothes it made for an interesting stroll. The afternoon was drawing to a close and more people were appearing on the street to either stand in groups to chat, or to promenade up and down the pavements and grassy central strip of the boulevard. Just as we had observed in so many other places.

The medina lay adjacent to the sea and was a larger if less grand and atmospheric market than Meknes. We wandered lazily through the winding lanes of stalls, remarking to each other about the absence of hustlers. Heather bought some small souvenirs for family and friends and we ate some kebabs and bread, washed down with bottles of cool Coke.

It was a pleasant time, without the stress of previous days and with the prospect of a comfortable and clean bed for the night. Then Heather saw one of those sights which brings one up short and reminds the traveller of the sometimes dreadful desperation that exists in developing countries.

A girl, aged in her twenties, was sitting on a pavement begging, a sight which we had seen many time before. But this poor woman was displaying her naked and entangled Siamese twin children to elicit funds though sympathy. It was a heart wrenching sight. Had the poor girl been rejected by her family for producing 'aberrant' children? What prospects did these dreadfully malformed and vulnerable babies have?

When rejection by one's home community is followed by a life of despair and no prospects, what hope is there? How can we, from the all too comfortable northern European countries, possibly understand what lay behind the sad eyes of the girl. Reduced to begging for a few dirhams and ignored by her own people.

It was a sobering and shocking experience, which left Heather in tears and myself with a hollow feeling in the pit of my stomach.

As we moved on, we had the guilty feel of people who realistically could do little to help that would be fundamentally useful. It certainly gave me a fresh perspective on Anna's views.

The sight of the sea raised our mood once again and we walked the promenade towards the huge Kasbah of the Udayes at the northern end of the shore. Its imposing walls and small passages offering a promise of curious exploration.

It was closed and as darkness finally fell we retraced our steps to the hotel through the balmy evening air. We dodged the still frantic traffic as we crossed busy streets and enjoyed stopping at the occasional roadside stall to see what was on display.

Back at the hotel, the pounding beat of nightclub music rose from a steaming doorway which led to the undercroft of the building. The night guard was doubling as a club doorman and was letting a steady stream of people go below. The problem was that the bike was parked right by the entrance and although it was chained up, was there for anyone to tamper with. After the bouncer gave his assurances that the hotel would ensure that nothing happened to the Triumph, we went to our room with a feeling of mild trepidation.

*

SARDINES AND WINE

The following morning, the bike refused to start; a totally flat battery. There was evidence that the switches had been fiddled with and the bike had been moved, so that the security chain was now taut against its anchor. The guard, who in the space of fourteen hours had transformed from guard to bouncer and back to guard again shrugged his shoulders and claimed to know nothing. "But it is still here, Insha'Allah" However, it seemed that early hours revellers had been playing with the bike, though how they'd managed to flatten the battery was beyond me.

A small crowd of excited youths had gathered to witness the fun of the English guy taking seat and panels off and scratching his head in puzzlement. But they were keen to help bump-start the bike.

With lots of laughing and shouting, the Triumph was manoeuvred onto the road and with shoving and further yelling, we wobbled down the road. I quickly engaged second and dropped the clutch. The engine roared into life with irregular popping and misfiring which died away as the generator started supplying current to the battery.

After escaping the traffic of the city, we turned north on the autoroute in the direction of Tangier. No real destination in mind, just an ambition to get somewhere near Ceuta before nightfall.

The motorway stretched ahead, the curiosities of the modern Moroccan six lane route rather as they had been the day before. Sheep, people, washing lines and crashed cars. Almost no other traffic though, so we settled down to steady mileage crunching.

"This is boring." said Heather an hour or so later. We had stopped for some coffee at a service station that was none too clean and offered only the view of a huge grass embankment on each side of the highway.

Looking at the map, she pointed to a coastal town nearby.

"Let's pull off at Asilah. I was looking at the book just now and it seems quite interesting."

Asilah looked to be an easy few hours from Ceuta and was possibly a good place to spend our last night in Morocco. So heading off at the next exit we took a short ride along a potholed road to check things out.

The town lay on the coast, about an hour or so's ride from Tangier. A quick turn around the medieval-looking centre revealed an attractive and traditional fishing port.

We checked into one of the empty tourists resorts, all of which were neatly positioned on the beach on the northern edge of town. The place was almost empty and a reasonable price secured a comfortable apartment by a large swimming pool.

Both of us were still suffering from the persistent and stubborn Berbers belly, so it was nice to spend the afternoon relaxing by the pool and doing very little. It wasn't too hot and a pleasant breeze drifted over from the beach as we sat on sun loungers and slowly sipped cool drinks. A very nice way of spending our last full day in North Africa.

"This travelling lark is all well and good." said Heather "But sometimes it's nice to just take in the beach and the sun somewhere comfortable. What is the attraction of spending all our time doing mega miles anyway?"

A good point. But I've never been the type that can sit all day in a sweaty tourist resort, either frying in the sun, getting shit-faced at the bar, or competing with Germans or French for sun loungers while hordes of screaming kids monopolise the pool. The worst kind of hell if you ask me. The open road offers so much more, in terms of what one can see and experience. There is also the spiritual fulfilment aspect.

"I dunno." I replied after some thought. "I agree that mega miles and frying in the sun on the open road is not always a huge amount of fun, but there's this whole sense of fulfilment, of seeing places for what they are, the experiences of people and cultures that an insulated package holiday will never give you. A sense of actually doing a journey; travelling to places as opposed to being transported from one situation to another without any feel of what lies in between."

Later in the afternoon, we walked along the beach and into town. Fishing boats in various states of repair were beached along the coastline. Small groups of suntanned men, stripped to the waist, were doing maintenance or preparing fishing lines. The bright coloured sand reflected a fantastic light from the sea, sharp and clear allowing distant views down the mainly flat coastline for miles. There was no hint of haze.

Felling too lazy for a long hike around all that the town had to offer, we instead sat on the sea walls overlooking the rocky coast. The town had a turbulent history, having been inhabited for centuries by Iberians who had been shipped in by the Romans. Aside from being at the centre of territorial disputes from the time of the crusades, it has hosted some colourful characters. One of the most notable was Er Raissouli, a Rif Mountain bandit who came to prominence in the early 20th century. For a time he held power in Asilah and used to force convicted murderers to jump to their deaths from his palace in the town. His own fate was sealed when he backed the wrong side during World War I.

The Moroccan Government has invested heavily in restoring the medieval town, particularly the Portuguese ramparts. The result is an interesting and surprisingly clean place.

It didn't take long for us to be latched onto by a local 'guide', but we liked Ali immediately. He wasn't pushy and was happy to wander with us, at our own pace, through the clean, though somewhat sterile looking medina – almost a caricature of a Moroccan medina... in Morocco. Ali fed us some grand tales about the history of the place and later invited us to take some tea in his home, a small, cool and carpet lined single room apartment by the old stone ramparts of the town.

Later, we settled down for a spectacular fish dinner at a table outside a restaurant which was run by a Spanish family. There was a pleasant aspect of the beach, with the tower of a medieval fortress and the ancient arched entrance to the medina adjacent to where we sat.

The owner was a keen fan of Moroccan wine and wanted us to try out the best he had to offer. At very reasonable prices for a half bottle, we set about an extensive wine tasting of different varieties, both red and white. I'm no wine expert, but the quality of this stuff was fantastic. Accompanied by excellent fried Sardines and Bream, our last night in this amazing country was a real pleasure and brought our first real pangs of regret about leaving.

The following morning, we set off with Gibraltar as our target. The map showed an interesting minor road which cut the corner of country between us and Ceuta. This quickly proved to be a smooth road full of excellent quality twisties curving its way through the picturesque Jebala range of hills. There was only light traffic and a great opportunity to explore the Triumph's handling for the last time in Africa.

We joined the coast road after Tetouan and finally, the Rock of Gibraltar loomed over the horizon as we approached the little enclave of Ceuta.

Moroccan exit and customs were in complete chaos, with hooting cars, heat and dust. Confused officials and hustlers were running everywhere. I took the opportunity to try and slip through unnoticed. Just as we were about to leave, policeman pulled us up, took a quick look at our faces and waved us through. Spanish border officials weren't the slightest bit interested in us. Continuing unchecked, we quickly traversed the town and headed for the port, where half an hour later, we boarded the fast ferry for Algeciras.

We sat on the open rear deck watching the Moroccan coast line sink away behind. A great plume of water from the catamaran's gas turbines curved away from the stern. Mixed feelings abounded, though it was too early for either of us to articulate them properly.

There was regret about leaving. It had been a terrific experience, though tempered by ongoing illness and the mistakes made when riding motorcycles in the overpowering heat of a Saharan July. We had seen the most wonderful things, but also witnessed moments of great sadness and despair among the people whose culture we'd witnessed first-hand.

"Morocco's great, but it's also a mess isn't it?" I asked Heather. She thought for a moment before nodding her head and saying "It'll be some time before I can really figure out how I feel about the place. It was great on one level, but on others, I just wanted to run for cover."

There was a delay at Algeciras as sniffer dogs ran about everywhere and customs officials searched every one of the long queue of cars that was leaving the ferry. The car in front was pulled up just as we entered a 'sheep dip' ditch full of chemicals, designed to sterilise Moroccan dust covered car wheels. Not fun if you're on a bike.

I stood up to my ankles in this evil smelling brew as customs officials searched the car and a sniffer dog burrowed under blankets. An officer pulled a house brick sized object from the boot of the car and held it up in front of the unfortunate and completely stupid car driver. His shoulders slumped and with his head down he was led away. The car was driven off by another officer allowing us to escape our chemical bath.

An hour later and we pushed our way to the front of a huge queue of cars that were waiting to enter Gibraltar. Spanish officials creating huge delays at the border – as is their wont when it comes to this disputed territory.

We followed a line of mopeds and other small bikes across the airfield and into the British enclave without any hold ups. We marvelled at English road signs and police in British uniforms complete with pointy hats.

A night at the Bristol Hotel was followed by a trip to hospital where dysentery was diagnosed. A prescription was followed 24 hours later by gradual relief from much of the illness and discomfort that had plagued us for nearly a week.

We left Gibraltar the following day and turned the Triumph's wheels northwards, with adventures still to come on the long European ride home.

Despite the mistakes we'd made, I couldn't help but feel a sense of satisfaction about having finally made it to Africa. I had spoken to Dave the previous evening. He was somewhere up the Spanish coast having had a successful few days riding the long coastal Moroccan route himself.

"It feels good to have some common point of reference with Simon you know." he had said over the phone. "At least when we mail the bugger again, we won't feel as though we've stayed at home and missed it all."

The Moroccan trip had been largely inspired by Simon and I figured that Dave was probably right. By virtue of expanding our own horizons and leaving the safe shores of Europe, Simon felt a little closer to us again.

But it was a trip that had taught us a great deal – and not just about riding motorcycles for long distances.

1992:
The long-suffering Bonnie in Wiltshire

1992:
Author being interviewed at a riders rights 'demo' in Bristol

1993:
Simon explains the facts of life to the European Commissioner

1993:
The 100bhp demo in Luxembourg

1993:
Author talking to
John Prescott MP
and Roger Barton
MEP in London

1993:
Making a point
at Labour's old
HQ in London

WHO
RULES
EUROPE?

1994:
Paris Euro
Demo gridlock

NATIONAL COALITION OF MOTORCYCLISTS
NCOM

1994:
Speaking at a
convention in
Pennsylvania
while Si looks on

1995:
Stop Anti Bike
Laws, Dublin

1995:
Portugal. Post meeting party.
Author with Simon and friends

1995:
Celebrating the success
of the all-Ireland 'Bigger
than Borders' demo.
Co Kildare

1996:
A fool with Dave French

1996:
Dave and author with fellow campaigners in Belgium

1996:
The Monster Harley, created to demonstrate the effect of a badly thought out emissions proposal

1997:
Glenda Jackson gave us loads of support for Bikers are Voters

1999:
Simon briefs us on the John T Overlander

India: Simon described this as one of the most inspiring moments of his trip

Public relations shot in the USA

2000: Triumph Sprint ST, a trusty steed for Morocco

2000: Anna getting fruit from prickly pears

2000:
Middle Atlas rock seller stall

2000:
Approaching
the High Atlas

2000:
Asilah

2004:
Simon in
central Africa

2005:
One of the last known photos of Simon, possibly taken in Nigeria

Riders' rights man dies

THE man who led the fight against the Europe-wide 100bhp limit in the '90s has been killed in a bike crash.

Briton Simon Milward, 40, was general secretary of European riders' rights organisation FEMA when it saw off the power limit threat, and he was credited with uniting riders against European meddling.

His other great victories were fighting off draconian noise limits and anti-tampering rules that would have made it impossible to modify your bike.

His close friend Craig Carey-Clinch, from Britain's

Motorcycle Industry Association, said: "We have lost somebody we just can't replace. He showed motorcyclists that we could make positive change."

Milward was killed in a solo bike crash while riding through Mali, Africa, on Friday, March 4. He was on a round-the-world journey he began in 2000.

March 2005:
Motorcycle News

Simon's memorial service, Simon's mum Jane Milward with brothers Shaen, Paul and Mark

John T who designed and built Simon's overlander

The inaugural meeting of Motorcycle Outreach. An illustrious crowd, including Barry and Andrea from Riders for Health

Preparing for a publicity shot. BMW came up trumps with the GS Dakars and other kit

Metal Mule luggage. Simply the best

Charley Boorman with the John T Overlander. He and Ewan McGregor gave us welcome support

PART THREE:
Into Africa Again

March 2005

From: Simon Milward
Sent: 25 February 2005 21:03
To: Craig Carey-Clinch; David French
Subject: Europe bound

Hi Craig & Dave

Sorry I've been a bit out of touch but now that my journey is coming to an end I have to think about real life things! I am kind of dawdling here in West Africa (Burkina Faso right now to be precise) but need to get on with it because the heat is building and I'm not even near to crossing the Sahara yet – a good few weeks away methinks.

Craig, I was thinking of coming with my bike to the motorcycle show at the NEC this year and was wondering what my options might be. Needless to say, I cannot pay anything. I could ask MAG or BMF if they would have me, MAG did of course prior to my departure. What do you think? My PowerPoint shows have been received raucously (!) around the world and would be more than pleased to do it at the Show, provided people could be drawn in to them. I'd be interested in tagging a fundraising side to it – I guess it would be the last of the Millennium Ride fundraising. We could even make the NEC the official end to the journey!! Hmm.

I did the presentation at a number of NEC equivalent shows in the US. Usually I do them for free and appeal for donations at them. Perhaps I could get some corporate donators lined up. It's true that in so many years gone by I have been going round the stall blagging freebies of different sorts! I'd have to get some pin badges or something made. I'd like to break that habit of going for small donations though, perhaps I should be tramping the corridors of the big bucks down London way. Your thoughts would be appreciated.

Take care you both, there shall be some good reunions later this year.
Simon
Simon Milward, on the road www.millennium-ride.com

*

To: Craig Carey-Clinch; David French
On Wednesday 02 March 2005 20:35, Simon Milward wrote:

Hi Craig

I have to get focussed on a few objectives for Europe as I finish my ride, and have a clear line between that and doing more serious long-term fundraising/promotion for Motorcycle Outreach Europe. Craig it will be good to work with you on that and look forward to discussing it.

Me back to Europe? Hilary offered to organise a welcoming in Gib, that should be about, phew, 1st April 2005.

UK, not till late Summer/Autumn since I intend to go via Israel and Scandinavia. Should be there for your wedding my man, congrats to you and Barbara. Ahhh that's lovely.

Dave I'd like to loop to SE Ireland from France in August/Sept time. (Can't go round the world and leave out Ireland of course). Do you think there would be interest to see my presentation there, and if so, could you put me in touch with yer people there please?

All the best guys and thanks for offering to help with bed etc and maintaining contact and interest and being good friends.
Simon
Simon Milward, on the road www.millennium-ride.com

*

BURGOS, SPAIN NOVEMBER 2005

Traffic roared by as I stood at the side of the lonely autopista. Motorists and their passengers sat hunched in warm coats and

122

glanced out at me in the brief instant that they were alongside. Probably wondering what on earth would possess someone to be riding a motorcycle on such a dank and bitter winter's day.

I drew my shoulders in, set my back to the icy breeze that blew across the wide open, undulating grey and brown plain which cowered under low and violent clouds. I scanned the road behind looking for signs of Dave.

Some minutes before, my riding partner had drawn ahead of me motioning to the wide-open aluminium box pannier on his bike. The lid had flown open, probably because Dave had forgotten to lock the box after our last fuel stop.

A quick check of its contents drew expletives. "Bloody jeans are missing," said a vexed Dave "it has one of those belts with a hidden money pouch, there's fifty Euro in there; gonna have to go back and try to find it."

Crossing the central reservation, Dave set off back up the road, caning the engine of his BMW 650GS Dakar in each gear as he went.

I sat on some Armco and rolled a cigarette. Dave was taking his time and I fell into thinking about the events that had brought us to this open and bitterly cold road. Forging southwards through the bleak and wintery Spanish countryside…

*

TRAGEDY, LOSS AND PURPOSE –
MARCH TO NOVEMBER 2005

From: Antonio Perlot
Sent: 05 March 2005
Subject: Fwd: Sad news – Simon Milward

Dear Colleagues,

I am sorry to be the bearer of such news, and hardly know how to choose my words. Upon our arrival at the office this morning, we received a call from a police officer in Mali, reporting that Simon Milward had passed away following a road accident. The accident took place on the afternoon of the 4th of March near the city of Kayes, and FEMA's was the only telephone number Simon had on him at that time. We do not have any other information for the moment.

We called Simon's family and the British Consulate in Mali and arrangements are currently being made in order to repatriate his remains to the UK. As colleagues and friends, we thought you would want to share our mourning. Please do not call the office this afternoon as this is all the information we have, and we would like to keep the telephone lines free in case of need.

We will let you have further information as we receive it.

Antonio Perlot

Secretary General, Federation of European Motorcyclists' Associations.

*

Nich Brown told me the news as I stood on Coventry railway station. It was a bright and sunny late winter's morning on the 5th March. One of those days where the gentle warmth of the sun brings promise of an early spring. I had been visiting the MCI office for one of my weekly meetings and was looking forward to returning home to Beckenham in Kent, my home since 2003. Not really looking forward to making another vain attempt to keep on top of the streams of email that flooded my computer daily.

"Oh hi Nich." I said in surprise as my colleague appeared suddenly and unexpectedly at my side.

His expression was grim

"What's up?" I added as a sudden sense of unpleasant trepidation gripped my stomach.

"Mate, you'd better come back to the office. I've had a mail from Antonio at FEMA. Something's happened to Simon."

"What do you mean something's happened to Simon?" I asked, already knowing the answer.

"Something happened in Mali. An accident. FEMA have had a call." He paused, "I'm sorry Craig, but they're saying that he died in the accident."

I stared ahead and only partially realised that I had reeled

124

forwards when Nich caught me. The sun was forgotten as numb despair took hold, the empty feeling of confusion before real grief sets in.

"But I only had an email from him the day before yesterday..." I blurted. Nich looked back at me grimly.

We hurried back to the office, where on Nich's screen I read the dread news from Antonio and then read it again.

What did I think? I don't know. Numbness continued; my mind paralysed with a lack of comprehension, emptiness and indecision.

I fumbled for the phone and rang Dave in Poland, where he'd been working for the last few years.

"Dave, check your email, something's happened to Simon.

I paused.

Look mate, there's no easy way of saying this. It seems he died in an accident in Mali."

Silence.

"What?"

I repeated the sentence that was to change everything.

Shock rendered him speechless for a time. There were then a few questions which neither Nich nor I could answer. He asked for Antonio's mail to be forward to him at work and then added. "I'll be on the plane to Stansted tonight, can you pick me up?"

That night, we sat in grim incomprehension at my home in Beckenham. I'd moved there to be with my fiancée Barbara Alam, who I had met some months after Heather and I had amicably gone our separate ways early in 2002.

Dave sat at the head of the table, mostly looking at the floor, a cold and almost untouched meal in front of him. Ian Mutch had joined us and spoke quietly about Simon, his voice barely containing his emotion. Barbara sat quietly and listened, upset for our sakes but also because she never had the chance to meet a person about whom I had spoken about so much. The four of us tried to figure it all out. An impossibility.

A call to FEMA had been an emotional experience. Antonio couldn't say much and Christina, Simon's former partner who also worked at the FEMA office, was inconsolable.

As the news spread, a paralysis settled over the operations of the motorcycle community, from the MCI through the riders groups and beyond throughout the motorcycling world. Simon had been well known right across the biking spectrum. The level of respect he was held in and shock at the news among both riders and hard-nosed industry types alike was profound.

He had been riding from Kayes in Mali towards the Senegalese border. A truck driver had found him lying in the road at a junction to a place called Ambidedi about halfway to the border. His bike was upside down beside him. Although a busy regional route, it was a poor unmade piste; like so many he had ridden along during the previous five years.

No one knew what had happened, and no one else had been involved. It seemed that he had just lost control of the bike for some reason.

The next day, things seemed to come back to life. Tributes poured into FEMA, along with a multitude of unanswerable questions. Motorcycling internet news groups were alive with comment, sympathy and speculation.

FEMA set up a website and opened a book of condolence, which rapidly began to fill with hundreds of entries.

During days such as these, people sometimes say things which stick in the mind, long after you feel that you've got used to things and moved on. Work friends at MCI, who had also known Simon well, Tom Waterer and Nich, had exchanged emails about Simon and copied me in on their thoughts.

Tom had commented how he had re-read a poem by Pilot Officer John Gillespie Magee, who while serving in the RAF as a Spitfire pilot in 1940 had written about his spiritual feelings as he flew in the clouds. Magee was killed in 1941. Tom felt that 'High Flight' in many ways also summed up Simon's spirit.

High Flight

Oh! I have slipped the surly bonds of earth
And danced the skies on laughter-silvered wings;
Sunward I've climbed, and joined the tumbling mirth
Of sun-split clouds – and done a hundred things
You have not dreamed of – wheeled and soared and swung
High in the sunlit silence. Hov'ring there
I've chased the shouting wind along, and flung
My eager craft through footless halls of air.
Up, up the long delirious, burning blue,
I've topped the windswept heights with easy grace
Where never lark, or even eagle flew –
And, while with silent lifting mind I've trod
The high untresspassed sanctity of space,
Put out my hand and touched the face of God

Pilot Officer John Gillespie Magee
1922–1941

I phoned Mark Milward, Simon's brother. I wasn't sure why initially. I suppose there was a sense of wanting to offer support. I had met Mark through Simon and both being beer drinkers, we had enjoyed some interesting nights out in Exeter several years before. On one memorable occasion, a visit to a real ale festival had been followed by an extensive drinking session in some nightclubs. But it had been some years since I had last spoken to him and both our lives had changed considerably. Re-establishing contact in the present circumstances was not ideal, but Mark seemed grateful for the call.

I offered support if it was needed. Simon had mailed me only forty or so hours before his accident and we had been corresponding about his humanitarian project on the Indonesian island of Flores. We had also spoken about his ideas for a new charitable initiative, which Simon had called 'Motorcycle Outreach'.

It turned out that Mark was keen for some help in trying to sort out where the Flores project stood, what plans Simon had and some idea of the money side of things. He indicated that there was general need to get some understanding of Simon's charitable work. We agreed to meet the following week.

That night, Guz Hurst arrived at our house. By coincidence, he had been in the UK on a visit from Australia and had heard the news when he had called me about coming down to London to visit Barbara and me.

Mutch had also stayed over. 24 hours on, we felt able to sit down together, eat and try to commemorate – or at least have a solid and in-depth talk about Simon's life. Not exactly an upbeat occasion, emotions were raw and dark moments would steal over us individually many times over the coming weeks. However, it was good to just sit and talk about our friend, make a toast or two and take comfort from sharing of each other's company and thoughts.

During the course of the emotionally charged evening, we started to think about what next. I suppose our conversation was borne out of a sense of helplessness, lack of closure and a feeling that Simon's life and energies should not go to waste. It was Mutch who found a way of articulating the thoughts that were slowly forming in our minds.

"Simon's way of things and personal energy isn't going to be repeated any time soon" he said, "But I don't want to see the trail of achievement and inspiration he left wherever he went go cold. There is no one person to fill his place, but maybe a bit of timely and sensitive networking could lead to a continuation of what he started and reinvigorate the health projects he was involved with. This in turn could help continue to generate material, political and moral support for his championing of justice."

He paused for a moment, before continuing.

"There are enough of us with enough links internationally and enough connections to make sure something tangible continues. Reading the book of condolence just confirms to me that Simon did have a genuine influence on people wherever he went." We nodded. FEMA had set an online condolence page the day before and it was quickly filling with tributes from around the world.

Mutch continued. "I understand he was talking about ideas

for what he wanted to do when the trip was over. Well it may not have ended the way he expected but that shouldn't mean his momentum has to stop. Simon managed to link riders' issues with broader justice concerns and I guess that's what I see as the crux of what made him who he was. A biker to the core, with a fundamental sense of justice. He did it very visibly – that's what we should aim to carry on.

"I'm thinking we should get a group of folk together willing to create a plan and pool resources for building closer links, web-based and physically, with the different parts of the world he visited. Bringing together the bike organisations to support each other and maintain awareness of at least some of the health and general justice issues he was interested in."

Little by little, things started moving. It took some days for Simon's remains to be recovered from Mali and there were several difficulties to be overcome, not least local bureaucracy and the police, who were investigating the accident. However, Simon was repatriated a week later.

His bike was another matter. It was all in one piece, but getting it out of Mali and back to the UK was not going to be straightforward. For a while there were question marks over where it was, though fortunately it turned up safely in a police compound. There was concern over the mechanism for getting it back to the UK. Africa was an unknown quantity for everyone and there was little in the way of knowledge about how things like shipping bikes would even work.

Bob Tomlins and Christina at FEMA were doing their best to help and Mark Milward even spoke to Harley-Davidson, who had been a constant supporter of Simon's efforts, to ask them if they had any West African contacts who could assist. However, it was the British Embassy in Dakar, Senegal who provided the most significant support and a few weeks later Simon's bike, the John T Overlander, was on its way back to the UK. Harley-Davidson settled the shipping costs.

Bob was working on putting som of Simon's financial affairs in order. Probate was an issue given that a number of Simon's affairs were in Belgium. Bob gave much needed support to Simon's family. FEMA also acted as a kind of firewall for the family, a place where people could send their messages of sympathy and of course sign the online book of condolence.

I was asked to look into Simon's charitable activities, investigate commitments he had made, how much money he had raised and for whom. It was already known that a considerable sum of money had been gathered. It was later discovered that he had cash on his person when he died which amounted to a few thousand US dollars – money which had not been stolen from him when he had been discovered lying in the road. So much for the, often instant, Western judgments of the integrity of African folk.

Simon had set out to support Riders for Health and Medecin Sans Frontiers (MSF) but it seemed that all of Simon's fundraising, after he had met Wily Balawala in Indonesia and founded Health for All, was geared towards supporting HFA in Flores. He had advised MSF that his support for them was on hold because of his new commitments.

There were also fledgling plans for several other projects in various South American countries. He had clearly been busy in the later years of his travelling and had evangelised as much about his idea of 'motorcycle outreach' as he had about his new-found Christian faith. He'd outlined some of these projects on his website and there was even a business plan for a project in Argentina.

While in the United States, Simon had constituted 'Motorcycle Outreach Inc' (MoR) as a low tax fund raising 'vehicle' with Rob Razor and Tim Owens from the American Motorcycle Association. A chat with Rob, a well-known and senior figure in the world of motorcycle riders rights and motorcycle sport, revealed that this American Motorcycle Outreach had around $2,000 sitting in its account.

There had been considerably more – Simon had raised around $108,000 in total – all but the current balance had been sent to HFA on Flores. Much of it used to buy motorcycles.

Motorcycle Outreach was dormant, awaiting Simon's return to start its charitable work again and Rob was happy to look after it for the time being. After further discussions, it was agreed that

Mark Milward would replace Simon on the MoR Inc nominal Board of Directors.

From all this, it appeared that Simon had created this low tax charitable structure and identified potential projects, with the aim of breathing real life into the 'Motorcycle outreach' concept on an international basis upon his return to Europe.

Simon had retained his interest in Riders for Health, but had not been supporting them with fundraising for quite some time. He had maintained a dialogue with 'Riders' and had liaised with them closely when Health for All was being set up on Flores.

However, there were differences in opinion about how to approach the idea of motorcycles and primary healthcare logistics. Indeed Simon and Riders did not always see eye to eye about how to do things. But mutual respect remained. Riders For Health founders Barry and Andrea Coleman were devastated by Simon's death.

Much later on, as Simon had travelled up Africa, he had the opportunity to visit 'Riders' in Zimbabwe which had reawakened his interest in Riders for Health and its work. This was because he finally had the chance to see it in action. Barry Coleman remarked a long time later, that if Simon had travelled the other way around the world he would have seen Riders in action before setting up the project on Flores, so avoiding various differences in opinion about how to run such a project.

The route of the final part of Simon's journey through Burkina Faso and Mali suggested that a visit to the Riders centre in the Gambia was also on the cards.

However, Riders For Health were quick to point out that fund-raising for them had not been part of Simon's later plans – he had HfA on Flores to worry about, plus his other plans for South America.

Dave and I travelled to Barnstaple to meet Mark Milward and to discuss these initial findings with him. Mark had changed a great deal since the last time I had seen him. He'd also married and had a family. Mark's voice always sounded uncannily similar to Simon and as we spoke, the vocal reminder of our friend was, on occasions, almost too much.

We sat in his kitchen and spoke about what had happened. Mark has a very direct way of speaking and like Simon, he takes a clear view of things, preferring to cut to the chase, rather than dither endlessly. Despite the sorrow of the occasion at hand, I found his attitude rather refreshing. I was reminded of Ian's comments of a few days before and the three of us fell to talking about what should happen next with Simon's vision.

Mark was emphatic that his motorcycle outreach dream should not die with him which, for Dave and I, were welcome words.

"But we've got to get the next few weeks about of the way first." said Mark, his voice dropping a tone and bringing us down to earth with a bump.

Visiting Mark was like seeing a bright light in a void of darkness. It was such early days, but a bit of Simon seemed to be still living in Mark, who although was unable to do much to help himself, was hoping that something would come along to keep Simon's vision alive.

On one level, Simon's funeral in Exeter on March 24th was a deep pit of bitter misery for all concerned. The service was lovely, but seeing Simon off for the last time was agonising. People came from all over the country to see 'Si' off and the hearse was followed from Simon's brother Paul's house by a cortège of helmetless bikers in the true tradition of riders rights. Simon would have been proud.

Despite the awfulness of the occasion, it was good to afterwards catch up with old friends and relive some of the best moments that we'd had with Simon over the years.

Prior to the service, there had been a family meeting at Paul's where the next steps were discussed. Those of us who had been involved in the events of the previous few weeks were also invited.

Bob Tomlins presented Simon's financial affairs as he understood them, but advised that caution and careful thought should be given to any future plans relating to Simon's mission 'legacy'. He stressed that it was important to note that pre-emptive activity could be unwise until legal issues relating to probate, Simon's personal affairs and potential 'cross-overs' between Simon's personal estate and the Millennium Ride had been resolved.

This was sensible advice on an immediate level, but I had noted a degree of caution from Bob when it came to Simon's charitable vision before. I was beginning to feel that necessary due diligence was one thing, but a 'do nothing without years of endless meetings and chat' approach was not going to be helpful. Dave, Mark and I were keen to keep momentum and wanted to work towards developing something that would maintain Simon's legacy. Bob did not seem comfortable with this.

However, Bob did have a point regarding the legal issues. It was agreed that much still needed to be discovered and evaluated regarding Simon's contacts, personal plans for Health for All/ Motorcycle Outreach and possible avenues for charity development.

In order to prepare for anything which may be developed, it was agreed that existing funds from Simon's efforts, which existed in various accounts in the UK and Europe, should be gathered together into one 'pot'. Simon's mum Jane had opened a deposit account for this purpose.

Everyone felt that that Health for All in Flores should continue to be developed if at all possible. Of particular concern was the long-term financial health of the Flores project. However, it was clear that much more work needed to be done before we could decide what options existed for continuing Simon's legacy.

Six weeks after the funeral, we once again gathered in Exeter for a memorial event to properly celebrate Simon's life.

The event was held in a leisure centre, which was full of people who had come along to meet, talk about Simon and hear those closest to him speak about his life and work. Rob Rasor had flown in from the States, along with other friends of Simon from America. Willy Balawala had also flown from Flores to be part of the event and meet everyone concerned in the future of HfA.

Simon's bike had finally arrived back in the UK and John T rode it to the event, where its battered form took pride of place in front of the podium. The backdrop to the event was an extensive montage of papers, photographs and mementos of Simon's life and his amazing round the world journey. Dozens of photographs looped on a big screen behind the podium, providing a moving backdrop to the speakers.

Speeches were delivered by Simon's family, FEMA folk and American visitors. But Willy made possibly the greatest impression, with his talk about what Simon had meant to him and what the results of his journey mean to the people of Flores.

Afterwards, we repaired to the 'Double Locks' an old pub by the Exeter canal and a popular place for local bikers. Food had been laid on and a convivial atmosphere of friendship prevailed as good times were remembered. For the first time lots of smiles appeared on people's faces.

The following day, May 8th, a second meeting was held to address the question of what to do next. This was an illustrious gathering. In addition to Simon's family, Dave, Barbara and I, Bob and Christina from FEMA were there. As was Rob Rasor and Willy. Ian Mutch also attended, as did Kate Kenlock, a person who had given Simon lots of help when he was still a MAG rep in the UK.

Although matters relating to Simon's estate were discussed, the main business of the day was to discuss what it would take to generate support from different parties in order to raise funds. The objective being to continue Simon's project work, both in Flores and in other parts of the world.

It quickly became apparent that there was real support for continuing Simon's legacy and that the best way of doing this would be to set up a new charitable organisation.

So, Motorcycle Outreach (MoR) was formed. Although it would be some time before the charity was properly constituted and there would be a long road to go down before we would be able to achieve half the things that Simon had planned, there was a great sense of relief. Plus, a sense of optimistic possibility as we closed that memorable session.

A final pleasurable moment for the day was the arrival of Barry and Andrea Coleman from Riders for Health. They'd tried to make the memorial event the day before, but were unable to get down to Devon in time. Although they'd also missed the meeting, it was good to see them and to receive their support.

*

Not long after Simon died, Dave and I had been talking in a quiet and inconclusive way about the idea of visiting the place where Simon had crashed. A look at the map revealed it to be some miles inside Mali from the border with Senegal, between the border town of Diboli and the large regional town of Kayes.

The trip looked daunting. The Sahara had to be crossed, several countries traversed, borders tackled. We had no real idea what the road conditions would be like, or what problems may be faced.

With the decision to launch the charity taken, the idea of the trip started to gain currency. Dave and I started to talk about using the journey as a launch event, a way of picking up where Simon left off. Not just charitably, but also physically – by riding the last stretch of Simon's Millennium Ride.

Opportunities to generate publicity and raise cash seemed high.

We discussed the idea with Simon's family and also with others in the group that was to become the core of Motorcycle Outreach. Support for the idea was strong and Kate even expressed an interest in coming.

As Kate, Simon's mum Jane and Barbara got on with the bureaucratic aspects of forming a charity, Dave and I finalised MoR's business plan. We also started to mould an offering for potential sponsors, for what was starting to be known as the Simon Milward Memorial Ride.

Kate had also been busy sorting through Simon's papers and along with Jane had catalogued an enormous amount of material. From this, they created a contact database of many hundreds of people who Simon had come across on his travels. We mailed these people, outlining what the new charity was about and mentioning the Memorial Ride plan. Strong support for our plans and messages of goodwill came back.

It seemed that both Motorcycle Outreach and the Milward Memorial Ride was gathering pace.

Dave was working full time in Poland again, so much of the organisation of the ride fell on the shoulders of Barbara and I. There was a huge amount to do. Visas to arrange, research into the route to be done, kit lists to draw up, legal documents to obtain. Most importantly, bikes to source.

I put together a prospectus for the journey. This included a detailed provisional itinerary, information about the charity and its aims, plus the background to MoR and Simon's vision. We had also booked a charity stand at the 2005 Motorcycle and Scooter Show at the NEC. The aim being to display Simon's bike, promote the charity and 'launch' the Memorial Ride.

The prospectus looked good and after Dave and I had agreed the main points, I approached Adrian Roderick and Tony Jakeman at BMW to ask for the support of BMW Motorrad. Given the overlanding heritage of the brand, it was clear to us that BMW's adventure sports bikes of the GS range were the obvious choice.

BMW gets lots of requests like this, but it probably helped to have done some proper research into our proposed route and to have a decent PR plan and narrative. Tony was certainly interested and we settled down to wait for a decision from the company.

All this activity, plus holding down my day job with MCI was bound to be stressful. It didn't help that we had to refine the MoR business plan several times for the Charity Commission. But these were heady days and it seemed possible to keep all these balls in the air and run a life, without too much caving in around us.

To add to the melee of things going on, Barbara and I were also planning our wedding. Tying the knot seemed a logical step in a relationship based on loving partnership, friendship and total trust. Our plans predated Simon's passing and despite all that was going on and thanks mainly to Barbara's abilities as an organiser, we were on course for a very pleasant day in October.

Time ticked by and we started to get concerned about BMW. Would they support us or not? Dave and I had asked for the loan of two GS650 Dakar's. We'd settled on these as being practical bikes for desert travel where the riders were highly experienced long distance motorcycle travellers, but were relatively new to the type of terrain that West Africa and the Sahara offered.

I deliberately avoided hassling BMW, but had just about reached the point when I felt I should drop an email to Tony, when the news came back from BMW. Not only would we get the bikes, but also BMW Rallye suits and a BMW GPS Navigator. We practically whooped with joy.

In the meantime, I had been searching for other sponsors of necessary kit. Scottoiler came on board and provided chain-oiling kits for the bikes, essential for ensuring that the chain would cope properly with long miles and grinding paste inducing sand and dust. Bike to bike radios appeared from Interide Communications.

After the bikes, proper luggage was the next essential item. It's quite possible to go round the world with nothing but soft panniers and a bag bungeed on the back seat. Enough folks have done just this over the years and my chaos of tired bags on our last Africa trip in 2000 had served me adequately. But such compromises are generally insecure and things are at risk of being nicked if the bike is left anywhere.

In many countries (especially our own), there's a risk of equipment theft and tampering with bikes (though we later discovered that this was rare in Africa). Damage can be caused just out of curiosity about the Westerners' beast on wheels, just appeared in an impoverished neighbourhood where the odd battered, African-manufactured Mobylette or, (more commonly these days) an imported Chinese scooter.

Hard metal luggage also helps protect equipment from all that the weather can throw at you. They can provide a degree of protection in a crash and are easy to bash back into shape in such crashes. Things can be kept locked out of sight and the boxes can also be used as impromptu seating or tables if required. The luggage debate perennially rages, but on balance I've erred towards hard luggage on most trips.

We were pointed in the direction of Paul and Ann Goulding. Paul ran 'Metal Mule', a specialist manufacturer of aluminium luggage for overland motorcycle travel. He was immediately willing to help once he'd seen our prospectus and PR plans. In the process, we gained two wonderful and lasting friends.

Tony Jakeman had sent us the registration details from the bikes and we set in train the process of obtaining 'carnets de passage' for each bike. The carnet is an important document that was vital for Senegal at that time. It effectively acts as a vehicle's passport and avoids having to pay excessive local fees at borders – or even demands for import tax. In Senegal, this is 150% of the new value of the vehicle, which in the case of the GS Dakar added up to about £7,500 per bike.

Senegal enforced the carnet with a vengeance during this period. Although we had heard of cases where people had got through the country without one, we were strongly advised that the hassle wasn't worth it.

The problem with the carnet is that it is only issued in the UK by the RAC. Only one person deals with them full-time and the fees are prohibitive. The RAC demand cash up-front to cover the face value of the carnet, or the payment of an expensive insurance policy. We needed two carnets, for bikes worth around five grand apiece. This meant raising cash or sureties of £15,000 just to have paperwork that allowed us to enter Senegal.

We blanched at this news and wondered how we would get over this huge hurdle. If we wanted to visit The Gambia, then we needed the Carnet. The Gambia is landlocked on three sides by Senegal, with the fourth facing the coast. This was clearly a major issue.

On other fronts, things were coming together fine. Two shiny new GS Dakars were collected from Vines BMW in Guilford and enthusiastically pored over and analysed by Dave and myself. Some initial riding to get the bikes run in revealed machines with excellent riding characteristics in a range of conditions. Comfortable, flexible and versatile, we knew immediately that we'd made the right choice in asking BMW to support our expedition.

We rode down to Sussex to leave the bikes at Metal Mule for luggage fitting. A lovely afternoon was spent with Paul and Ann enthusiastically discussing our plans for the journey. We were also able to pick their brains about their own trip across Africa some years before.

We continued making plans. Maps were obtained and routes discussed. We had six weeks to get to the Gambia and back. The basic plan was to take the ferry from Portsmouth to Bilbao and ride across Spain before crossing into Morocco via Ceuta. We would then head straight south down the country, linking up with the Atlantic Route south from Agadir. Then down through the Western Sahara.

Mauritania contained a question mark. We'd read much about the planned new tarmac road across the desert from Nouadhibou in the north of the country to Nouakchott, the capital. Rumours about how complete it was varied. Some claimed it was almost finished; others spoke of miles of bad piste between completed stages. There was no real consistency in the reports that we were receiving. Even the excellent Horizons Unlimited, the overland travellers' website, could provide little in definitive information.

The alternative route was the old Atlantic beach route. This was an arduous two-day ride across stony plain, soft sand and then down the beach itself. A prospect that I did not relish given our tight timetable.

We felt that the new road – assuming it existed – was the best bet and resigned ourselves to dealing with whatever we discovered when we entered Mauritania.

Numerous people had warned us about the border crossing from Mauritania into Senegal at a place called Rosso. Comments ranged from 'It's hell' to 'I had to buy my passport back from these crooks at the border'.

Rosso lay on the road that we had to take, but an alternative was suggested which would take us along a 100 kilometre piste from Rosso to a place called Diama Dam. The border crossing here was reputed to be far more relaxed.

Once into Senegal, we intended to visit a travellers' campsite called Zebrabar, a place which was reputed to be like a tropical paradise. We figured that a place that sounded like this would probably be in order after days in the desert.

The final outward stretch of the journey would take us through Senegal, via Kaolack, down to The Gambia and onto Banjul. This is where we would meet Barbara and Mutch, who had already decided to fly out and meet us so that we could all visit the Gambia Riders for Health centre. Andrea and Barry from Riders agreed to set up a visit from us with the local Gambia Riders team. The plan was then to ride east, enter Mali and visit what had become known as 'Simon's place' – the site of his accident.

How much planning and preparation to put into a journey is often a matter for fierce debate. I generally tend to prefer to have some sort of loose daily plan, a general idea of the route to take and a rough view on where to sleep that night. Some folks make no plans at all and let their wheels take them where they will. Others plan everything from breakfast though to what time they will go to bed.

Our planned expedition was heavily supported by sponsors who had been convinced by our prospectus to loan us equipment worth many thousands of pounds for us to achieve certain targets that we had proposed. Our sponsors were helpful and very supportive, but sponsorship does not come from a sense of altruism – sponsors expect something back in PR and marketing terms. They also expect to know what's happening and when. They do not appreciate fundamental changes of plans without being consulted.

Because of this, I felt that we had a sense of responsibility to have a reasonable plan and create confidence that we would do as we said we would and achieve the targets that we had set.

In PR terms, both for the sponsors and for MoR, we needed to ensure success and minimise the potential for problems by mitigating potential risks on the journey. For me this was no holiday. It was a journey undertaken in respect for a friend passed on with the aim of providing PR coverage for our new charity and provide value for those who were risking both equipment and credibility by supporting our efforts.

It started to become clear that Dave saw things slightly differently. He had initially made no comments about the route or any of the preparation work and sponsor relationship building that we had already done. He also seemed happy with itinerary and the aims of the journey. But for some reason his views started to change. I started receiving emails suggesting wildcard routes taking us way off the beaten track. I felt that these ideas could throw announced intentions way off track.

I began to feel uncomfortable. Was Dave about to throw a spanner in the works by insisting on doing something far removed from what we had told our sponsors we would be doing?

It all came to a head one evening during one of Dave's regular planning visits to London.

"This is my holiday that I'm using up here." he said "If you think I'm gonna stick rigidly to some itinerary, then you've got another think coming."

I pursed my lips feeling slightly alarmed, despite the months of planning which he had been deeply involved in, Dave had given no indication before now that he felt so strongly.

"So what are you suggesting then?" I asked.

"Just that if I want to take off in a different direction, or change the plan en route then I will. OK?"

This started a row.

"I can't go telling sponsors one thing and then go off and do something else." I said. "They expect things to happen as we explained it to them. They would not have offered us all this kit and the bikes if I'd had gone to them with some vague plan of the two of us floating about in West Africa with no proper planning, or a recognisable itinerary."

We argued the toss for a while, but the basic issue was clear. I saw the trip as being as much about duty and responsibility as I saw it as a new adventure. Dave saw it as a holiday, a chance to explore Africa at his own pace and didn't want the responsibility of answering to sponsors.

"Well dammit." I said. "There's no way we can do this trip without the sponsors. We ain't got the bikes and we ain't got the support. I for one do not want to waste the opportunity to maximise the PR that we get from a sponsored trip, so that we can get the word about MoR and Simon's trip out to a wide audience."

"Well I could do the trip just as well on my V-Strom and there's no reason why your Harley wouldn't make it."

"That's not the point." I retorted. "This is not what we agreed and you've said nothing before about wanting to swan off and do your own thing before. You've had plenty of opportunities to say something before I went and secured all the support that we have."

Wisely, we moved onto other topics of discussion, but I retired to bed that night feeling worried about the whole thing. Was Dave going to insist on derailing our, until now, carefully prepared plans?

The next morning Dave seemed to have a change of mood.

"Look, I'm still not happy about being dictated to by sponsor requirements, but we'll get this thing done OK – and keep the sponsors happy, you'll see."

Relief flooded through me. The issue had not gone away, but I was glad that Dave had considered what I had said.

"Thanks mate." I replied. "You know, there may be chances to take some loops or adjust the route as we travel, but for the time being let's just focus on making the plan that we have work, is that OK?"

It was and I figured that we'd deal with any issues about the route as they came up. Sometimes, it's best to deal with a problem by letting it lie until a solution presents itself and this seemed to be one of those occasions.

We couldn't plan for every eventuality anyway, to do so would have been impossible and ultimately disappointing. It seemed best to let this problem go and let the road unfold before us, dealing with any issues as we travelled.

This was also the day that the bikes came back from Metal Mule. As Paul wheeled the immaculate GSs from his van, fully kitted in bright shiny new luggage, we both felt for the first time that the trip was really going to happen.

Jabbering away at each other excitedly, we circled the bikes talking about all manner of things as we analysed options for loading gear and fitting additional equipment.

We took a 'shakedown' ride to Guildford where Vines had asked us to come in and pick up our Rallye suits. The bikes handled well and we took the old A25 road across country, via Westerham and Reigate. Stretching the legs of our bikes and enjoying the curious looks of other road users as the fully kitted GSs, with their slab sided boxes, passed them by.

The visit to Vines was an amusing hour of trying our suits on. The only colour left in stock was red and white and we laughed at the sight of each other, kitted out like Duplo Men in our signal red attire. They were excellent outfits though. Pockets in the right places, lots of air venting and also weather and armour protection. Just the job for a major overland trip in extreme conditions.

Just about everything else had now been organised. Visas had been obtained for Mauritania and Mali, though a visit to Brussels had been necessary for the Mali visas. We had sorted out medical supplies, had sat in doctors surgeries and visited the Nomad Travel Centre for various jabs. We'd received a pile of essential spares for the bikes and fitted the Scottoilers, radio and video equipment to the bikes. The latter had been supplied by bikecameras.com.

Our PR was also bearing fruit, with good coverage in the press and messages of support coming from Ewan McGregor and Charley Boorman of 'Long Way Round' fame. World motorcycle endurance Guinness World Record holders, Kevin and Julia Sanders also offered words of support and gave useful advice based on their own travel experiences.

But the Carnets still remained an impenetrable barrier to our plans unless we could come up with the financing needed to secure the documents.

Barbara had been dealing with Paul Gowen at the RAC, 'Mr Carnet' as many people know him. Paul is the kind of chap who is both empathic and comes across as really understanding overland journeys and the state of things in different developing countries. He had given us a great deal of help with the Carnet application and had discussed with Barbara at some length the options available for financing.

Lodging straight cash with the RAC was not an option – we didn't have 15K. The insurance option also required cash up front, several hundred pounds in fact, but the majority of this would be returned at the end of the journey. The final option was a bank guarantee and it was this that Barbara settled upon.

Even getting one of these meant several leaps through hoops. Not least trying to find someone at Barclays Bank who knew what a Carnet was, what specific guarantees we required and who was authorised to arrange one.

Several phone calls later took Barbara to the Bank's business centre in Birmingham and to someone who not only understood what we were after, but had also heard of a Carnet de Passage. A few days later, Paul Gowan phoned Barbara with the news that the guarantee had arrived and that both Carnets would soon be with us.

"You'd better not lose these, or screw up the border procedures."

Barbara warned Dave and myself in an email. "We'd have to sell the house to pay the guarantee if an administration of a country you visited cashed them in."

Then we got married. In a chaotic timetable of frantic activity and hassle, the wonderful day was an interlude which will always fill me with the most joyful and serene of thoughts and memories of friendship and beauty. Dave was best man. The service, reception and party at the Georgian mansion at Buxted, in the depth of the lovely Sussex countryside, marked a lifetime highpoint. Buxted was also a perfect setting for the start of married life with my lovely Barbara.

The tale of that day is for another time, but as a gathering of clans and friends, little could surpass it. It was the best of times which Barbara and I were grateful to share with our families and also with those others who are closest to us.

Our final commitment before 'The Off' was ten days at the Motorcycle Show where, sited conveniently alongside the huge BMW stand, we displayed Simon's bike and one of the fully kitted and prepped Dakars. Simon's bike had made it to the NEC as he'd planned, but not in the circumstances any of us would have wanted.

New adventure contrasted with the tangible evidence of long and hard global travel that was clear for all to see as the thousands of show visitors viewed Simon's Overlander. Displays celebrated Simon's achievement and announced new life for Motorcycle Outreach.

We held an official launch for MoR and the Simon Milward Memorial Run. It was a well-supported event. Senior people from BMW attended, as did many folks from what can be called the 'overland community'. We met Sam Manicom for the first time, the overland adventurer and writer who would give us a huge amount of good advice and friendship in the years ahead. Jane and Paul Milward were also there, the pair of them spending several days at the show, looking after the stand and talking about both Simon and the forthcoming journey with enthusiasm. This was appreciated as the motorcycle show can be exhausting for exhibitors.

On the last day of the Show and four days before Dave and I were due to leave, Barbara and I headed up to Birmingham to relieve Paul and Jane and break down the stand. We loaded the car and I climbed aboard the Dakar and rode out of the halls. We headed for Stratford on Avon in the gloom of an early dusk, where we checked into a hotel for an evening without hassles. An opportunity to set aside a little time for each other.

It was a pleasant if sometimes poignant evening. We tried not to talk about my imminent departure, but it hung over us like the kind of cloud which may or may not hold rain. Excitement at the start of a new adventure on one hand, concern about forced separation and the possibility of travel problems on the other.

We knew we wouldn't be apart for long, given that Barbara was due to fly to The Gambia with Mutch for the Riders for Health visit. But the long days and miles until then weighed heavily.

For the first time, I found myself feeling a little nervous about the whole thing. These were thoughts that I quickly dismissed. Worrying wouldn't change anything and we'd planned and prepared as much as was humanly possible.

What would be would be.

THE 'OFF' 14TH NOVEMBER 2005

My eyes opened and for a while I lay looking up and the ceiling, feeling warm and comfortable, not wanting to break the spell of that relaxed, just-woken 'fug'.

The previous afternoon Dave had flown in from Poland with a ton of equipment and riding gear. Our enthusiastic greetings when I met him off the 'plane was soon overtaken with the hundred and one final little things that we needed to discuss. The journey from Stansted Airport to Beckenham resulted in a long list of last minute things that needed to be done.

Evening dinner was accompanied by lots of wine as we celebrated the start of the trip. Mutch came over as did Fil Schiannini, who worked with Kevin and Julia Sanders from GlobeBusters. He manufactured custom 'Green Leopard' earplugs as a side-line and he had offered to kit us out with a pair of these each.

We went over our kit, talking excitedly about the journey and debating how best to compact the laid out equipment into the Metal Mule boxes in the most efficient way.

It reminded me of another night in Brussels, so long ago that it seemed to be almost a lifetime away...

I didn't say anything, but I expect that Dave had the same thought at the same time. He sat quietly for a moment and then looked at me and smiled.

"Shame we're not doing this to go and actually meet Simon." He said.

The need for coffee shook me out of my morning fug and I went downstairs to find Dave already brewing a pot of coffee. Oli, Barbara's son, was frying eggs.

One coffee turned into three as we went over the final preparations again.

The phone started ringing. Press calls, people wishing us luck, a call from the Met police to ask us if we'd like an escort out of London. There were also work calls and emails as I desperately worked on completing remaining MCI business before a six-week absence.

Dave was busy loading the bikes, checking and adjusting things. He came out with the occasional comment, or grunted as things went the way he wanted.

People came and went. Mutch arrived and bantered in his usual amusing and slightly eccentric way.

The clock slowly turned inexorably towards the four pm start of our adventure and the 70-odd mile ride to the ferry in Portsmouth.

As dusk settled, the sound of revving engines heralded the arrival of several police bikes. Neighbours curtains twitched as they doubtless speculated upon the imminent raid and arrest of the international criminals who lived on their street. Smiles all around as mugs of steaming tea went into the hands of the Metropolitan Police's finest.

The minute hand of the clock started its climb towards the hour of our departure. We pushed the bikes out onto the road and clambered into our gear. Equipment was checked, straps tightened. Loads checked for security.

Another friend, Steve Manning, had appeared to photograph the occasion.

The hour struck four pm. Goodbyes yelled as the convoy departed and headed out of Beckenham. Mutch and Barbara rode their bikes with us as Dave and I headed the small convoy of motorcycles, shepherded expertly by police outriders.

Out of London via Biggin Hill, down the escarpment into Surrey and onto the M25. Regular well-paced riding and curiously well behaved traffic as drivers took unusual care in the presence of so many traffic cops.

We Joined the A3 and the road into Guildford. Friendly greetings from the staff at Vines, a quick coffee and a few words from Vine's ever supportive Duncan Bell. Then Dave and I mounted our Dakars, to leave our escorts behind and head south to the port.

Barbara stood in the middle of car park, smiling and waving in my rear view mirror, but unable to hide a pensive and sad demeanour. Tears, barely held back behind her shining eyes. A low moment that I tried to put behind me as we picked up speed on the A3, Portsmouth-bound.

Our ride in the darkness built speed. Free from sponsors, escorts and well-wishers, the two of us opened our throttles and let the bikes take us south, with increasing joy in our hearts at the realisation of our plans and the start of new adventure.

Portsmouth and the mammoth shape of the Bilbao-bound ferry towered above us as we coasted into the port. After pulling up in the waiting area, I saw the shapes of Paul and Ann Goulding who were waiting to bid us farewell. We enjoyed pleasant conversation over a final coffee on UK soil as we waited to board the ship. We thanked them both for coming all this way from their home to wish us well.

Then the tannoy announced that it was time to sail. After final goodbyes we trundled aboard the ferry, tied the bikes and struggled up to our cabins, hauling the metal boxes up lifts and along narrow passages.

Later we sat in the restaurant, with good food ordered and a bottle of wine opened. We sighed relief and relaxed as the lights of Hampshire cruised by the windows and the Pride of Bilbao gathered knots and headed out to sea.

*

THE STORM

Pitching and rolling filled my dreams. Like a scene from one of Hammond Innes' finest sea faring thrillers, my world churned around about me in a chaotic tumble of thoughts and sensations. Consciousness returned and I became aware of a cupboard door banging and curtains swaying across the windows.

The ship lurched violently to one side and I involuntarily rolled over to the edge of the bunk.

I sat up feeling woozy, vacant, and looked out of the spray soaked window at the Maelstrom beyond. Huge broken topped waves marched across the ocean leaving a deep swell behind them before they crashed against our hull. The low dawn light was masked by threatening clouds and mountainous waves reached towards the horizon. We were protected from the wind in our comfortable cabin, but the low moaning of forced drafts of air could be heard beyond our door.

The low throb of engines resonated through the deck of our cabin.

Dave stirred.

"How long has it been like this?" I asked.

"Well, I woke at five and the ship was already bouncing about." He looked at his watch "Hmm eight am. Still early. Do you want breakfast?"

"Not sure." I replied. I don't get seasick, but I sometimes find myself arriving at the portal before serious nausea and by sitting up I had stirred those unpleasant and tiring feelings. "A coffee would be grand though."

I sent Barbara a text from my phone which, curiously, seemed to be working OK. 'All well, big storm, bit yucky, but OK.'

She immediately replied. 'Use tablets.' OK, what tablets. A

quick rummage in our medical supplies, which contained enough kit to deal with a major outbreak of plague, minor war, pestilence and epidemic, produced some medication which were designed to make life more comfortable.

We clambered along pitching corridors to find coffee and some food. There weren't many people about at the early hour, but green faces were a common feature on those folks that we did see.

Coffee and a small amount of breakfast was slowly relished and we wondered what to do with our day. The main problem with storms is that unless you've got some vital task, or you're a working member of the ship's crew, there's actually bugger all to do. Movement can be difficult in conditions such as these so, as a mere passenger, all that's left to do is a lot of sitting about while waiting for the sea to moderate.

We tried wandering the ship. Difficult and slightly risky on the stairs. We lingered for a while at a large window which showed alternating views of the open sky and the deep blue as the ship pitched from side to side. A middle aged couple staggered drunkenly out of the lift just behind us. The woman, seeing a bin positioned strategically by the lift doors, stumbled a pace or two towards it before noisily throwing up, only just managing to direct her vile brew into the bin.

"Nice." said Dave. "Let's get some more coffee and try going out on deck."

This turned out to be a good plan. Despite the storm, it wasn't cold and the spray didn't reach the top deck. We sat in splay-legged deckchairs, designed so that they didn't tip over during rough passages and sipped our coffees. We gazed out over the stern of the ship as the horizon pitched up and down perhaps twenty or thirty feet at a time.

Dave checked his GPS.

"We're just passing the Ile d'Ouessant."

This put us somewhere off the far north western coast of France and would explain why the sea had mounted in ferocity since the early hours, as we headed southwards. Exposing our flanks to a storm that we had previously been forging straight into the teeth of.

Time passed and we sat talking about nothing much as friends sometimes do. Occasionally people would come and go, but mostly we were left to ourselves and to the elements which, being warmly bundled up in our coats, we were thoroughly enjoying. The clean fresh air filling our lungs and no pressure to do anything at all lent a nice feeling of escape.

As the day wore on the sea moderated and more people began to appear. Inaction forced by a rolling and pitching ship was replaced by a sense of boredom. That afternoon we spent time going through kit and repacking so that certain items became more accessible if we needed them while travelling.

The sea calmed further, so that by dusk, only a gentle swell remained. We took another walk on deck to witness the sinking sun break through the wrack of cloud on the horizon. It cast deep red hues across the ocean towards us.

And then, nothing to do but to descend a few decks to the bar, for the first of many sundowners that we would enjoy on the journey. Later, we feasted on the truly exceptional nosebag that P&O offered on this ferry route.

*

MIND GAMES

Dave's bike appeared in the distance, his headlight getting larger as he sped out of the gloom towards me on the autopista. He slowed towards the hard shoulder and drifted to a stop behind my bike.

"Can't find the bloody trousers." He looked pissed off. "That and my bloody GPS means that I'm having a great day." He cast me an accusatory glare which I avoided by turning away to zip up my kit and put my helmet on.

The GPS incident was my fault. Dave had sent a mount over to London which would allow the device to be fitted to his Dakar, plus the necessary wiring. But without realising that the power adaptor, which is used to power up the unit via a car cigarette lighter, also functioned as a transformer. I'd wired his GPS directly to the bike electrics, with predictable results from feeding a one or two volt piece of kit with a circuitry-frazzling twelve volt blast.

To add insult to injury, we'd blown up a second GPS, which Dave had bought in London, before I realised my mistake. A blunder which was now costing my companion real money. It can't have helped for him to see my BMW Navigator faultlessly tracking our journey and wired correctly to my bike. We would get to Ceuta before Dave could finally sort out his GPS arrangements.

A day that had started well, with the ride from the ferry onto Spanish roads and an exhilarating ride up into the mountains on the Madrid road out of Bilbao, was turning into bad tempered misery. The cold clamped down on us and difficulties and errors evolved into barely concealed anger both at our circumstances and at each other.

We set our bikes into the wind and set off with the Dakars creating the characteristic raw thump-thump of the big single as both bikes accelerated away. Both were running fine and had good acceleration, despite the weight of humans and luggage that they were carrying.

We passed Burgos, stopping briefly for fuel and a welcome coffee, the warm air of the café bar contrasting strongly with the chill of the outside world. A television blared in the corner, very much as they do in most Spanish bars and many restaurants. We enjoyed strong coffee and chatted while absent-mindedly churning our feet in the carpet of cigarette ends and ash which liberally covered the floor. Then we went out into the cold again to take on the frosty challenge of our ride south.

Slowly we built up speed. A cautious sixty mph cruising speed was gradually replaced with a more satisfying seventy mph; the bikes not affected by being allowed to breathe a little freer.

Past Lerma and on towards Aranda de Duero, the road marked the way to our adventure. There wasn't much traffic and the views were excellent. But it was freezing cold. Jack Frost crept his way into our riding suits and another coffee stop beckoned.

But the more we travelled the more we settled into our old routine when we rode together. I led, trailblazing a Spanish route which we had both done many times before. Dave rode behind me, sometimes close to my rear wheel, sometimes dropping back for half a mile or so.

We crossed the undulating hills and brown grasslands of the Sierra de Pradales and started the long steep climb towards the towering Sierra de Guadarrama, which lay like a huge barrier across our path. The range divides the northern regions of Spain from the central region, which baked under a merciless sun in the summer months.

As we climbed the cold became more intense. Freezing fog patches gave way to denser gloom as we entered the low cloud base. Our visors fogged up and our pace slowed as we reached the summit. We were mindful of dangerously driven cars which still hurtled by at high speed, despite visibility that could be measured in feet rather than yards.

Then through a tunnel and onto a steep descent, picking up speed again. We were cautious of icy patches on the road, but soon emerged from the cloud to appreciate the opening vista of dark mountainous country and habitation dotted about the landscape. A brooding layer of black cloud overlaid the vista.

We pulled into a service station to fuel up and grab a bite. Both of us chilled to the core, but now feeling exhilarated by our ride. Hopeless attempts to heat up some pre-packaged food in a small portable grill doing nothing to dampen our enthusiasm and Dave took a photo of me trying to chew a frozen sausage.

Onwards to Madrid. Cloud, chill winds and freezing fog rapidly gave way to low bright winter sunshine which bathed the still undulating countryside with a sharp glare. Trees, walls and buildings cast long shadows of stark contrast.

Ploughing determinedly into the maze of motorways which criss-crossed Madrid, progress was made as the Dakars were swiftly piloted through the urban network which cut a way through densely populated suburbs and city. Randomly navigated traffic filed along its multi-lane routes.

We attracted stares and the occasional hoot from the many that saw our heavily laden, brightly coloured, bikes and the pair of us in our fresh red and white Duplo man suits. I wondered what those who took an interest in us would have thought about the idea of taking two wheels to our far distant African destination.

We curved away from the fume filled knot of city roads and onto the motorway southwards, signposted to Cordoba and the last long stretch before our destination for the day; Valdepenas.

The terrain slowly levelled out into the plains of Castilla La Mancha, a baking cauldron of relentless heat in the summer, now brown, cold and desiccated. Bare trees and bushes sat in a landscape which was cooked in the summer and freeze-dried in cold winters of windswept chill.

The sun fell low in the sky and browns gave way to a sombre grey light as we rode along a motorway that led through an almost featureless region. I shivered and checked the GPS with a keen eye on the distance to our destination.

We had nowhere in mind to stay, this wasn't the kind of journey where every stop was planned in meticulous detail. Instead we had set ourselves rough daily targets with the intention of casting about for accommodation once we had achieved our aims for the day.

We stopped briefly to check out a hotel which had indicated its presence on my Navigator. It advertised itself as a Parador. I suppose I could have stopped there, but it was expensive and isolated. Dave was having none of it and to me the interior represented a faded representation of an Eastern Bloc building of the 1960s. All faded ribbed wooden panelling, low, plain tables, poor abstract designs and a foul smell of stale cigarettes – off-putting even for a smoker. We pushed on.

Dusk was settling as we rode under a motorway bridge to see the bright lights of Valdepenas open up before us. Well, the lights of expressway truck stops, fuel stations and the few bars which served the small regional centre of this important wine growing area of Spain.

Valdepenas is hardly an architectural or historical gem, but it would serve our transient intentions for the night. It had the bonus of being well placed for a hassle free start to our final day in Spain.

A roadhouse offered basic but comfortable accommodation, a pleasant bar and restaurant attached a perfect accompaniment.

We were both on a high. The day had gone well despite the earlier tensions, washed away by a fantastic mileage munching ride and the semi detached companionship of the road. We'd enjoyed the psychological security of the companionship, but with the welcome solitude of personal thought and time to be in touch with one's self.

We settled in the bar and two beers vanished in quick succession as we watched the final vestiges of daylight fade from the cold blue sky. Trucks roared past the roadhouse and their tail lights disappeared into the night as they headed on their way to distant locations in this vast and often empty country.

Another beer and we repaired to the dining room for a meal of soup followed by roast chicken in breadcrumbs and sauce.

A few mouthfuls into this second course and the feeling hit me like a sledgehammer.

A wave of mild nausea followed immediately by a sharp sense of foreboding, anxiety and panic. I was mentally seized in a vice like grip and I stopped eating and sat back staring ahead. Consumed with unexpected and alarming inner feelings.

Dave glanced up from his meal.

"You OK?"

"Er yea, er huh, yea fine mate."

I was anything but.

Somehow I made it through the rest of the meal. The nausea had passed almost as soon as it had swept over me, but the prospect of sickness had not left my thoughts. Anxiety settled within me like a stifling blanket of fear and refused to budge.

What the hell is this? I asked myself.

I tried to put a brave face on it as we finished the bottle of good wine that we had ordered. But it must have been clear to Dave that something was preoccupying me.

An early start the following morning, meant early to bed and I made the excuse of checking the bikes and having a final cigarette to give Barbara a ring in London. I paced up and down outside puffing away, with a feeling of anxiety which I felt was leaking from every pore.

I told her how I felt, but aside from offering comfort, there wasn't much to be said. She remembered an episode in the Alps the previous year where a long day's high pressure riding followed by too much rich food and wine had left me looking more than a bit green for an hour or so. But that was a momentary sickness which had generated more in the way of ironic laughs and ribald humour than anything else.

This was quite different.

"Look, you're tired, go to bed. You'll be better in the morning."

I wasn't. The following morning was grey, dull and slightly drizzling. Breakfast and a nice early start saw us heading out onto the road before eight am. However, all I could manage was a coffee and a nibble on the corner of a piece of bread. Wordlessly, I stumbled around, packing kit, adjusting straps, not saying anything. Totally consumed by my inner torment.

I'm Ill; I'm not ill; I'm going to be ill; I'm going to be fine; what about the road ahead; the road ahead is fine; I'm ill; I'm not; we'll crash and die; we won't crash and die; I'll overheat and die; you won't; there won't be a road in Africa; sand will cover everything; there'll be malaria, there'll be sickness and dysentery; the bike will break down; there'll be nowhere to stay – and on and on and on; a droning mental monotone which seemed to be drilling itself into my brain.

Ever varying combinations of irrational fears running over and over in my head, overlaid with feelings that varied from mild anxiety to almost blind panic.

I began to feel that I was in danger of being too terrified to go on.

And it had all been brought on by essentially nothing at all. This was a new experience for me. The only times I had felt anything like this in the past was when about to take to the air in passenger jets – another environment which engenders irrational doom-laden inner thoughts and fears.

I love flying, but hate being a passenger on a commercial flight. How odd is that? Indeed, the prospect fills me with fear and creeping anxiety days before boarding a scheduled flight. As an airline passenger I am nervous, anxious, barely in control of my fear. I only fly when there are no other options.

Yet the logic of this is completely daft. Present me with an old piston-engined, propeller driven aircraft and I'm yer man. I'll gaily take to the air in anything old, or basic. I even have flying hours under my belt. Only a month before heading off with Dave, I had added an hour or so to my piloting experience by taking a dual control 1938 Boeing Stearman biplane up over Kent and the Weald. A magnificent flight with a raucous radial spinning in front of me as I swooped low over the beach at Ramsgate and flew high over the Thames Estuary.

Bucking and weaving through layers of thin cloud at 5,000 feet in an open cockpit gave a sense of freedom and exhilaration unmatched elsewhere in human experience.

Fears are often utterly irrational and totally perplexing.

And here I was, in southern Spain, two days into a six week trip down the west coast of Africa, seized by something that had come from God knows where. I could rationalise, but fear still had me totally in its grip.

But go on we must. There was no turning back. Why should I turn back anyway? No reason 'But what happens when you get sick and the bike breaks?' asked the voice in my head.

With grim determination, I turned the bike out onto the highway and headed south. Dave followed close behind, probably wondering what the hell had got into me.

In all other respects the ride was, if anything, an improvement on the previous days thrash down fairly bland motorways. Not long after we left Valdepenas, the road started to curve and weave its way through the eastern tail of the Sierra Morena, climbing ever higher through wooded mountains.

Low cloud created a softer light. Dull, but atmospheric. It was also much warmer than it had been on the previous day. The rising mountains stood out in sharp relief, each fold of the land providing contrast and clear perspective.

The motorway became a slower route as we curved through long mountain passes, the road surface become a patchwork of variable quality tarmac and concrete. Near Santa Elena we passed a roadside café full of trucks, slowing briefly as we hesitated about whether to stop or not.

Deciding against this we roared off once again only to pull in a few kilometres further on in a high lay-by, where a short stone tower offered mountainous views over the pass and sight of the northbound motorway, which was at a much lower level.

It was a good opportunity to do a bit of leg stretching and to get some photos. It was still dull, but not cold. Aside from the nagging knot of fear inside me, I was enjoying a good start to the day's ride.

With my mind no longer preoccupied with riding, the mental demons came flooding back. Casting them aside as much as I could, I focussed on chatting with Dave and on taking some refreshment from our packs.

We continued southwards, noting that we had passed into Andalusia. As we rode, we emerged from the Morena to rolling plains at a higher level than we were during yesterday's blast across the barren plains. Green-clad farmland marched by as we rode on a route which was turning steadily westwards.

Later, we turned south and were soon surrounded by vast acreages of olive groves and grape vines. Every so often a small rustic stone building stuck its roof above the fields of olives and wine. Occasionally there were one or two men tending their horticultural charges.

In the distance we could see the Sierra Magina coming into view, more dramatic vistas, the city of Jaen nestling at their base. A good place to stop for a spot of food and coffee.

The service station was like any other that you come across in Europe, providing coffee and pastries to sustain us for more road miles.

Except that I couldn't get a thing down my throat apart from several small cups of coffee. The fear had me in its grip and it wouldn't let go. As the day progressed my mental turmoil was getting worse, not better. I figured that these stupid feelings would pass as we progressed. But instead, the unshakeable anguish was generating a sense of physical malaise.

A dark void of turmoil distracted my mind and made it impossible to talk. Dave sat silently again. Heaven knows what he thought was going on in the mind of his silent companion.

There was nothing for it though and we pressed on, having first taken some pictures of the nearby city set in its dramatic mountainous backdrop.

The sun was gamely trying to make an appearance and every so often shafts of light broke through the comforting gloom to cast a warm light across the landscape and onto the nearby mountain ranges. Sharp contrasts of brown and grey colours, enhancing the already beautiful scenery.

The Sierra Nevada shoved grand peaks into the sky south of Grenada as we approached. Our bikes made steady progress as we bypassed the city and turned west. The Sierra de Almijara laying to our left as we anticipated the turn-off to Malaga some kilometres ahead.

Jeez, it was cold. The temperature had been steadily falling as we rode on higher roads and the air became cooler. The green swathes of farmland gave way to scrub and huge prairie fields lying fallow for the winter. We looked forward to our final major turn south on this route, figuring that lower levels would be much warmer as we descended towards the tourist flesh pots of the Costa del Sol.

We stopped for coffee and a final warm up at the Puerto de las Pedrizas. The road was already dipping downwards and I figured that we'd enjoy the descent into warmth.

"Remember the last time we were in these parts?" I asked.

Dave grinned.

"Yep, bloody traffic chaos a bit further on."

"How are you feeling anyway?" He asked.

The demons were still crawling around my brain, but The Road had taken hold and I was starting to enjoy the day a little more.

"Fine. I reckon we'll soon see the sea, always cheers me up."

Half an hour later, we were diving in and out of heavier traffic, heading westwards with determination as we sought to escape the congested misery of the Malaga bypass.

As predicted, the ride down miles of winding mountain motorway was accompanied by rising traffic levels and increasing warmth as we descended from the high plains.

I was starting to miss the emptier motorways of inland Spain and much easier riding. But then we rode by the final exit to the resort and lane discipline more or less reasserted itself.

Cold riding had been replaced by pleasant ambient warmth which was enough to make me want to shed a few layers. Cliffs in gold and yellow tones washed with the mid afternoon sun rose away from the road to the right. To the left, the Mediterranean winked and glinted in the sharp light of the winter sun. Sun which also shone into our faces, partially obscuring the road ahead.

Some kilometres later Dave pulled his bike alongside and motioned for me to pull off. Glancing at the map and GPS showed that Marbella was only a short distance ahead.

We pulled off the motorway and soon found a fuel station, adjacent to a shopping development and Dave went in search of a sandwich.

"There's a shopping mall just over there, think I'll go looking for a GPS." he announced.

"Grand, gives me a chance to enjoy some peace and quiet and a bit of sun." I replied.

We parked the bikes under a tree next to the mall and Dave strode off in his usual purposeful fashion. His red and white Rallye suit trousers looking incongruous against his tee-shirt in the warm sun.

I got another drink and relaxed against the wall, enjoying the various comings and goings from the nearby mall entrance. Sometimes families babbling way at each other, with hassled fathers being harangued by stressed wives. Sometimes groups of teenage folk of both sexes, dressed stylishly, carrying mobile phones. Some also carried the kind of minimal crash helmets that one sees in these parts.

Mopeds and scooters were everywhere, zipping in and out of the car park, parked haphazardly in any convenient spot. Young men and women came and went by bike, greeting each other in excitable Latin fashion.

Dave's disembodied voice unexpectedly burst from my pocket. "Can't find a bloody electronics shop!" he declared, making me jump. I'd forgotten about the two way radios, which we had last used fairly unsuccessfully in bike to bike mode the previous evening.

"Bugger the electronics shop." I replied; "You should see the girls out here."

"Pretty good in here as well." he shot back. "See yer in a sec."

He came back, not with a GPS, but with yet more coffee. We soon climbed aboard the BMWs and headed westwards once again. This time forward motion assisted by the buzz of too much caffeine.

The sun was sinking as The Rock of Gibraltar appeared ahead and the final miles of our European ride opened up around the Baha de Algeciras. The dual carriageway gave way to road works and broken tarmac as we entered the faded and battered port of Algeciras and finally arrived at the ferry port.

We grinned at each other and shook hands. Spain crossed in two hits. Perfect – all going to plan.

The demons were resting. But not for long.

The gas turbines of the rumbling Sea Cat gained power as we slipped from port. We stood on the stern enjoying the evening light and taking photographs. I looked across the bay at Gibraltar's lights, which were starting to wink against a darkening sky. They seemed warm and welcoming compared to the dark unknown ahead. What awaited us? 'Good times' I told myself as the demons threatened to take hold again.

Dave was busy taking photos of the vista, some great views were opening up of the bay and the mountains behind Algeciras.

Southwards, we could see the mighty Rif rising from the sea. A promise of adventure, but what else? I suppressed a cold shiver as Dave slapped me on the shoulder.

"Turn this way for a pic and fer Christ's sake smile will yer!"

*

MEFLOQUINE MISERY

Gradually loosing 'way', the catamaran coasted into port. The long plumes of spray, testament to the power of its propulsion system, gradually reducing to churning white soup below the stern. Darkness had almost fallen as we emerged on our bikes from the car deck. We clattered our way down the ramp and onto African soil for the first time in five years.

Ceuta greeted us with palm lined roads and its usual mix of heavy traffic and mopeds. The fortress walls rising above us as we 'puttered' slowly along the port road looking for the Hotel Africa, where we had stayed before.

Dave swerved into the kerb as he spotted the now familiar sign.

I looked up at the building. Faded paintwork, broken windows and a generally tired air about the place was not what I remembered. Dave went inside only to emerge a few moments later.

"They'll take us OK, but this place is a crap hole now. Full of dodgy characters and they're not the same people who used to own it."

"OK, let's press on into town." I replied, "We should be able to find an alternative."

It was good to be back. I remembered how much Ceuta had impressed me before. In the evening light, the sea reflected the lights of the enclave in a romantic fashion as we rode up into town, soon finding ourselves in the old Spanish centre of this tax free haven.

The problem was that we couldn't see many hotels. We tried a guesthouse or two, but all were full. Hotels seemed thin on the ground.

We rode around a cobbled square which seemed to be a Ceuta focal point. Palm trees lined the square and a pleasant small park lay at the centre. At the east end was a large Parador, a luxury hotel. We stopped, there was no intention of paying inflated prices, but Dave figured that it was a good place to ask for help.

It was. After an attempt to get Dave to part with lots of Euros for a night of style in the Parador, the receptionist directed us to the slightly more modest Tripp Hotel a few streets away. Much more business-like, even if the price was not far short of what we would have paid to stay in the Parador.

We checked in.

"Just like any other European business-box." I sniffed disapprovingly. "But it'll do the job." Dave didn't object, though he added a few choice words to describe his low opinion of the place. This was not Dave's style at all.

But we'd arrived late and accommodation was clearly an issue in Ceuta unless booked well in advance. I wasn't about to start engaging in a fruitless conversation about the best way to choose travel accommodation. It was dark and we were hungry.

And in any case, the demons had emerged with the darkness and were once again plaguing me with promise of illness, crashes, death, dehydration. Grinding me down with fear and terror.

Eat? That was a laugh as far as I was concerned. We wandered towards the port and finding nothing suitable in the restaurant stakes, we settled on a corner café, which also did a reasonable menu.

I've heard it said that any restaurant which shows photographs of its menu should be avoided at all costs. This place, run by a grubby looking Arab was full of faded pictures of various dubious gastronomic delights, making the food appear unappetising and cheap. 'Cheap, but not necessarily cheerful', I thought.

I wasn't hungry, the strangling knot of fear in my stomach had removed any urge to eat. Dave ordered beers and studied the menu. I swallowed my beer like a man just emerged from the desert, hoping that the cheap alcohol would settle my jangling nerves. I slumped into the back of my chair consumed with dark thoughts and fears.

"Order something or you'll definitely be ill otherwise." my companion ordered.

I pulled myself together and ordered a pork dish. "Last of these for the time being." I muttered and managed a smile.

Dave raised his bottle of beer in response.

Later, we wandered the streets, admiring the mix of architecture and the vibrant night life. The evening was balmy and pleasant. But we were tired and having no street map meant that we lacked points of reference. The result was a lot of stumbling about to no real purpose.

We gave up and settled in a small bar on a paved avenue, which was lined with small orange trees, the fruit winking from boughs just beyond our reach. At least this was more relaxing and we spent some time soaking up the general ambience. After another beer Dave suggested going back.

I stumbled along after him, increasingly in a world of my own. Surges of terror, horrible images in my mind of what the future held. Heaven only knows what was happening to my mind. I was very scared and fear built upon to fear to the point where by the time we entered the lift to our room, I was so terrified that I immediately wanted to escape the enclosed space.

I tried broaching the subject with Dave, but it just seemed too difficult. I was certain that he'd never understand. A mistake.

My mind was a blur as I checked over our kit, which had been exhaustively hauled in their metal boxes from the hotel's garage below. I filled out my diary in a state of apprehension as Dave quietly made a few notes of his own and settled into his bed with a book.

There was a long conversation with Barbara, burning a vast hole in my bank account as the local cell phone provider gleefully applied banana state GDP sized roaming charges. I tried to settle in my bed, but was too terrified of my state of mind to relax.

Another call to England, the soothing tones of my love.

I tried to sleep.

A void of terror settled as the light went out. Every combination of fear and terror of the awful things that could happen to me burst forth like a scene from one of the more horrific of William Blake's 'Dante's Inferno' etches.

My turmoil filled reverie in darkness was interrupted by my phone pinging into life with a text message.

'Don't take any more Lariam and call me in the morning.' Was the terse message from Barbara.

A vague memory of reading about the possible side effects of the malarial prophylactic Lariam came to mind. Psychological effects had sometimes been reported, or something like that. I'd taken a further tablet from the course of treatment only two days before.

I fell into an exhausted sleep.

Strangely and unexpectedly I slept deeply and gained a lot of new energy from it. But the hell continued in my sleep. Dave finally woke me up after a vivid dream where we had both spent several hours murdering someone and dismembering the body in a spectacularly gruesome fashion before hiding parts of the unrecognisable corpse under the bed in our Ceuta hotel room. The blood splattered scene would have made Tarantino proud.

"Come on we need to get breakfast and hit the road." gurgled my dream-state version of Dave, who was talking through mouthfuls of oozing and dripping blood and the loose strips of raw and quivering flesh that he was stuffing into his gob. His bright red eyes flashing insanity and demonic thoughts at me.

The image faded as I opened my eyes and saw a clean and fresh Dave standing over me, looking rested and relaxed. He'd even showered without waking me up.

Daylight brought a semblance of sanity and coffee brought a sense of greater wellbeing, though I still couldn't face a proper breakfast.

Dave wandered off to continue his search for an electronics shop, the hunt for a new GPS still very much on. I got a bottle of water and made some phone calls from a pleasant pavement alcove which looked over the port. Keeping in touch with real life and motorcycle industry responsibilities back home.

A call to Barbara revealed that she'd spent half the night researching the effects of Lariam and looking at alternative malaria tablets. She said that the way that I'd been talking on the phone had alarmed and frightened her. This had got her thinking and a quick search on the net had brought up pages and pages of personal experiences of Lariam side effects. Some accounts were extreme and on occasions resulting in long term debilitation.

My apparent state of mind completely matched some of these experiences.

I felt relief that there was perhaps an explanation of the way I was feeling. Months of high pitch activity and organisation built around a busy set of work commitments – plus all that had to be done to arrange our wedding – had probably created a sense of exhaustion and stress. All of which only served to enhance a classic dose of Lariam side-effects.

Yes, I was relieved, but this knowledge still didn't make me feel much better. The terrors were still there, but at least there was some explanation for them now.

Barbara suggested alternative tablets and rang off.

I looked out over the port feeling a new sense of purpose. I now had a fairly reasonable explanation of what was going on, the only question was whether it would be possible to cope until the side effects started to subside.

I was doing my best to suppress an urge to get back on the ferry and hightail it back across Europe. But I knew that to skulk back to Beckenham, a failure, with ambition and travelling credibility destroyed, would do much longer term damage than even the awfulness that I felt at that moment.

Dave reappeared triumphantly clutching a box and a bright green GPS.

"Got one!" he exclaimed "And I ain't letting you get anywhere near it this time!"

We both laughed – a good moment.

Several chemists later and I gave up on trying to find replacement Malaria tablets. The shops only seemed to sell the combinations that were no good in Sub-Saharan Africa. Pharmacists didn't have a clue about the names of drugs that Barbara had provided.

I sent a text to Barbara, who quickly replied that the Lariam would do its job for about a fortnight. She said she would buy a course of the more expensive daily Malarone alternative and bring them to The Gambia with her.

By now it was mid-day and with the bikes packed, we headed round the bay towards the border with Morocco. The sun shone rays of warmth as we left town and passed by dusty tenements as Ceuta fell behind.

The road hugged the east side of the Spanish Moroccan promontory as it curved round a bay of bright shining water fringed with mountains which marched down the coast and faded into the midday heat haze. It was a fresh, mild and cheerful day with only a few clouds wandering slowly across the skies.

The border post loomed a mile or so in the distance, a clutter of buildings and some tall gantries marking the entrance to Morocco.

We slowed as the roadside filled with cheap tumbledown Moroccan style shops and the road became busy with people and vehicles.

The road opened out at the Spanish exit point. We were waved through, then on past a throng of people busily moving around the gates to the Moroccan customs post. Some had a dark Spanish look, but most were Moroccan, dressed in flowing djellaba. We'd learned that the robes were also sometimes known as the gandourah on this western side of North Africa. Plump women in white robes hustled about haranguing menfolk and appearing to be selling fruit. We hadn't even left European territory yet.

Instead of the signs taking us to the long low building with small windows as it did in 2000, the road took our bikes to a new border post adjacent to this. A more modern arrangement, with several vehicles lanes and two prominent glass booth checkpoints near the centre lanes. This new tableau was semi shaded under a large set of gantries covered with corrugated iron.

We stopped and looked about. No hustlers waving white bits of paper this time. A few cars, half a dozen men standing around, a small queue at both huts.

I got off the bike, feeling a bit thrown by the new sense of order which seemed to have come to the previously chaotic border.

A weasely-looking Moroccan in a brown robe and close fitting cap sidled over.

"This your first time here?"

"No." replied Dave

"It's a bit different here now though." I added. A mistake.

"I am a licensed guide." Weasel announced, flashing a photo ID card at me. There are a few of us here, we work to help you."

Dave and I knew what this probably meant. But to me , the chance to be doing something productive seemed to drive away the ever present waves of personal anxiety. So I entered into a fruitless debate with Weasel about our probably not needing him at all.

At some point another 'guide' came over and told us to move our bikes and park them on a different lane.

"Look Dave." I said after we had parked. "Give me all your papers, I'll sort this lot out."

He looked at me sideward.

"Well don't get ripped off then." He handed his package of paperwork over.

I set to trying to get what I needed without using Weasel. Not easy. I hunted up and down for the white customs forms, but the only people who seemed to have them were the 'guides'.

Weasel hassled.

"Our job is to help, you will not get very far in my country if you don't trust people." And so on.

In the end, I took two of his white forms and admitted defeat.

Give the man his due though. Things quickly swung into action. No one else hassled us and within a few minutes, I had both passports stamped at the first glass booth.

Unfortunately registering the bikes was not so straight forward. Both were registered to BMW Motorrad and not Dave and I. Having collected the green forms required for registration at the second hut, I started to fill them in with Weasel offering advice for every line.

"OK, give me the papers." said Weasel when the forms were complete.

He looked them through and then looked at the letters of passage that BMW had provided for the bikes.

"Ooh this is a problem, this is a major problem." Weasel groaned, wagging his head sadly in a pantomime of affected concern. The words 'this is a problem' being of course a euphemism for 'hurrah all my Christmases have come at once, now open your wallet effendi.'

"No problem last time." I said, casting him a fierce stare.

"I'll talk to the man, but he is corrupt you know, he will need something. I will sort it out and make sure you are treated fairly."

He turned on his heels and scurried off to one of the old border post buildings, with our papers I was left standing bemusedly clutching my pen and wondering what was going to happen next.

I wandered over to Dave.

"I think the buggers are gonna exploit us over the ownership details."

My companion cast me one of those looks which he is good at, kind of inscrutable, but carrying a certain wave of annoyance with it. This time, the unspoken sentence was 'I bet I could have done the job without this hassle'.

167

Pre-empting any comments I added:

"You try avoiding these bastards. Next time, we come with a supply of white forms."

Dave looked away and opened a bottle of water.

Weasel appeared silently by my side.

"OK all sorted, you can register your vehicles now."

He gave the papers back and I waited at the small queue by the small window of the second glass booth again.

The official took my papers with a glance from one good eye. The other had a nasty sty which gave his face a lopsided look. A caricature of dodgy officialdom.

But within seconds, papers with stamps on them were created, passports were again annotated. But instead of handing them back, they were passed to Weasel who was waiting at the side entrance to the booth.

He scurried off towards the old buildings again with me in tow wondering what was next.

"You need insurance?"

"No." I replied, we already have this." I pointed out the Green Card, with Morocco clearly indicated.

"You need money?"

"Yes, but I can see the bank, so I don't need help with this."

He smiled broadly, revealing a black tooth.

"Then we are done! There is only the issue of the consideration…?" He glanced at me furtively.

I Knew this was coming.

"OK, twenty Euros for the lot."

He looked aghast.

"Do you know what I had to do to get permissions for your vehicles? There are people who need paying, you must give me 150 Euros per bike."

"What!" My mind reeled. "No way, twenty for everything is fair, 150 each is not reasonable."

We argued for some minutes. Our vehicle papers seemed to be held with a tighter grip as each moment passed. Two of Weasel's colleagues came over and lent a supportive presence to the rip-off merchant.

We haggled, but this guy was not going to shift his position unless I offered something. This was the old barter game 'on mescaline' and I wasn't winning.

The rip-off loomed. Weasel knew that he could keep us here all day if he wanted. There was no skin off his nose if we spent the day at a stuffy border post. I contemplated trying to grab our papers and start a noisy row, but a policeman stood nearby was regarding me with a look that suggested that trouble was not a good plan.

In the end we settled on forty euros each. Still an outrageous sum. I was livid, but paid up.

Dave was stunned and incandescent.

"Bloody hell, what the hell was going on?" No way would I have paid that and yes I would have spent all day here."

"Well I'm not doing that." I snapped. "You spend all day here if you want. I came to do a journey, not spend my life pissing about at border posts."

There didn't seem to me more to be said. We mounted our bikes and after a cursory glance at our luggage from another policeman, we were waved on our way.

It had taken under an hour to complete formalities this time. Ripped off? Yes. Could it have been avoided? Not sure. I felt that Dave would have struggled to have avoided a wallet emptying on that particular day. The trick is to try and get the famous white form and appear to know what you're doing before you get hustled. Then steel yourself to be as impervious as possible to some fairly strong arm persuasion tactics.

I learned a lot from the episode and later discovered that vehicles can be pre-registered with Moroccan customs online. The 'guides' are still there and difficult to avoid, but I've never since paid more than a token tip for 'assistance' at Ceuta about five Euro for genuine help. On one more recent trip, Barbara and I got ten bikes through in one block for around twenty Euro in total.

A few weeks later, a much more experienced overlanding friend was stung for sixty euros which made me feel less of a complete 'numpty'. But it was an episode which left a bad taste and annoyed my friend.

But part of the problem was probably my underlying mental

state. This was leading to an eagerness to just get the bloody border post out of the way as fast as possible. Making me partially blind to what was going on.

Exiting the border though the well-remembered gates, the throng of chaotically parked and battered Mercedes taxis was there very much as they had been five years before.

The same crowd of shouting street traders, hustlers and merchants milled around. Displaying their wares and trying to catch our eyes as we slowly rode through the dusty clearing at the gates and joined the road south.

But this time, we joined a road which was smooth, fairly new and wide open ahead.

We picked up speed as this new highway cut past Fnideq and Riffen and not down the old slow road through both places; the very chaos and decay of which had generated such a culture shock in 2000. We could see that buildings were painted and the cars were in better condition. This was a relief.

Within a kilometre or two, the road opened out into a dual carriageway. Not European class, but a good steady surface which saw cultivated fields and surprisingly new looking farm buildings shoot by us as we settled to a comfortable cruising speed.

The boys on mopeds waving trees of Cannabis were absent. There was hardly a donkey cart in sight and the smattering of four wheeled traffic was more or less new. Not the experience we expected at all.

Then we came to the first of many roundabouts. I slowed, with Dave following, as it appeared ahead and I set myself up for my usual line: Then grabbed for the brakes as my eyes widened at what I saw.

The high walled centre of the roundabout had been essentially dumped in the middle of the carriageway, with new roads roughly cut at 270 and 90 degrees. The road markings went straight under the centre of roundabout as though it had been just teleported in. There was nothing to indicate that there were lanes leading around to the right. Just a small strip of tarmac pointed the way and this needed to be taken at ultra-low speed.

Heeling the GS over, I prayed that there would be no diesel.

After a few seconds bumping around the badly designed obstacle I found myself back on the highways south with a frantically beating heart.

I pulled into a disused petrol station and stopped the bike.

"Bloody hell!" exclaimed Dave. "That was a bit rough."

He laughed and tore his helmet off his head.

"Just goes to show that you can't relax. Mind you the road is generally much better now innit."

We passed the water bottle between us and chatted for a while. The expensive border humiliation seemed to have been set to one side and I wasn't going to raise the subject again.

We were stopped near some farm buildings. The countryside in all directions was green and an impressive variety of crops mingled with the palm trees that lined the road. Many were in flower, belying the season. Ahead of us marched tall, rugged hills, with fields of growing produce leading to the base of these. In the distance we could see higher peaks which were indistinct in the afternoon haze.

"This is a much better ride than last time." I said. "I reckon we'll be passing by Tetouan in about thirty minutes. We should be on course to make Rabat by tonight if we press on."

Dave agreed.

"But I think we'll be needing our waterproofs." He motioned at the sky, which was beginning to fill with black clouds that had emerged from the mountainous peaks ahead while we were stopped.

Climbing into rain gear, we once again set off.

Several dangerous roundabouts later and the road turned into single carriageway. From time to time, we saw police checkpoints, but no one took the slightest interest in our approach. The road turned inland from the sea which had appeared on our left every so often and we left the Mediterranean behind as Tetouan approached.

The city had not changed a great deal from the last time we had used the road. The same chaotically positioned maze of dense mud splattered white buildings covered the land away from the main road. The sprawl stretched away as far as the foothills of the growing mountain range a mile or so behind the city. There was the same air of impoverishment and I noted the broken roads, alleys and tracks which led in and out of the centre of town away from the highway.

Old cars competed with donkey carts for road space. Gandourah robed people thronged the pavements and bustled around the market stalls and shops, which had precarious stacks of goods spilling out onto the street.

There was the same pungent aroma of sewers which had wafted across our nostrils on the last journey and we stuck to the main road around the outskirts of town.

The main difference this time was that the bustle and hustle seemed to have more purpose. There was more activity. More shops and traders. Each road intersection had a neatly dressed policeman waving his arms and wielding his whistle.

The whole feel was much more 'alive' than before.

We took the Tangier road out of town and started to climb towards the Rif mountains. Heavy lorries thundered up and down and the general standard of driving was as poor as I remembered from before. 'same driving, newer cars' I thought to myself as I swerved to avoid a car which had put its brakes on in front of me.

Then the rain came. Heavy splatters were soon replaced with great sheets of water as the black clouds unleashed their dense cargo upon us.

At El-Fendek I pulled off the climbing road into a layby to look at the map. I was keen to find the back road which would take us along a mountainous route south easterly towards the Rabat-bound motorway. The same road that Heather and I had used when coming up from Asilah.

Dave stopped beside me and giving me a weary grin through his rain splattered visor, wrung his gloves out, a steady stream of grey water emerging from the waterlogged leather. Another heavily laden lorry thundered by, grinding along in low gear as it climbed the steep hill.

Beyond the road, low clouds marched across the surrounding mountainous countryside. Rain laden mists creating an atmospheric view of partially cultivated moorland and hills behind. It all looked rather like parts of the Lake District or North Wales. Despite the rain, this was an enjoyable ride.

"Gotta watch out for diesel." yelled Dave as another lorry roared by.

"OK, we'll be off this road soon anyway."

A little later and we turned down the long twisting road south, which led us over high moorlands, though low mountainous passes and past numerous farms. Flocks of sheep and goats milled about under dry stone walls, shepherds standing peering at us from under the pointed hoods of their cloaks, their charges standing with heads down against the downpour.

This was a minor route and for a time, the surface was indifferent. Much as I remembered from my previous ride along this way on the Triumph Sprint. But as we rode, the rain started to ease off and visibility improved. Soon we were able to see a long distance ahead as the road curved through what was now moorland terrain.

It was an excellent riding road, lots of slow twisties which brought out the best in the bikes. The single cylinder BMW GS 650 Dakars were not best suited to motorway mile crunching, but on roads like this they excelled.

Dave signalled to pull over at the end of a long steep climb to a sort of moorland peak. A glance backwards showed a breathtaking view of the high moors, with the mountains we had so recently negotiated now some way behind. A thick carpet of cloud still lay over them, with dense flat bottomed 'cells' of darker storm clouds hanging over the higher peaks.

I motioned to our now mud splattered bikes. "Look a bit more the part now don't they." I said. Dave took some pictures of the first mud of the trip. "Now these look more like overlanding bikes heh?"

The comment reminded me of an earlier conversation. What is an 'overlander'? had been a subject for discussion over one of our numerous cups of coffee.

Dave was scathing about the whole concept of calling a long distance trip 'overlanding', though he was being very tongue in cheek of course.

"Surely any kind of trip by road is 'overland' I'm overlanding when I go out for a pint." He laughed.

"Yup, but the term kinds evokes the idea of some serious distance." I countered. "'Overland' means, well, a major trip across a series of countries, not just a 'tour' which as a description, evokes gentle mileages and a five star stop every night."

"Yeah, but a tour is a tour. It can be across to Germany, or to The Gambia. It's still a long distance trip. 'Overland' is a term designed to make out that it's something special."

He had a point, but biking has so many genres and expressions which describe different aspects of the biking lifestyle or even biking subcultures. It was no great surprise that a new term had entered the biking lexicon to describe what was essentially adventure motorcycling.

'Overlanding' was a useful way of setting relaxed motorcycle touring aside from longer term transcontinental motorcycling, where more personal risks were taken in unfamiliar environments and new cultures explored. To me, the idea of a 6,000 plus mile trip to The Gambia and back was pretty special.

But Dave's contention that all these 'tags' in the motorcycle world were ultimately a little bit silly had a certain resonance. It reminded me a little of the whole 'heavier' end of the biking scene that I had briefly been on the periphery of in the mid-1980s. Back patch clubs would use the term 'MC' to describe their motorcycle club. But the description 'MC' was also a tag to indicate identification as an 'outlaw' bike gang. Disputes between such clubs could and still do have ugly and sometimes violent endings.

Standard, every day motorcycle clubs used the term 'MCC' to indicate that they were in a 'motorcycle club' but not at the outlaw, extreme end of the club scene. At one time I had been a member of a few of these. The Flyers MCC in Bristol had been one of the best. A great crowd of folks, whose club was taken from them, when the local heavies, an 'outlaw' MC, decided to bust up several of the friendly local MCC clubs as part of a moronic and small minded campaign to stamp a territorial presence in the city.

Club politics. I'd had enough of all this by the late 1980s. Life is too short.

The road now took us steadily downwards, straightening out as it did so. The moor opened out into a broad plain which may have been used for cereal crops in the spring and summer months. In November though, it was not much more than a bleak plain full of dead stubble and forlorn grasses.

Then ahead of us, at the end of final kilometre long straight, we saw a huge scar in the land which marked a freshly upgraded motorway intersection.

We turned our bikes south on the route to Rabat. Behind us, we could see the new stretch of multi-lane highway which led to Tangier further north.

Afternoon was drawing on and a glance at my bike's clock revealed that we only had just over an hour of daylight left. I started to speed up unconsciously and before long, both bikes were eating up blacktop at a respectable rate of knots.

The motorway had a different feel to the previous time I had been on this very stretch. More traffic, no livestock, very few pedestrians, just the odd character waiting patiently to walk across. We stopped for fuel and an excellent cup of milky coffee at a modern, but scruffy and unhygienic service station.

As the sun westered, it broke through clumps of cloud to cast an eerie cold glare across the flat landscape and farmland which fringed the empty motorway. Cool light contrasted with dull and chilly shadow. The atmospheric sunset was a welcome contrast to rain, but it was a spiritually chilly end to the daylight and I looked forward to turning off towards Morocco's capital.

My mood fell as the light faded. The demons which had spent the day in quiet abeyance came back to life like some kind of Transylvanian horror. The light dimmed in the sky and as I peered through the gloom ahead, the fears and panic returned.

My mood was not helped by sharp rain showers which reduced visibility to almost zero. Dave stuck steadily behind me, his headlight a comforting presence through the spray and gloom which I irrationally feared to lose.

An unlit overhead sign pointed the way to Rabat, a quiet motorway intersection leading us westwards. Full darkness was upon us as the gradient took us downwards towards the distant sea.

With the coming of darkness, my mind went into chaotic free-fall. As far as I was concerned, my wheels of terror were leading me to an unknown and dreadful fate. Waves of panic swept over me and rationality twisted itself out of all recognition. My brain seemed to be locked into some kind of surreal storm and I was only dimly aware of the increasing traffic and the appearance of the odd street light, as the smooth dual carriageway led us ever nearer the city.

We were approaching a series of intersections and I fought to regain control of my thoughts as I chose the route into the 'Centre-Ville'. Traffic slowed as we started to come across traffic lights and finally in the distance, the lights of the city shone. The brightly lit walls of what I assumed to be the old city standing out against these.

The now busy road climbed towards the old town. As we passed another well-lit junction, where traffic was husbanded by a neatly uniformed policeman, the thought flashed in my mind. 'I can't carry on, I'm going mad, I'm better off dead'.

In an instant something became clear. An unexplained mystery, which had years ago filled a close-knit group of friends with deep sorrow, came into sharp focus.

Many years before, I had spent some great times with a group of characters who were all part of a British motorcycle owners club. We had rallied and partied together, taking enjoyment from our bikes and the good companionship of friends. Great memories of the West Country as a young man in my twenties. Living for the moment, enjoying life, focussing only on the good times ahead with my group of like-minded friends.

One day, one of them, I'll call him Pete, announced his intention to ride around the world on a pre-1950 British single. It seemed a mad proposition, particularly back then, but Pete knew his stuff and he knew how to prepare.

He thought of every issue that could arise with the bike, everything that could possibly break or wear out. He prepared complete kits of parts and tools for every individual problem. These were all put in dozens of numbered boxes and left in his mum's attic. The idea being that if, say, he holed a piston, he could phone his mum and say 'Send me box ten.' He'd then hunker down, wait for box ten to arrive, fix his bike and carry on.

About six weeks before he was due to leave, Pete's closest friend, we'll call him Andy, decided to join him on his endeavour. Andy had a pretty much identical bike to Pete and they both figured that they'd have more than enough parts between them to successfully complete the journey, which they both reckoned would take five years.

There was a huge party to see them off and they both left with a fanfare and coverage from the local media. The idea of two characters riding around the world on such old bikes was certainly news worthy and lots of people came to see them off.

They dawdled in Europe for some time and we received only the occasional report from them. But we figured all was going well.

Then one day, a bolt from the blue arrived. Andy had got as far as Casablanca. There had been no warning that anything was wrong, but one morning he was found hanging in his hotel room.

Pete didn't come home, indeed I never learned if they were still riding together at the time. All we ever learned was the basic awful news. It was devastating to hear and we found it difficult to comprehend, why Andy, so full of life, had decided to end it all in a place so far from home.

Pete continued his journey and two years later arrived in Australia, still riding the same battered and patched up old thumper. Three years after Andy died, I'd moved out of the area and unfortunately lost touch with folks.

And now, riding up that final hill into Rabat, I understood in a flash the kind of mental turmoil that could have lain behind Andy's suicide. It was a moment of clarity which both calmed me and made me want to weep. Understanding and long buried sorrow washed over me in what was in a weird way, some sort of comfort. My view was blurred by tears and for a moment streetlight glare assumed crazy patterns as I peered ahead.

I felt calmer as I pulled over at the first hotel I saw, the Annakhill. The road had led us into an older quarter of town not far from the Boulevard Mohammed II. The hotel didn't look special, neither did it look cheap. It stood alongside a busy, but clean street which was not unlike any European city street. Pedestrians wore mostly western clothing and cars rolled by steadily, but without the usual blowing of horns.

I wasn't in the mood to spend hours hunting for cheap hotels and good deals, I wanted to stop. I'd glimpsed hell, been reprieved and now needed to rest and take stock.

Dave didn't make a fuss about finding somewhere cheap and sorted out the room for us. The bikes had to stay on the pavement, but the enthusiastic staff were happy to lay on a night guard for a few extra dirham.

The room was comfortable and a hot bath made me feel more human. We pottered about with our stuff and studied the map.

"We've made good progress." grunted Dave. "Where to next?"

"Essaouira." I replied. The small port was a fair distance ahead. "Motorway most of the way to Marrakech." I said, motioning at the map; "Then a straight run west to the town. It'll take all day though." Our itinerary meant sticking to the faster motorway route, which would save time compared to the more direct 'National' road.

Dave nodded his acquiescence and we went down for dinner.

The demons were still with me and I was still suppressing an urge to cut and run home. But things seemed just a bit more manageable after my earlier revelation. I was beginning to recognise that my brain storms had a reason and this was fuelled by my natural tendency to worry too much about things.

However, it was still difficult to consider eating anything substantive, there was simply too much anxiety still flowing through me.

As a result, I was once again nearly silent over dinner. Dave didn't do much to break the silence and things felt awkward between us. He dealt with the situation by getting stuck into a tagine and I ordered an onion soup and bread which turned out to be the best onion soup that I'd ever tasted. A few beers and sleep beckoned.

THE OTHER SIDE

The next morning, I finally broached the issue of my feelings with Dave. I also told him about the urge to abandon the expedition that I'd been fighting.

"I'd never let you forget it if you did that." he said gruffly "And I'd never let anyone else forget either."

I glanced at him and he gazed back as inscrutable as ever.

"Well thanks for all your understanding." I replied peevishly, too mentally screwed up to realise he was actually doing me a favour.

Dave seemed fairly nonplussed about the whole thing and the subject was dropped. I felt that he didn't really have any terms of reference to deal with such descriptions of personal chaos and probably saw the whole thing as personal weakness on my part. My private hell was to remain private it seemed. I craved more understanding.

This was coming from Barbara, but I couldn't keep ringing her up and brain-dumping. It was costing a fortune.

Unbeknown to me, Dave had been quietly sending text messages to Barbara, telling her not to worry, that I was dealing with things, that all was going to work out OK, that he'd look after me. He also told her not to mention that she'd heard from him.

Dave clearly cared more than he was letting on, but why keep it a secret? What was the point of this 'iron man' shit anyway? Perhaps he felt that the best help he could give was to put my fears into perspective by being dismissive.

It was a lovely morning though. As we loaded the bikes, dealing with 101 excitable questions from the hotel staff, the early sun shone down through an avenue of buildings and along the street. The air was fresh and we launched our mounts into building traffic, seeking the way out of Rabat.

An hour later and we were clear, having run down through town and out to the coast road. The streets bustled with colour as we rode by. A multitude of shops, street traders and suited office workers shared pavements with djellaba-clad men going about more humble daily business.

We took the old coast road towards Casablanca. The city soon gave way to long beaches lined with the occasional large house or small groups of huts, the road protected by banked boulders. Atlantic waves crashed on the nearby shore as we drifted along. A sharp breeze blew low clouds from the west.

It was our first view of the Atlantic, which would be our companion for much of the journey. We stopped to take photos, a fresh wind blowing off the sea.

At Skhirat Plage we turned inland to join the nearby motorway and once again picked up speed and headed south.

The mood of the day was better. The clouds slowly lifted and the day became bright as the sun poked through the grey cover. Just being on the road, doing something with purpose was enough to drive the demons back to their den. I fervently hoped that they would stay there.

At Ain-Harrouda, the motorway split and we took the southerly direction towards Marrakech. My (non) Michelin map outlined a new motorway leading most of the way to the famous old Moroccan city.

We stopped for coffee and a snack at a service station. Here was a place where the modern world was about to drive out a more traditional way of doing things. A vast building site heralded the imminent arrival of a BP service station of the kind seen just about everywhere now.

Holding on for a final few weeks was the original service station. A series of small shops and a café which was locally owned and did a good range of meals and snacks in a more recognisably Moroccan style. We sat at a table outside and watched the world go by for a while.

"Why does progress mean ripping up and destroying what was there before, even when there's nothing wrong with it?" asked Dave.

"Take this place. A perfectly OK service station, with everything that you need for a rest stop. Full of people, lots of social interaction. Now they're gonna tear it all up and open a photocopy of the bloody place just down the road from my apartment in Poland."

I agreed and pondering this, studied the grey sludge in the bottom of my coffee glass. Something about Morocco was being lost compared to the last time we had visited. Yes, things seemed a bit cleaner, there was less obvious poverty, cars were newer, but something essential about Morocco felt threatened – at least in this region near the major cities. I wondered what it was like further inland.

Before we took to the road again, I wandered around the back of the buildings and took a leak in a pungent public toilet. Coming out, a pathetic sight greeted me. A gorgeous adult collie dog was standing in a parking space looking up at me, with open, friendly and serene eyes and wagging his feathered tail gently. A heart-warming sight ruined by the dog's hideously broken and twisted front leg. A ghastly injury which was an insult to the otherwise lovely picture of a healthy and clearly very tame example of man's best friend.

It was desperately sad. There was really nothing I could do about it. Approaching any dog in Morocco is largely regarded as a bit unwise, given the low but latent risk of Rabies in the country. With the Moroccan attitude to animal welfare being what it was, I would be unlikely to enlist the support of any of the service station's staff.

Feeling profoundly depressed, I tore my gaze away from the insulting view of the poor animal and went to join Dave. The image of that lovely dog, ruined by injury and unlikely to find a home and someone to care from him, was to stay with me for quite a while. I still sometimes find myself thinking about the poor animal.

We took off southwards once more and travelled a motorway that went through increasingly open and straight country. The more varied coastal countryside gave way to the flat agricultural plain of this part of the interior.

The traffic, which had never been heavy, became much lighter as the kilometre posts indicating the distance to Settat steadily reduced in number.

My map showed the path of the new motorway heading dart-straight towards Marrakech. As we by-passed Settat, the well-used surface gave way to brand new black tarmac, crossing brand new bridges and fringed with freshly dug embankments.

There was now no traffic. The last cars that we had seen were leaving at an exit just before the town. We opened up the Dakars and stormed up a long incline and around a sweeping curve.

Flashing lights ahead gave warning of trouble and as we slowed we could see the motorway disappearing into a freshly dug gash in the land. This headed towards the jagged maw of massive earthworks in the side of a hill.

The road diverted onto a single carriageway road and as soon as I could, I pulled in.

'Bugger'. I thought as I contemplated my now useless map.

"So Brigadier." asked Dave with a hint of sarcasm, using the nickname that Ian Mutch had awarded to me some years before. "Where's this new motorway then?"

"Don't blame me, not my fault that the map must have been teleported out of the future." I replied feeling a bit crestfallen at the implied criticism of my map-reading skills.

"Ah don't worry about it." Dave laughed and slapped me on the shoulder. "Kinda buggers up your tidy plan though, eh?"

I rummaged in one of my boxes and pulled out the Michelin map of Morocco – the one I should have been using in the first place.

"No motorway here." I said "but the road looks straight enough. Will be slower going though." I added as a stream of slow moving lorries thundered by. I hate getting stuck behind lorries. You can't see ahead and all kinds of crap gets blown all over you or kicked up from the road and spat at you by large tyres.

We lingered for a moment to take a drink.

"Neat bit of road, that last stretch of motorway." Dave commented. "All new as well. The pace of development here is amazing. Must be foreign investors looking to make some bucks."

"Well if it does something to put an end to those terrible diesel drenched main routes that we used last time, I ain't complaining." I replied.

We were in a fairly featureless area. The plain was interspersed with a series of low hills which were smooth and light brown in the winter sunlight, the grass of the previous spring burned to arid stubble in the fierce heat of the previous summer. In the distance, we could see more substantial hills starting to poke their heads above the horizon.

The change to the old fashioned main road meant a more technical ride for us both as we continued south and diced with the numerous lorries which were plying trade between the north and south of the country. There were fewer of the diesel and fume belching lorries that we encountered in 2000. In general, the vehicles were of more modern European types. But they still represented an ongoing obstacle and were sometimes erratically driven.

I settled into a routine of working my way past truck after truck, speeding along the empty stretches before judging when best to 'take out' the next lorry, or series of lorries. It became an enjoyable diversion from merely eating miles on an empty road. But after a time, I yearned the more relaxing open route that motorways offer, plus the luxury of being able to take the time to look properly at the countryside around.

Being mindful of my companion as I roared past each truck was of paramount consideration. I waited for Dave to follow each overtake before moving onto the next one. Dave was not as adventurous as me in taking opportunities when they presented themselves. Yes, he was being rightly cautious, but sometimes he'd linger in the dust cloud of a smoke belching behemoth, when he should have an opportunity to get past. Waiting for him, when the road ahead beckoned, became irritating as the day progressed.

Every so often we'd pass through roadside towns, a series of dusty single storey buildings hard up against the side of the highway. These were poor places in faded whites, with small windows and dark doorways. Many with a blanket hanging over them to keep dust and flies at bay. Sometimes an old man or woman sat outside, gazing at the world go by. Occasionally, we'd shoot by a pavement café with white plastic tables and chairs outside, shaded from the sun by ubiquitous Coca Cola awnings. Sometimes, a roadside shop displayed fruit and veg on wobbly wooden stalls.

These did not look pleasant places to live, eking a precarious existence from passing traffic. Trying to raise children against a backdrop of streams of polluting traffic and hoping that life would get better.

As the forthcoming motorway marched ever southwards, even this poor way of life was under threat. In Morocco, motorways may slash journey times city to city, but risk throwing some onto humanity's rubbish heap as a consequence.

Some kilometres later, we slowed as the road passed through the larger town of Skhour-Rehamna, good tarmac giving way to the kind of broken and potholed surface that reminded us of our previous journey. A babble of djellaba-clad men and shapeless women, veiled in cavernous black, moved in and out of the suddenly dense traffic. Roadside shops sold a kaleidoscope of wares and produce and many restaurants cooked brochette from numerous pavement barbeques. These cast great palls of fragrant smoke over the town and passing traffic.

It was a scene that took us back five years. I slowed and motioned Dave to come alongside. "Just like the Morocco we remember." I shouted.

Dave flipped the front of his helmet up and grinned agreement.

Leaving the town, the road soon started to climb a steep incline as it took on the taller hills of the Reham Na. The change in scenery was welcome, but this was to be only a short break from the monotony of the plain. Before long, we were taken back to the now familiar slightly rolling land.

The road was now completely straight, heading into the distance, allowing greater visibility to pass the endless lines of trucks Progress only interrupted by opposing traffic and the hazard of the occasional junction to a side road.

As we drew nearer to Marrakech, the peaks of the High Atlas started to emerge from the distant haze, the mountains taking on a purple tinge as they rose in the afternoon sunshine. I felt relief. Fuel was starting to run low and I reckoned that we could both use a coffee stop.

Our plan was to skirt the edge of the city and as we approached, untidy civilisation seemed to spring up all around. I was glad that we had decided not to stop here for anything but fuel and refreshment. The whole area around this side of town was one massive building site. Blocks of apartments were springing up as land was being claimed from the brown earth of the surrounding countryside.

New development contrasted with the more familiar sights of traditional Morocco as the fast developing city ploughed its wealth into a real estate boom reminiscent of the Costa-del-Sol.

Time was wasted seeking the N8 westwards. Maps were of no use as fresh signs took us along new roads which led through acres of carefully marked building plots. I was relieved to finally pick up the main route, signposted to Agadir.

Dave trundled along resolutely behind, as we once again picked up speed and headed away from Marrakech. A visit to the old city once again set aside for another time.

The new route had an entirely different flavour. The streams of trucks were complemented by large numbers of crazily driven cars which weaved in an out of the traffic. They took alarming risks when overtaking in the face of speeding oncoming traffic.

I swerved to avoid a car which pulled from a junction onto the main road at high speed without looking, glancing in my mirror to see Dave pull off a sharp avoiding manoeuvre immediately behind. This was scary stuff and I became much more cautious about overtaking trucks – the fun of earlier in the day now becoming a risk-laden dice with danger.

At Chichaoua, we continued straight on for Essaouira, while the main road curved south, taking the suicidal fleet of cars and thundering lorries with it.

Relief was profound as a clear route opened ahead and the road started to go uphill and curve around a steeply undulating landscape.

Sidi-Moktar was a pleasant revisitation of the rustic townscape and chaotic civil life that we had seen earlier in Skhour. The road climbed still further beyond.

Round the top of a tall hummock of land and a view opened out before us which made me immediately pull over, switch off my engine and remove my helmet.

The land fell gently away towards the west. The low sun of late afternoon shone under a vast blanket of black cloud, casting light on a scene utterly devoid of any kind of vegetation or building. We had entered a totally desolate region of brown stony high prairie.

The light cast a warm glow over the stone which contrasted warmly with the dark cloud.

"Some spot this." said Dave, clearly impressed.

We climbed off our bikes and stretched our legs, revelling in silence of a traffic free road and the utter stillness of the calm approaching evening.

We took some photographs and Dave was unable to resist a quick ride on the stony ground, getting a first feel of off road riding on his laden Dakar. His antics raised a few laughs and a chance to take some more pictures as he felt his way across the rocky land.

But the sun was getting ever lower and by my estimation, we still had about seventy kilometres to ride before we reached Essaouira. We set off once again for what we hoped would be the final stretch of riding that day.

The road continued downhill and within a few kilometres, the arid ground gave way to farm smallholdings, fields laid out by dry stone walls. The agricultural year may have been over, but a few fields still contained scattered vegetation. Others had livestock, goats mainly.

Darkness fell and with it our speed, the route ahead becoming indistinct. I did not want to be caught out in the dark like this. On an unknown road, with many potential hazards – we had already seen some stray goats wandering on the tarmac while it was still light.

I settled down to a dogged plod through the growing darkness and tried not to let my mind wander. Dave's headlight remained close behind, but as I rode, it seemed to split into two, then three; the new lights growing ever larger. As I came around a corner a straight section opened ahead and a modern coach came thundering past. The single word 'Essaouira' was on its side, just legible in the periphery of my headlight's beam.

I opened my throttle wide, aiming to catch this huge battering ram of a vehicle. I hope that Dave would take the hint and follow. The coach was all the protection we needed from the evening's hazards. We could hide close behind, while it carved its way along the darkened road, lighting the road and deflecting anything which would stand in its way.

We found ourselves eating the remaining distance at an impressive rate. Despite the lack of forward visibility and hazardous proximity to the speeding coach, I felt safer riding like this than I felt when feeling my way ponderously along with little idea of what was ahead.

In a short time we entered the town of Ounara, where the coach finally got far ahead of us. Ounara was just waking up to its evening and the wide main street was fringed with a variety of well-lit pavement cafes.

Dave pulled alongside.

"There's a sign for a campsite, let's stop here and go for a meal."

I pretended that I hadn't heard him and pulled away on the road west out of town.

Camp? I wasn't keen. The last thing I needed after the hundreds of kilometres that we had ridden that day was to argue with a dodgy campsite owner. Then fumble with a tent in the dark and spend my night trying to fend off hustlers, scroungers and the rest of the hassle that is well documented by those who camp on official Moroccan sites. (though in fairness, this mainly seems to happen to mobile home based travellers.)

After a ride as long and as good as today's, I wanted a good meal, perhaps a beer and then a proper bed in a private room.

We were fully kitted out for camping, we had tents, doss-bags, even cooking gear. But I've never been the type of person who sees earning the camping merit badge as being an essential part of motorcycle travel. If I can afford it, I prefer tents with four walls, a roof and made of stone or brick. I saw camping on a trip like this as being reserved for those days where there was little alternative, or if we found an especially picturesque and remote spot where we would not be disturbed and had already obtained supplies for the evening.

I pressed on, feeling guilty about ignoring Dave, but also resolute in my aim to reach Essaouira and get a good night's sleep somewhere comfortable.

Dave followed as we headed out of town and along bumpy roads that curved gently downwards past walls and small holdings with the occasional light which shone out at us as we went by.

Through the darkness, I could make out trees and bushes at the side of the road.

Then at long last, the road fell sharply away and we relied on engine braking to take us down the hill and around a bend, where a large dirty sign announced that we had reached our destination for the night.

The brightly lit sign of the Hotel Mirador drew us like moths to an unshaded light. We stopped and looked at the large complex by the side of the road at the edge of town.

"Should we press on into town and see what we can find?" said Dave. "We could try that place where I stayed in 2000."

"To be honest mate, it's been a long day, this place looks secure, so why not just stay here?" I replied. Dave shrugged his shoulders. "Unless you've got any great objection…" I added.

But the Mirador was expensive, guestless and alcoholically dry. Dave had been right to suggest moving on. But we were soon checked into a very comfortable room by the side of a magnificent pool, which reflected shimmering light from regularly placed wall lanterns onto the surrounding complex of rooms.

Dinner held further compensations as an excellent meal was served in an imposing dining hall ornately decorated in Moorish style reminiscent of the Alhambra in Spain. The walls were replete with complex plaster mouldings and carefully illustrated columns which rose to an intricately moulded and artistically designed ceiling.

We were alone among all this splendour. Sitting with our meals and bottles of mineral water, we were both captivated by our surroundings and spent time sharing discoveries of new features with each other.

We awoke to a cloudless blue sky and gentle warmth that we had not felt since Marbella. A lazy breakfast was followed by a mile-long leisurely stroll into Essaouira as we looked for somewhere to have coffee.

The plan was to spend some time exploring before riding 170 kilometres of mountain and coastal road to Agadir, where a day off was planned.

The quiet coast road took us along a pleasant sea front, fringed by a perfect beach of white sand and gently breaking sea. Then onwards towards the cluster of white buildings and battlements which marked the centre of town.

Several small hotels with excellent views were strung along the road and Dave threw me a 'told you so' look.

Alongside one of these, was a small café and the sound of a steaming coffee machine reached our ears. We settled at a table which offered an uninterrupted view of the beach and were soon enjoying tall glasses of Café Latte prepared with an Italian coffee machine and served by a diminutive Hindu woman.

"What a contrast of cultures." grinned Dave. "Wait until I tell Mutch."

I smiled. "Yes, he'll be totally confused by the concept of a bit of Africa, India and Italy all in one place, miles from home. Beats the hell out of the Islamic Republic of Leyton that he keeps waxing lyrical about."

The morning was spent in the pleasant fug of a relaxing and almost dreamlike state after our long days on the road.

Our feet led us to the edge of the old town, where whitewashed and battlemented walls rose above us. The path seaward tool us to a large stone built medieval harbour which was protected on three sides by high sea walls. It was the focal point of one of the town's main industries.

Essaouira port contained a mass of small blue sardine boats, mingled among larger trawlers which had been built to traditional designs using local materials. These trawlers plied in and out of port, loaded with large quantities of equipment and tackle, crewed by at least nine or ten men and boys. All crawled over their vessels preparing tackle. Cleaning things, or diving in and out of the fish holds for various reasons.

A gaggle of people quickly gathered around each new arrival and fish was unloaded by a team of men who cast small baskets loaded with fish in a human chain that led from the boat to ice packed crates. Trucks waited nearby for their loads of fish.

The small blue boats were also busy unloading. Many were crewed by teenage boys, who waded among their slimy cargo as they loaded baskets and threw them up to shouting men on the quay side.

A group of old heavily shawled women moved around watchfully, looking for chances to pick up and pocket any stray fish that fell from the crates.

The strong light of the morning picked out the bright colours of the boats and people, throwing them into sharp relief against the long shadows which were cast by ranks of large boats. Some of them were out of the water and lined up on the broad quay for maintenance and repair. A few were old hacks, hulls worn and faded by years of heavy seagoing service. Others were being newly built. There were also vessels taking shape from curved keels, with fresh wooden spars giving shape to the new trawlers, but looking like the ribs and spine of prehistoric beasts.

We walked into the town itself and explored the ancient but clean medina. Not many people were around at this hour. Stalls were opening. Larger shops and cavernous warehouse-like buildings opened their doors to reveal a wealth of intricate wooden ornaments and furniture.

The medina seemed to give way the deep narrow avenues of the Portuguese designed fortress, small doorways in thick stone walls leading to the compact workshops of journeymen and artisans.

We sat on the high battlement, looking out to sea, a mild swell occasionally sending spray high enough for us to taste the salt on our lips. A line of canons shared the battlement, their barrels reaching out over the ocean. Seemingly yearning towards a distant past when they were more than mere ornaments. Languishing quietly and symbolically still guarding the town.

I noticed a group of boys, riding the waves on inflated truck inner-tubes and fishing with single lines.

I fell in love with Essaouira.

Riding away from town later that morning, I felt pangs of regret at leaving and looked forward to returning in a few weeks. We had already decided to spend a day or two there again on the return ride.

The road to Agadir was a more minor back road which curved its way higher as we headed south and into the last outcrops of the High Atlas. Mighty and dominant inland, not much more than low rocky hills at the point where the mountain range sank towards the ocean.

This was good riding country. An even and clear road led us along short straights and curved around hills. Small buildings and farms were spaced evenly and the occasional quiet village added some colour and variety. Herds of goats and the occasional group of camels were tended by men in muddy and stained robes.

The road became more twisty and less predictable. But as it rose and fell, curving around rocky outcrops and tumbling into deep valleys, the ride became more enjoyable. The terrain, although largely arid, had a sparse covering of small densely branched trees. Then I slammed on the brakes and squealed to a stop.

A goat in a tree? Hang on, there's two; no three goats in that tree …

Dave pulled up behind me looking just as surprised.

A small herd of goats were gathered at the base of one of the small trees and three were pulling at the braches above with their mouths. Nearby, a lad in his teens sat with a long stick over his knees and his head swathed in a dark cloth. He regarded us with interest.

"Ah!" said Dave "I've read about this somewhere, the goats are farming something? Look at the guidebook."

I descended from the bike, removed my helmet and pulled a bottle of water from my bungies. "Well, it seems like a good moment to stop anyway."

The book solved the mystery. The trees were 'Argan' trees and the goats were eating its fruit, having been encouraged by the goatherd to jump up and root among the branches. Apparently, the goats semi digest the hard shell of the Argan seeds, enabling the locals to process them further and distil Argan oil, which is prized in Morocco.

"Hmm, goat shit oil." I said. "What a job, rooting through crap to find the seeds, not my cup of tea."

"Maybe not, but it seems to be their cup of oil!" laughed Dave.

We went on our way.

The Argan trees became denser in number and we started to see the occasional roughly built roadside stall, with large glass jars of oil placed for sale to passing trade. Old women tended these stalls and mostly sat under adjacent trees. Sometimes they'd wave a jar as we passed by.

We stopped again in a dramatic location half way up a winding stretch of road. There were rocky outcrops on one side, but the other looked out over a stony, rolling and tree filled set of small semi-arid valleys which took the eye towards a distant glimpse of the sea.

"Grand spot." muttered Dave and set to with his camera taking pictures from all angles.

I sat under a tree, enjoying the shadow cast by its thick, if quite short bole. I lit a cigarette and sat back in the pleasant warmth.

A waving arm at the top of the nearby outcrop caught my eye. "Hey!" came the distant call and the arm grew a body as a teenage boy detached himself from the ground. Another youth stood up and the pair of them started down towards us.

Something felt wrong.

"Hey Dave, it may be an idea if we press on."

Dave pointed a finger towards the clambering youths, who were steadily getting closer as they climbed down the outcrop.

"Ah, they're probably just fine."

"Probably. But let's go anyway OK?"

Dave shrugged. "Sure, got my pictures anyway."

The sight of us putting out helmets on spurred the two boys to scramble towards us faster and now we could hear their cries.

"Hey, hey, Arretez! hey Cadeau monsieurs!"

Dave had already pulled away and as I fired up my engine the first lad reached the edge of the road about twenty yards behind me. For the first time I noticed that he carried a thick, knobbly branch. He broke into a run as I pulled way and his face became a mask of anger and the stick rose as he shouted after me.

The road continued to head in a generally southerly direction and we continued to navigate around outcrops which grew steeper as we travelled. Soon we were running through an area of high cliffs and the occasional small tunnel, where the route had been lasted through a particularly rocky patch of country. The sea came into view more often and it seemed that we were soon to break through to the coast.

Another sharp corner and a large dirt layby came into view. Dave, who was leading, pulled in and stopped.

"You ride up and down and I'll get some pictures of you." He commanded. "The angle of the sun and the gradient of the road are just right."

Bowing to his burst of artistic flair I rode up and down a few times, disappearing around the bend where we had come from before turning around and coming back to offer more flash-card filling opportunities.

As I came back into Dave's view for the final time, he was no longer lying at the side of the road, but was busy packing his camera. A youth had appeared from nowhere and was clearly trying to get something out of Dave in a fairly animated fashion. As I drifted by, the boy suddenly made a grab for Dave's water bottle from where it was bungeed to his bike and Dave quickly pushed the lad back.

As quick as a flash, Dave was on his Dakar and starting after me. We both accelerated away. Dave's habit of not taking his helmet off for short stops had been a good policy on this occasion.

We rode through some more sharp bends for about two kilometres and rounded a final curve to find a dramatic landscape opening before us as the road came through an opening in the cliffs and out onto a high coastal road. This gave a clear and elevated view of the sea ahead.

We pulled into another layby and enjoyed the view for a second before climbing off the bikes. The land fell steeply away from us towards the sea, across a landscape green with wild grasses and reeds, with the occasional sand dune showing its yellow head above the waving grass. The coastline further along the shore could be clearly seen, with rocky promontories marching southwards into the distance and the road curving around them. Sometimes near the sea, sometime higher up.

It was our first sight of the proper Atlantic Route of African overland fame.

Dave let out a long breath.

"What a view!"

"So what happened back there?" I motioned over my shoulder.

"Well, this kid appeared out of nowhere and starting haranguing me for bloody 'cadeau'. Then he made a grab for me water.

They're a bit bloody eager around these parts aren't they, that first kid seemed to be going for me with that big stick."

"Yup, can't figure it, it's reasonably prosperous around here, must be the Moroccan version of bored youth. If this was Dublin they'd be wearing hoodies and nicking yer mobile phone." He smiled at his deliberate generalisation

Our conversation was broken by the roar of an engine as a fast driven silver VW Golf hurtled around the bend behind us and spitting gravel locked his brakes in what seemed like an emergency stop into the layby.

The driver's door opened, releasing a cacophony of rap music and a lean Moroccan in his twenties jumped out. He was dressed neatly in a white shirt and black trousers and bounded over to us to shake hands.

"Hey, wotcha doing here guys!?" he said in fluent English. "Saw your bikes kilometres away and I've been catching you up ever since. Gave the girls a hell of a fright I did."

I glanced at his car. Two young women had carefully climbed out of the cramped interior and were stood looking bored. One occupied herself lighting a cigarette.

"Ohh, just taking a ride south." said Dave. "What's going on anyway?"

"Ah, I work in a night club in Agadir and I've just been up to Essaouira to pick up my friends. Do you want to come to my club for some free drinks tonight?"

Dave and I glanced at each other. This was a westernised Moroccan version of the usual scam, only with slicker PR. The guy was obviously used to dealing with holiday Brits on the piss in Agadir.

I found the whole thing amusing and spent some time swapping anecdotes with the fluent young Moroccan. He seemed to be a budding member of a new breed of entrepreneur, westward looking and disregarding of old social and religious norms.

Eventually the trio squeezed back into their car. Rap pounded forth again from open windows and they disappeared with spinning wheels in a large cloud of dust.

We set off, heading south once again and enjoying the mild air and cooling breeze. The road wound its way down to sea level and then climbed again as it found it way round a high rocky promontory. The surrounding country was green and full of vitality. Refreshing after a morning in the dry hills.

We took coffee in Tamri, a large village not far inland from a natural estuary. A traditional Moroccan community with market stalls, smoky street barbeques, laden donkeys and the usual dynamic hubbub that we had come to expect.

As we approached Agadir, villages joined into small towns. Some were ordinary communities, others catered for surfers who came from all over Europe to enjoy the famous winter swell of the Atlantic coast. One place was so full of surf shops, bars, hostels, VW camper vans and languid, tanned, blond haired European surfers that I almost imagined for a second that I was in Cornwall.

Just outside Agadir the road widened into a dual carriageway which went past tenement housing on one side and a large factory on the other. Crowds milled around intersections and filled slow moving busses which seemed to appear from nowhere.

We climbed a steep hill and rounded a corner to see Agadir's beach stretching before us, circling a wide bay. High up a hill on the left, the walls of the town's ancient battlemented Kasbah could be seen.

Riding into town, it wasn't long before local residences gave way to lines of large hotels and resorts. These fringed the seaward side of the main road through town. Small parks and lines of trees appeared and well-dressed cops directed traffic at intersections. All felt ordered and, well, Western.

A day off was planned so after riding up and down the main Boulevard Mohammed V a couple of time, we settled on the least garish and touristy looking large hotel. Walking into the wide foyer covered in dust and grime, the reception desk staff greeted us like long lost family and we were soon ensconced in a large twin room, with a view over the pool of the half empty resort style hotel.

Off-season prices meant good value for accommodation that was fairly up market and after a beer in the bar, we set off towards the sea front looking for some action.

With no early morning start to drive us back to our room early, we stopped at several bars on the way towards the tourist beach area. It was a balmy evening and sitting at tables outside, we enjoyed our drinks and watched the world go by. A street scene more reminiscent of Ceuta than Morocco. Figure hiding robes and shawls had given way to jeans and short sleeved shirts among the men and western attire among the women.

Many were tourists from Europe, lots of English was spoken, but also French and German from groups of young or middle aged holiday makers.

The beach front was well-lit and lined with restaurants. Some were Western food chains. We settled for dinner at a place which served good brochette and large beers. It also advertised full English breakfast, including fried bacon, a surprising culinary ingredient for a Muslim country. Dave theorised that Agadir sat in a sort of self-containment bubble, which the rest of Morocco tolerated due to the income from tourist Euros, but preferred to forget about for the rest of the time.

Later we sat in the large and comfortable bar of our hotel, working bottles of Flag beer into ourselves and staring with wide eyed incredulity at a dreadful karaoke act that was playing out before us. Bad renditions of truly awful 1980s hit parade singles bellowed from worn out speakers, while the gathered group of drinkers laughed at whoever was looking for beer-induced moments of local fame.

Penetrating hangovers the following morning led us to take a long walk after breakfast. We hid our eyes from the bright morning sun with sunglasses and set off through the town and towards the port and Kasbah. The general idea being to see what else Agadir had to offer aside from beaches and beer.

Dave did some shopping while I found an internet cafe and caught up with our sponsors by email. I also posted an expedition update to PR man Dan Sager, an industry colleague who had agreed to cover some of the press work while we were in Africa.

We again joined forces and sat at a cafe by the town's mosque, injecting more coffee into ourselves in a vain attempt to soothe our pounding heads. Later, we strolled down the beach towards the port and passed a new development of London 'docklands' style apartment buildings.

Behind this, lay the huge port of Agadir, which thronged with people working, or hanging around in the hope that work would come their way. We wandered down the kilometre long quay, taking pictures of men at work unloading older style fishing boats. These were much the same as those at Essaouira. Some were uneasy at being captured on digital 'celluloid', but most just smiled or waved a fish for the benefit of the camera.

Further down were large ocean going trawlers. Rusted and battered by high seas, these were lined up at right angles from the quayside in groups of ten or more. There must have been over 100 ships, all of which were laden with neat equipment, aerials and modern electronic navigation aids.

Some were silent and still, others bustled with crew loading supplies and busy with maintenance tasks. Senior crew members watched activity from the wide ships bridges, radar receivers and old style 'Navigators' span on their masts.

Dave went off to take some photographs of people packing fish into crates, while I chatted to some dockworkers who were gathered on the quayside. Some were cooking sardines which were clamped in small grills and roasted on charcoal braziers. They offered me a few cooked fish and I managed get permission to board one of the larger boats to take some photographs. It was a rusting hulk which seemed somewhat derelict.

Entering the Bridge housing, I startled an old man in oily clothes. He turned out to be a caretaker and was happy for me to wander about the ship and take my pictures. He told me that the ship had been recently decommissioned and was awaiting a buyer.

Dave had joined me and motioning to the warped decking, which was full of rust holes, commented that the ship had seen hard times. "I suppose there comes a point where no amount of improvisation can get around the fact that the whole deal is falling to pieces with rust." He added.

Leaving the port we took one of the small yellow 'petit-taxis' to the old Kasbah high above the town. Sitting at a commanding position on top of a steep and rocky hill, the road up wound around and around the hill as it climbed. Dave snapped away while I enjoyed the experience of not being on a bike for once.

The driver leaned back over his seat towards us, chattering away about all manner of local gossip as he drove. Only half an eye on the bumpy road and one hand on the wheel as he used the other to smoke a noxious cigarette.

Arriving with a squeal of well-worn brakes, we paid the taxi driver off. Ignoring a group of spitting camels which were there to serve the tourist trade, we wandered up a wide path, where vendors were selling local crafts and entered the Kasbah through an ancient gate in the high sand coloured walls.

The Kasbah was a focal point of the old town of Agadir. At one time it was probably a very interesting and picturesque old Moroccan sea side city, which dominated the area with its battlements and defences. But in 1961 a disaster visited, which must have seemed to its inhabitants to be the wrath of a vengeful God. The city was destroyed in a huge earthquake.

Destruction was total and the loss of life was of biblical (or Koranic?) proportions. About 18,000 people were killed, with many more dying of disease afterwards. The destruction was so complete that rescuers had little choice but to treat the whole site as a mass grave and buried the lot under tons of stones.

Only the Kasbah walls survived and these now served as a memorial to those who had died. Agadir was rebuilt as a new town and tourist resort below the hill on the coast. But every day some of those who remembered that terrible tragedy still visited the Kasbah, mourning the victims of the horror that visited years before; I saw one old woman sitting by a rock where someone had laid flowers. A passing local said that she had relatives who were believed to be buried near the spot.

It was sobering stuff and as we sat on the high walls, looking at the dramatic views of the sea and mountains behind the new city of Agadir, we tried to imagine just what it must have been like. The day that the earth moved and death strode through crashing rock and the cries of the desperate.

A further taxi ride and gassing by cheap cigarettes didn't appeal and as the afternoon was a pleasantly warm mixture of sunshine and light cloud, we decided that a walk back to the new Agadir was in order.

A small track wound down the hillside away from the Kasbah and as we walked the heat rose, but not unpleasantly so. It was a stony path, lined with shrubs, small cacti and the occasional stunted acacia-style tree. As it wound down towards the main road below we stopped for photographs and lazy conversation. Sometimes a goat would cross our path, or the occasional beast would pop its head up from behind a rock and bleat a greeting at us.

Later in a beachside bar, we enjoyed slow beers and snacks, watching holiday makers play with their children on the wide sandy beach. We revelled in the fact that our own expedition held so much more than their undoubtedly pleasant one or two week escape from the chill of Europe.

*

INTO SAHARA

We were away before first light the following morning. The day's riding was going to be one of the longest on the journey and this would be our first day in the Sahara. There was an air of anticipation as we fired up the Dakars and headed out onto the main road south.

Agadir's south side was packed with messy residential districts and even this early in the morning, traffic was starting to build as we negotiated congested roads and looked for the turn off to Tiznit. Away from the holiday resort area of town, Agadir became a mirror of many other provincial Moroccan towns – with the semi ordered bustle of everyday life spilling onto the litter strewn streets.

Finding our route south, we were glad to break free of urban sprawl and head into more open country, along a route that was sometimes lined with ordered rows of trees. We passed small villages and agricultural buildings, making fair progress in a part of the country that has the kind of vitality which comes from commerce and agriculture.

Tiznit is a significant regional town and the guidebook outlined an interesting history. But all we saw of it were new urban developments which lined the main road as it brushed the eastern edge of town. It was a shame not to stop. Tiznit was the last large town before we entered the desert and is an interesting southern trade centre, with ancient thick city walls which were built to surround the twelve Kasbahs which existed there in the late 19th century.

We were now at the start of the long lonely road which would take us into West Africa. For roughly the next 1000 miles, there were few road interchanges that led anywhere but into the desert towards remote settlements. Our road was the only fully sealed road south and the sense of adventure rose as the Anti Atlas, our last mountain range, appeared in the distant haze.

The land was starting to take on a distinctly brown hue, appearing burned and desiccated. Green grass had gone, to be replaced with desert scrub and small trees. This wasn't the desert yet, but the increasingly barren hills held promise of what was to come.

For me, excitement was still tinged with the feelings of paranoia and fear which had dogged me since Valdepenas. As each day passed, I was coping better and getting on top of the feelings, but they stubbornly refused to go away. This meant that I was still not getting the best out of the journey. My days were still spent hiding from fear and erratic thoughts, but this was now interspersed with ever longer periods of relaxed clarity.

The walk from Agadir's Kasbah had been one such moment and others had been offered by the change of scenery and pace during our day off.

The previous evening, we had settled in the hotel bar, feeling a little tired, but also refreshed by our trudge around the town. Dave was not really one for rest days, but I've always felt that it's important to take time out from riding once a week or so.

"Look at it like a job." I suggested. "You wouldn't work much more than seven days without taking a rest would you."

"But this ain't a job." my friend replied. "Travel is leisure and relaxation."

"Yes, but without a chance to do something different, you would eventually just tire of the pleasure." I argued. "Besides, even the best journey takes a lot out of you."

Dave was still sceptical, but as we quietly debated the issue, drinking beer and generally chilling out, the clatter and bangs of falling equipment drew our gaze. A local chap had tripped over the step up to the bar area, his arms full of boxes of what turned out to be PA equipment.

A complement of hotel staff were quickly on the scene and with much jabbering and exclamations the scattered gear was retrieved and more equipment and large loud speaker bins started arriving.

"Looks like we could get to hear a band." Dave noted. "I'll get more beer."

I idly watched the gear being set up and didn't immediately notice the quite classily dressed young woman sit down near our spot on the fairly luxurious sofas that were littered around the place. My attention was then caught by an altercation from the bar, where Dave seemed to be in some sort of dispute with the bar tender.

"Can you light my cigarette please?" came soft and well-spoken tones of the girl. She was standing over me. I offered my lighter and she sat down by me and started to converse. Where was I from? What did I do? "Ooh a moto from England!" All that sort of stuff.

It soon was clear what was going on, particularly when she crossed her legs and leaned towards me.

Well, I wasn't going to shoo her away just yet. She may have been plying her 'trade' around the local hotels and I certainly wasn't interested. But she spoke well and it made a change to talk at length to someone else aside from 'yer man', my sometimes dour Irish mate.

Dave interrupted the conversation by thumping down two brimming glasses and a plate of olives.

I offered the plate to our new friend, who daintily took one and cast an enquiring gaze at Dave.

"Ah, this is Dave, he also rides bikes and, er, drinks beer…." I offered. The girl smiled but didn't say anything.

Dave grinned broadly. He'd sussed the girl out as soon as he saw her.

"So what brings you to this hotel?" he asked her.

"I have friends that I meet here."

"Ah, OK then, right you are!" His grin got broader

"So are we going to stay for this band then Brigadier?"

"Actually, I've got a horrible feeling that it's Karaoke, not a band. Should be a bit of a laugh."

We drank our beer and talked to the girl. She was adept at not telling us anything substantial about herself. She was from Agadir, but spoke mainly about seeing friends. Definitely a bar fly who pulled the odd trick. But bright and engaging and good company for half an hour. She used her phone ringing as a reason to make her excuses. Neither the Irishman or myself were up for any custom this night.

The memory made me smile in my helmet as I rode. That and the dreadful caterwauling of the evening's Karaoke, which drove us from the bar and onto a restaurant for a good meal and a bottle of wine.

We pulled over someway along a gently climbing straight section of road, adjacent to a brown hill that raised its enormous smooth hump from the bone dry floor of the surrounding land. A scattering of huts sat on its lower slopes, not dwellings, but more in the style of small shepherds' huts.

We took a drink of water and consulted the map. Tan-Tan was our lunchtime destination. It seemed that we would make it, provided we kept going at a good pace.

A battered Renault stopped sharply by us and English language greetings came from within. The old Renault hatchback was covered in stickers and graffiti, with this quickly explained by the Dutch couple who owned the car.

They were taking part in the Amsterdam to Banjul Challenge. I'd heard of the Plymouth to Banjul Challenge and this Dutch version was in the same mould. The challenge involved driving old cars across Europe and through the Sahara to Banjul in The Gambia – our own destination – where the participants auctioned their vehicles to raise money for Gambian charities.

Our new Dutch friends had crossed Europe at a huge rate of knots and only the day before had been in the north of Morocco. They estimated arriving in Banjul in less than ten days.

Both were enthusiastic and upbeat, nice people to run into on our long day's ride. They gave us some phone numbers and asked us to keep in touch and then roared off up the road, crashing their gears at each change, wheels leaving a huge cloud of dust.

Dave shook his head.

"Totally different kind of travel, almost like they see Africa as a playground."

This was an interesting comment. I'd seen a programme on the TV about the Plymouth to Banjul lot. Their hectic drive was in aid of charity, but was presented more like a gung-ho 'raid' on Africa more than anything else. A group of their cars had famously broken out of the customs compound at Rosso in Senegal after being held up hours by corrupt officials. However, they'd soon been caught, with the episode only serving to make this border more awkward for others.

It was darkly rumoured that overland travellers owed the Senegalese insistence on the Carnet de Passage to the first Plymouth/Banjul Challenge, whose participants had left dead and dying cars scattered around the country, sold to locals for a song. But despite this, there was something quirky and exciting about the Challenge and I'd often considered entering myself. 'Rally raiding' has some strong attractions and adventure motorcycling is by no means the only way to see the world.

The Amsterdam based challenge consisted of several groups of cars, all leaving at different times over the few weeks that we were also in Africa. Whatever the reputation of the Challenge series from different countries, it was good to see friendly faces as we travelled. We kept running into teams all the way to The Gambia. They were great folk, who made the desert in particular seem a less empty place.

We were just donning our helmets again, when out of the south came a couple on a battered Yamaha XT600. They pulled in to say hello and presented a picture of long years spent on the road. The bike looked tired and was clearly the veteran of many running repairs and 'needs-must' bodges. Everything was covered in a thick layer of caked oily mud and dust. Their luggage was battered, faded and worn. Bags were held on with rope and bungies and a worn out spare tyre hung from the rear of the bike.

The rider was a middle aged German whose piercing eyes shone from a tanned and worn face, his unkempt long beard giving him a wild man look. His and his wife had the brown leathered look of people who had been in the sun for many months. They were clad in faded and patched riding gear that had seen hard miles.

But both were pleased to see us and Dave with his better understanding of German pumped them for news of the road south. "The new road in Mauritania? Yes it is opened, it is good. Borders? No problem, but don't go to a place called Rosso on the Senegal border. Many bad men."

It turned out that they had both been on the road for a couple of years exploring Africa mainly. But all good journeys do come to an end and they were putting in long miles each day to get back to their home in Germany and a long awaited family reunion. They anticipated being home in just over two weeks. A nice run compared to our somewhat fierce itinerary.

A cheery wave and the starter motor slowly churned their old and faithful XT into misfiring life, its tired battery only barely able to turn the engine over. The motor barked as the clutch was fed out and this pleasant mannered and well-travelled couple thumped off in the direction that we had come from.

Soon after, we found ourselves behind a stream of lorries grinding along in first gear as they shared our climb up the increasingly mountainous road which marks the start of the Anti Atlas, Morocco's southern barrier against the Sahara. Round the steep bends we went and the road rose ever higher. We took opportunities to get ahead of the bellowing engines and clouds of diesel whenever they were offered.

The dramatic landscape of the Anti Atlas gave us one photo opportunity after another as we continued south. Between lorry queues we dived and swooped around curves. We gunned our engines on straights and laboured our sturdy beasts up steep inclines and over the top of small passes where further breathtaking vistas waited to greet us.

The Anti Atlas may seem barren on the map, but the reality was mixed agricultural land enclosed in small holdings of dry stone walls, cultivated trees and plants mixed with cactus and scrub like trees of infinite varieties and colours. Goats shared habitation with humans and small towns doubled as truck stops for the never ending fleets of trucks that plied the route north and south. Low palls of smoke from numerous barbeques hung over the road at these places. Giving us notice of another exercise of dodging carelessly manoeuvring trucks.

Then the road started to descend. The view between the hilly peaks was now filled with harsh yellow light, heralding the open desert ahead. Our route now winding downwards between bastions of rock which sometimes forced the road to hang out over deep valleys. Overtaking the sixteen-wheel leviathans now became much more risky and we elected to burble along behind in low gear and to enjoy the last few miles of the last mountainous roads we would travel for many weeks.

Just before Bouizakarne, we emerged from the Anti Atlas and a harsh arid and blindingly bright vista opened up. Bouizakarne itself was a staging post' of a town, the low yellow buildings and battered infrastructure set in a dry and sandy landscape. The first place we had seen that resembled a proper desert town. We quickly rode through and left the place behind us, setting out along a straight, flat road into a much more empty landscape. A vista now relieved by only occasional modest cultivation.

A stop for fuel and we headed onwards, though the bustling town of Guelmim which was dominated by the red tower of a large mosque. Then finally out into the Sahara Desert.

The road stretched ahead through a harsh view of rocky yellow and light orange desert and huge folds of desolate land. The first few miles quite intimidating and setting off an inward desire to return to more green and pleasant places.

But onwards we rode and our bikes climbed over giant humps of land and followed the road along vast valley floors, which sloped smoothly upwards to rounded ridges that hosted only a few stunted bushes. This was an empty place indeed.

Traffic levels had reduced, so that we only saw the occasional fast driven car. Though good numbers of medium sized lorries still could be seen and overtaken when safe.

This part of the journey didn't make for particularly pleasant riding. It was a harsh and empty introduction to the desert and the area felt forsaken – a new kind of culture shock. From time to time I could see the remnants of abandoned farming and once ordered fields. Was this an area which had succumbed to desertification? Or was the agricultural season so short as to provide only the barest of existence to the people who lived there?

With so much of North Africa a barren desert, it seemed that only the mighty Atlas stopped the rest of Morocco from being buried under sand. Thinking about my previous journey to the edge of the Sahara, it certainly seemed that anywhere east or south of the Atlas was pretty desolate.

But this time it was our task to breach the vast emptiness of the Sahara and discover what lay beyond.

Tan-Tan appeared on the edge of my GPS screen and as we approached, I remembered seeing a photograph of the famous 'Kissing Camels'. Now ahead and slowly filling my view were the two tall camels, reaching out across the road in a parodoc attempt to give each other the 'eye'. It was an amusing sight and as many travellers before us also did, we stopped to take the obligatory pictures of the twenty foot tall concrete beasts. Posing in a slightly awkward fashion as we snapped each other. Capturing evidence of our 'official' entry to the Sahara.

The Amsterdam/Banjul folks also had the same idea and we spent some minutes in the company of a couple with a battered Volvo which had been painted in a Zebra design. It gently dripped water from somewhere underneath while it stood.

Tan-Tan was our half way point for the day. Although we didn't stop in the town, the main road through revealed an interesting centre of local civilisation, with a medley of traditional donkey and cart and motorised traffic. Bustling and colourful local commerce ranged along a thoroughfare of painted kerb stones. Lush palm trees lined part of the route. Modern and traditional buildings, painted a stucco colour, jostled for space and a couple of attractive looking restaurants. A few hotels sat at the street's edge.

After passing over a dried oued, the road passed through an arch in a crumbling town wall, marked with reliefs of ancient design. Beyond this, buildings quickly thinned out. Out of town we went, passing areas which had been earmarked for development. A large sign was crudely hammered into the ground, proclaiming that new housing and business was coming Tan-Tan's way.

The road now swooped and climbed over dramatic folded land, vast humps of rocky country, which opened new vistas of brown stony land as it took us directly west. The sky ahead was bright and the blue of the coast appeared on my GPS as Tan-Tan Plage drew closer. Then a curve to the left at the turn off for the small coastal settlement and the Atlantic came into view. A calm unending seascape lapping onto a sandy shore at the bottom of a seemingly never ending thirty foot cliff of stony hard packed sand. Marching headlands led the eye into the distance and inland the sharp yellow sun-haze gave view of a flat and featureless 'hamada' – the local term for the astonishing plateaus of jumbled rock, scrub and occasional sand that we were to ride through.

We rode the bikes off road and onto a small sandy track so that we could get close to the cliff edge and look out over the sea. I immediately fell off in the soft sand, the Dakar's road tyres losing all semblance of grip and dumping me into the pillow like embrace of a small forgiving hummock of sand and dry grass.

Laughter as I picked myself up. We both walked the few yards to the cliff edge, where crumbling packed sand and soil cautioned us from getting too close to the view below.

"Grand spot." remarked my companion with overwhelming understatement. The view was incredible and the contrast between cool blue sea and hot yellow land was as harsh as an impressionist's painting.

I felt peace and calm in the stillness. Almost nothing could be heard. The few trucks on the road rumbled by, their engines and tyres muffled by the sand almost to nothing in the small distance that the sound had to travel to reach our ears. A gentle breeze stirred the air and an occasional chirp of some foraging bird could be heard from the beach below.

We walked along the cliff edge for a while, giving respect to the dangerous underhanging edge and keeping ourselves at a distance to avoid mishap. The surface of the sand had settled into a thin crust which our boots broke, leaving a clear impression with every step. It was like walking on a mattress, or on the surface of the moon and the urge to tread gingerly was irrationally strong.

The contrast of desert and sea under a burning azure sky created a great sense of peace. "People go all their lives and never see a view like this." Remarked Dave, also somewhat in awe of this new landscape which, with variations, was to be our companion for the next 800 miles.

For the next hour or so we rode slowly drinking in the undulations of the land. Feeling sorrow when the road turned inland for a while, joy when our path took us close to the sea again. Photo stops became numerous as we found new features to capture in our lenses. We were now well and truly in the open Sahara desert.

Distant mesas came into view inland. But very low ones, perhaps twenty or thirty feet in height – enough to add a further contrast to the view and interest to our ride.

The emptiness was curiously intimidating; all those miles between us and civilisation could be an uncomfortable thought. But on our many stops, peace stole over me and suddenly the desert was a wonderful place to be. I could appreciate that what appeared at times featureless when riding was in fact a vastly contrasting land of colours and textures, with small plants and wildlife eking a living among the sand.

I thought of Michael Asher and his incredible journey by camel across the Sahara from Chinquetti in Mauritania, to the Nubian Desert in Egypt. He and his new wife Mariantonietta Peru were the first recorded westerners to take on this challenging adventure. All those days of steady walking must have shown them desert features that no motorised overland traveller could even imagine seeing from behind the handlebars of a motorcycle, or the steering wheel of a four wheel drive. Asher's account of adventure and adversity in his book 'Impossible Journey' is one of the most powerful I have read.

We wasted time burbling slowly through this wonderful landscape and as we lazily rode, the sun sank lower until it filled our view of the world ahead. The road was now pretty much arrow straight as it tracked the cliff and took us towards Laayoune, our destination.

Dave indicated that he would like to stop at Tarfaya to see the memorial to Antoine St Exupery. He was the pioneering aviator of the 1920s Aero-Postale, the colonial French air postal service. But it was getting late in the day and there were still many miles to Laayoune. The sun was now a harsh orb in our visors, huge and inescapable, its rays burning though the protection of our sunglasses and leaving a harsh imprint on our sight. I dipped my head to avoid its relentless glare and a glance in my rear view mirror showed Dave riding one handed, the other shading his eyes as best he could from the sun's harsh attack.

We stopped at a gas station just outside Tarfaya. As the oily-overalled attendant sloshed poor quality 'Super' petrol into and all over our bikes, I looked towards the town, a rough piste leading from the road by the Garage towards the settlement. The sun had now sunk lower and was no longer bothering us.

"It would be a shame to miss it." said Dave. "We could find somewhere to stay here tonight, or camp."

I pursed my lips and considered this for a moment. "Could do, but we'd be over 100 kilometres short which we'd have to make up tomorrow. Besides, it's gonna be dark in about half an hour so no time to appreciate it really. In any case, we'll be back here in a few weeks, why don't we go then?"

Dave expressed disappointment. But staying in Tarfaya, burning an hour at the memorial in the morning and starting late, would leave us with less time to cover a larger distance to Dakhla, our destination for the day. Stopping now just didn't seem to make sense. Obsessed with the itinerary perhaps? But I was concerned about margins for error further south.

Dave seemed less concerned about that. Indeed, he made comments from time to time over the preceding days which added to the feeling that he still thought less about arrangements and commitments for this journey and favoured instead using these nice bikes that we'd been lent for a blast around Africa on our own time. I had huge hidden sympathy with the sentiment – what bliss that would be. But I was absolutely not going to stray from the commitments that I'd given to BMW in particular.

It seemed that this trip was in danger of revealing inconsistencies in our approach that could threaten to spoil the years of easy travel that we'd enjoyed together. I hoped that this wouldn't be the case.

But the fact was that Dave still viewed the journey more as a holiday, while I viewed it as a kind of mission, with expectations which needed to be met in return for all the good will and help that we'd received from individuals and companies who had made the whole thing possible in the first place.

Out there, in that remote place, where all senses and emotions are heightened, I was irrationally starting to feel as though Dave was cheapening the whole purpose of the journey. Devaluing everything I had done and all the effort that Barbara and I had made to put him in a position where all he had to do was to get off a plane from Poland and ride a motorcycle.

But in fairness to Dave, aside from his sideways comments and occasional disappointed demeanour, he was generally happy to let me lead the way and set the agenda.

This was Lariam induced stress again. Dave was my buddy, my main man, my soul brother. Here I was thinking uncharitable and very unfair thoughts about one of the people I loved the most. The voice in my head told me; 'Put up with his irritation Craig, he won't let you down and you're too 'wired' anyway. You have been for weeks'.

We set off towards Laayoune again, but only after Dave extracted a promise that we would spend quality time in Tarfaya on the way back. I readily agreed. In any case, I was also curious to see this remote and lonely memorial to an aviation hero. Just not today.

Darkness fell quickly. Within ten minutes of leaving the gas station, the bike's headlight was taking over from the sun as the main source of light on the road ahead. As it steadily grew darker, the desert receded and our vision became increasingly 'coned' in the pool of light from our lamps. There was some illumination as we passed by the group of buildings which marked the border of Morocco. A border that was only nominally recognised by Morocco, which had annexed our next country years before.

The Western Sahara took us in its embrace via its lonely road. Another country behind us as we pushed out into the disputed former Occidental territory of the Sahara Desert.

Lights ahead gave warning of approaching traffic. A group of headlights came closer into view, followed by a train of other headlights which dazzled my vision and left me guessing the path of the route ahead as a stream of lorries roared by us heading north. This wasn't usual commercial traffic – that had dried up when darkness fell. These were army trucks and as their tall bulk streamed by us in the opposite direction, I could glimpse figures sat in the back of each truck, the occasional cigarette glowing in the darkness.

These convoys became numerous. Shattering the darkness, blinding us. Fast driven and disorientating as I navigated the way ahead, Dave sticking close by me now.

The problem was that even when I wasn't being blinded by yet another convoy of army trucks, I couldn't really see the road ahead very well. I had not a clue about what lay ahead, whether the road would become potholed and at some point cast one of us off our bikes into the darkness – or into the path of a convoy. I now regretted not fitting auxiliary lights to the bikes.

The kilometres counted downwards as we came nearer Laayoune. The truck convoys continued to assault our sight and left our eyes dazed and peering ahead into blackness. An eternity of danger and tense concern. The road almost unseen ahead, guided our wheels. Thankfully, no potholes appeared.

Finally, the lights of civilisation started to wink dimly ahead, a few bright ones masking a mass of illumination which started to become clearer as we approached the edge of Laayoune. I felt huge relief as a marker post told me that we only had five kilometres to go.

The police pulled us into a checkpoint at the edge of town. A friendly cop and a more business-like and suspicious plain clothes guy with him. The 'spook' examined our papers in depth. But both were courteous and gave us directions into town and indicated where we could find a hotel.

A short ride down in incline and a huge stone arch marked our arrival at the Capital of the Western Sahara. Then we crossed the 'Green March' bridge, named to commemorate the mass migration of Moroccans into the Western Sahara many years ago.

211

We rode under the protective illumination of regular streetlights and breathed relief as we came into the city to be greeted by the familiar sights of people, traffic and human habitation.

It had been an epic day. Just about 600 kilometres and a great achievement. But the last hour or so of riding in the dark had been pretty scary and reminded me why everyone strongly advises against riding in the dark in developing countries.

We booked into a place which we quickly renamed Hotel Stench. The plumbing didn't work properly so water kept backing up in the pipes and the whole place stank of excrement by the following morning. But if one ignored the smell, it was comfortable and cheap. Dave shot some film on one of the video cameras and with the day's journey ended, we felt upbeat and came up with some amusing comments for the lens.

The 'dry' bar downstairs didn't inspire, so after a short walk through dusty and run down streets, lined with hastily thrown up concrete blocks of apartments, we headed up a hill towards the more interesting looking centre of town.

Attracted by a sign for a bar and restaurant, we found ourselves spending the evening in what was billed as Laayoune's Parador. Dinner was unremarkable, but the hotel had a nice courtyard among palm trees and fountains. With the tensions of the day now gone, it was nice to sit there quietly sipping our beer, listening to the trickling of water into a small pool.

As well as being the Capital of Western Sahara, Laayoune also sits strategically at the heart of the country, straddling the only sealed route north and south and well connected by air, sea and land. The country is disputed territory between Morocco and the Polisario, an independence group who hold vast territories in the east of the country and across the border with Algeria, where their people live in long term refugee camps. In November 1975, Morocco took over the country and marched-in thousands of civilians (voters) during the so called 'Green March' and has since invested billions in the country's infrastructure. Rabat's aim is to ensure civil support for Moroccan rule in a UN-brokered referendum on the future of the country to be held at 'some point' in the future.

Until a few years ago threats of Polisario attacks meant that the Atlantic route could only be travelled as part of an army convoy, but a lasting truce now makes this unnecessary. The country remains flooded with troops and UN 'Observers'. From what we could see, the UN types seemed to do little but hang around in restaurants in Laayoune and Dakhla. Or drive around in Land Cruisers. 'Observing'.

The result of the truce and uneasy peace has been unfettered 'Morocco-isation' of the territory by the Rabat government to create what we were told was a tax-free haven of new towns and villages. The Capital enjoys huge investment to create solid modern infrastructure and a very odd feel.

We kicked the ethics of the situation around between us for a while. Rabat was determined to keep the territory and their treatment of the Polisario deserved close scrutiny. The long standing refugee status of the disenfranchised Polisario people has been largely ignored by the international community for far too long. But on the other hand Morocco's investment in the country and the development of the Atlantic Route, though self-serving, had brought notable improvements to the territory.

It seemed to me that the Polisario deserved better than being dismissed as mere terrorists. From time to time the outside world gets to hear about the miserable conditions that the displaced indigenous peoples faced in the Algerian refugee camps. But however strong the Polisario's case for independence may be, total independence for Western Sahara is unlikely to happen. Pragmatism suggests that the Moroccans and Polisario need to come to some sort of arrangement which can bring the people home and perhaps have the territory jointly governed. Let both sides be winners.

If that could happen, then perhaps the UN wouldn't need to hog all the hotel rooms and restaurant tables in Laayoune – a space or two for the overland traveller would be nice…

MINEFIELDS AT DUSK

Our first excursion into serious dune territory led to Dave banging away with his camera with enthusiastic zeal. I couldn't blame him. The rolling area of soft unblemished sand dunes which we encountered just outside of town early the following morning was impressive.

Leaving my bike, I walked across the virgin sand, the sight of the road quickly left behind as I strode. Soon all I could see was undulating sand, with Dave walking about, with an accentuated 'Basil Fawlty' gait. Leaving footprints and measuring camera angles. It was a faintly Luna landscape and sand was wind blown into crazy shapes – a reminder that away from the road, there was a real live desert out there.

Less impressive was the huge phosphate ore plant which disgorged stinking smoke and dust at El Marsa few kilometres later on. A conveyor belt ran from the coastal industrial complex into the deep desert. A piece of real estate which was significant enough for the map to note its presence. The road circled the plant. Through large gates in its perimeter wall, I could see blackened filthy workmen toiling among the dust and grey rocks, feeding the huge hungry and belching beast of factory workings like worker ants. Life for them looked miserable, with little to look forward to.

We pushed past this grim spot as quickly as we could.

The road continued southwards through the hamada of stone, dust and sand. Sea on the right, sand and rocks on the left. It became mile after mile of monotony, broken by stops to sit by the cliff edge when the road ran near the sea.

I really wanted to press on. The views were magnificent at times, but it was a long and lonely road. The day's destination was Dakhla, 460 kilometres away and I wanted to get there before nightfall.

My companion felt differently though and regular photo stops became the order of the day. Sometimes with good reason as the landscape threw up an interesting set of dunes or mesas. At other times, stops seemed a bit pointless, or for no real purpose.

Once again I was being irrationally impatient, particularly as I had my own reasons for wanting to stop from time to time.

Either for a drink, or to let that desert peace and stillness steal over me again.

The residual effects of Mr Lariam ensured that riding this vast emptiness remained slightly intimidating. The slightest thing or mild irritation would create their own tensions or paranoia. I spent long hours listening to the beat of my engine, wondering if it sounded OK. Or I'd worry about dire things that could happen down the road; robberies, break downs, illness, heat stroke. Despite the fact that worrying about these things wouldn't solve anything and that they probably wouldn't happen anyway. Dave's presence whenever we rode alongside each other was a huge help though.

Dave would sometimes ride close, other times let distance fall further between us until he would occasionally pass out of sight. When we stopped we didn't talk much. I would sometimes feel tense in his presence, particularly after yet another photo stop for a seemingly pointless bit of sand. Sometimes he would look at me impatiently. There was much that we weren't discussing that perhaps we should have.

Or perhaps not. Was the tension real or imagined? Above all else, we got on with the ride and continued to work well as a team. Long familiarity with each other overcoming whatever did – or didn't – lie beneath.

But on other occasions through the day, we'd slip once again into more familiar easy companionship as we discussed a panorama that we'd stopped to take in, or saw some other feature of the land that we liked. Or do something slightly daft together which made us laugh. Occasionally larking about in the sand with our overloaded motorcycles. Perhaps we really were both too tense and reading things into each other's behaviour which we shouldn't have. Indeed, was Mr Lariam slightly affecting Dave? He later reported that he'd had disturbed sleep and bizarre dreams.

Despite times of seeming monotony in our riding, the landscape constantly changed, with plains of dunes contrasting with wide mesas, plunging cliffs and deep chasms in the desert floor. The ocean was never far away and the occasional shipwreck added colour to the beautiful coastline and vast miles of sandy beaches. Sometimes we could hear the sea moving and murmuring when we took time out from riding. Sitting on the cliff edge enjoying the peace and slightly cooling breeze.

Despite the emptiness, we never seemed to be quite alone. The road was fairly busy with commercial traffic and we saw many beaten up old trucks transporting fish from Dakhla to the markets in the north. Strangely, there seemed to be many people who lived on the cliffs, eking out a precarious existence from fishing, with long and very basic fishing rods. Sometimes we'd be stopped on the side of the road taking in the view, when some character would come walking or cycling by muttering a greeting as they went. Very strange given the vast distance between any kind of organised habitation. In over 300 miles we saw only a handful of villages and only two towns of any size.

Police and army checkpoints were frequent. Bored officials would take down passport details in minute detail in old exercise books and the atmosphere was mostly relaxed. There was one exception.

The road took a dive through a low cliff and for a short time we ran along the ocean's edge before the road climbed again onto the coastal plateau. A campsite was nearby, full of French registered motor homes. Once on the plateau, we were flagged down by a group of policemen who manned a checkpoint. A small stone building which housed a police post stood nearby and the red Moroccan flag with its star hung limply from a pole.

Most of the cops displayed a relaxed attitude, but they sent us into the building where an entirely different character lorded it over a tall counter. He was an albino black African an unexpected sight in an Arab dominated region. His demeanour suggested trouble. Flashing eyes and a curt manner as he demanded our papers.

I tried to explain what each document related to as I had done many times before. But he slammed his fist on the counter and exclaimed. "You stand still there and don't say anything!"

A few small glass tea cups jumped as his fist came down, disturbing their dark viscous contents and the numerous flies that were buzzing around them. I shut my mouth as commanded and waited.

Albino scrutinised at length each of our documents in turn and then demanded a 'fiche' from us, the one thing we didn't have. A fiche is essentially a photocopy of our passports and driving licenses, with the Moroccan ID number written on the back. We had yet to run into problems with this, but could see why it was desirable to have them handy for checkpoints. The fiche saved time waiting for some bored official to laboriously copy details from our identity documents.

Albino started to make a loud fuss about the missing fiche and complained about having to write everything longhand into the ubiquitous filthy school exercise book.

"This will take time; this is not in order." He snarled.

It seemed that a small 'inducement' may help oil the wheels of desert bureaucracy. Reaching inside my pockets for one of the cheap biros that I had brought to use for minor 'cadeau', I produced a budget 'Bic' with a flourish.

"Will this help?" I asked.

Albino's eyebrows shot up.

"Certainement!" he exclaimed and set to writing in his exercise book without a further murmur.

Dave cast me an amused half smile.

Albino was clearly happy with his gift. Tea was even offered. While we had been waiting a German registered motor home had arrived and the driver came into the office as we left to be greeted with a renewed snarl from the Albino.

"Seems that the guy has a bit of a chip on his shoulder." remarked Dave.

"Bet he has a huge biro collection." I laughed. We mounted our bikes and got out of there as fast as we politely could.

At Boujdour we stopped for coffee and snacks. The small regional town bustled with commerce and thriving businesses lined the road through town. Local income seemed to come from bureaucracy, fishing, and serving the needs of the people passing through on the long stretch between Laayoune and Dakhla.

We sat with our drinks and watched the world go by, particularly the brightly painted, old and heavily overloaded trucks. With cargo piled to twice their height, they wheezed along the road belching diesel fumes. Tired suspension crashed down onto chassis bump stops with every pot hole.

The setting was almost picturesque. Boujdour has a fishing harbour, a lighthouse and a long deserted beach south of the town. Its centre is not totally unattractive, with more modern Moroccan buildings in white and occasionally with balconies and colonnades.

The coast at Cap Boujdour is famous for treacherous winds and used to be renowned for shipwrecks. The most famous was that of the US brig 'Commerce' which was wrecked in 1815. The Captain, James Riley, and other survivors underwent great privations and an escape from slavery to trek the 1200 kilometres to Essaouira and safety. Riley later published an electrifying account of his ordeal in 'Sufferings in Africa' a book that strongly influenced a young Abraham Lincoln.

We pressed on southwards through the unforgiving hamada. The seascape added interest, but when not in view, the overwhelming emptiness and oppressive 'deadness' of the country weighed down upon me. But despite the feelings of exposed nakedness before the desert and sky, I felt a degree of fulfilment that I had never felt before.

It is said that people find God on long desert journeys. There are many accounts about this. Simon had certainly found God in an overwhelming fashion as he travelled around the world. His handwritten diaries clearly revealed the influence that his faith was to have on almost every aspect of his life and every decision that he made.

Our journey may have been short on time, but it was long in miles. Miles which allow the mind to wander, nowhere more so than during our five day journey across the desert. I began to think about the nature of God in a way that I hadn't done since I was a teenager.

There was no blinding revelation in store for me, as I've always had a strong personal faith in the immortality of the human spirit, but I did find that I was appraising my long held faith, as my temporal being cruised along in an environment which exposed me to a world that was unfamiliar and where the future was uncertain.

By 2005, I'd not been a regularly practising Christian for many years. Indeed, I remain cautious of the concept of traditional organised religion, despite becoming involved again in local church matters some years after Dave and I made this journey. Often moulded in times past to suit cynical, even brutal ideologies or social conventions. Even the benign Church of England, my own church, was born from the desire of a king to divorce.

That said, I take the view that militant secularisation, humanism and atheism lack credible answers to many Big Questions, including those which surround the decline of moral and ethical standards in society. I am given to wonder if benign religious recognition doesn't indeed have a place in society. It's an issue that I've debated internally for many years. I am also curious about the seeming fear that atheists have for faith based ideas. They endlessly attack religion with a surprising vigour and fervour which suggests discomfort with the entirety of their own arguments.

Atheism seems to project itself almost as a religion in its own right – surely then, a self-defeating philosophy.

Some blame religion for the ills and wars of the world. But this view fails to appreciate the innate tribalism that exists within humankind. No religion or religious fundamentalism would not mean no wars. Other reasons would be found for conflict. Age old tensions between the West and the Arab world would find expression in other ways. Indeed they often do.

Therefore I've quietly held onto my faith, even if it had been rarely practiced for much of my adult life. I've also held onto the notion of good and evil and a value system which exists to guide one towards a moral life. I'm not sure that I believe in the idea of 'God' as a person. No – to me, 'God', if you can call 'him', 'her', 'it', is more a guiding force which brings peace and fulfilment in a troubled world. My broadly Anglican Christianity sits in the background to these beliefs. The Mormons hold the view that 'as we are now God once was and as God is now, we can become'. It's a statement that works on many levels and to me says that it is up to us to decide what kind of person we each become.

Some would argue that spiritual strength comes from within and 'God' is merely an excuse, a prop, a construct which doesn't exist. I can't subscribe to that seductively convenient view. It seems more like an attempt to explain the unexplained in merely human terms; a way of not facing up to the fact that that not everything can be explained by science and logic.

Such folk also argue that the end of life means the end of the spirit. That we do our time and when we die, that vast sum of experience, learning, knowledge and personal gain ceases to exist. Only living on through the transient memories of family and friends.

This seems completely illogical. If there's no point to developing ourselves as individuals through our lives, when why do we have the power to do this? Why do we bother to learn new things that are purely about developing personal intellect, or learning life lessons which often have value to no one but ourselves? Surely, if all consciousness ended at the point of death, then we would be little more than semi mute beings. Scrabbling around, living in basic shelters and competing with each other for food and mating partners. Our sole objective in life being to perpetuate our species. Wouldn't that be more scientifically logical if the individual spirit also ended when our time on this mortal coil came to a close?

The wholesale rejection of spirituality by vast sections of society has perhaps been partially responsible for a rising tide of social selfishness. 'Grab it while you can' attitudes, social disorder and disrespect of fellow beings. After all, it all ends when we die, surely it doesn't matter if we selfishly do exactly as we please while we are alive.

For me, Christ as a prophet certainly existed, in the same way that Mohammed also existed. Both enlightened remarkable beings who proclaimed messages which have often been abused and manipulated by those who claimed to be their followers. The excesses of the Medieval Christian Church and the fundamentalist interpretations of Koranic teaching are extreme examples of the perversion of sound doctrines. The calls for a more moral and spiritual existence that were made by those remarkable prophets often set aside, or mere lip service paid to the concepts they taught.

As I rode, I pondered this and my own beliefs, finding that a sense of peace came from these mental debates. An exercise that led to a strengthening of my own convictions. Not a revelation from 'god'; more an affirmation of my personal, if slightly non mainstream, faith.

I suppose an agnostic or an atheist would say that I'd subconsciously summoned a personal comfort blanket. But I know otherwise.

It was warm, but not uncomfortably so. Increased aridity meant that I had started to ensure that I was drinking regularly. The wind seemed to suck moisture from the atmosphere and my face felt increasingly dry and wrinkled. I'd read somewhere that the Western Sahara is one of the driest places on the planet.

We occasionally passed townships which seemed new and empty. They were bright and clean; incongruous compared to the usual beaten up and dirty settlements that we had become used to. I made a mental note to check one of these places out at some point in the journey.

Already the sun was sinking toward a position directly ahead of us – promising a burning late-day glare before it sank towards the horizon.

Fuel stations were rare but regularly placed and were focal points for vehicles to stop for a while, even if no fuel was needed. For us they represented something different to look at after miles of desert travel. One place had a restaurant in grand, but grubby style, with a high domed interior and many tables occupied by diners. There were also private alcoves where women took refreshment, while their men mingled more publicly. Passengers from a coach parked outside were taking a lunch stop.

Thousands of flies buzzed about inside, but the place offered a range of meals and drinks, with plenty of seating in the decorated and picturesque dining hall. Numerous ceiling fans stirred the dry hot air.

We set off again. Now the sun burned ahead and like the day before, I did my best to mask my eyes from its unrelenting glare.

But Dakhla was near and we finally arrived at a road junction without any real warning that we had reached a major intersection. The road south was a more minor road. I hoped that it was tarmacked as far as the border, though the map seemed to indicate this.

The main road curved to the west and down towards Dakhla. A gas station stood nearby and a police checkpoint was adjacent, from which a cop emerged to quickly check our papers.

The guidebook described Dakhla as feeling like the last place on earth. The ride into town certainly reinforced an impression of reaching the end of the world.

As we left the checkpoint behind, the road fell through some high dunes to reveal a dramatic view of an ocean bay with a backdrop of more tall dunes. The sea was dead calm, reflecting the sun and the huge, almost white, sand dunes marching along the shore.

The long peninsular which is partially occupied by Dakhla, dominated the distant view. The road took us arrow straight down to the shore line and then up once again, away from the lonely bay, to track the top of this huge promontory of sand for a final forty kilometre ride into town.

We arrived as the last light of the day fell from the sky and slowed our bikes as the familiar style of Moroccan arch appeared over the road ahead. Beyond it, a mass of new white and terracotta painted utilitarian 'block' buildings sprouted from the desert floor.

The Hotel Doumes took us in for the night, a plain but welcoming place on the main 'drag' into town. After we struggled upstairs with our heavy luggage, we settled into a clean room, which was basic but comfortable.

Our bikes outside had attracted a great deal of interest from local youths, who were either standing silently gazing at them, or making excitable comments to each other. The hotel receptionist assured us that in Dakhla our bikes would be safe and that there was someone who would watch over the bikes all-night in any case.

As we left to walk into town, a couple of French registered Land Cruisers pulled up, a group of explorers who were focusing their efforts on desert travel in the south of the Western Sahara. With almost military precision they unloaded their gear, which was packed into large aluminium boxes. They loudly hauled their loads into the hotel – lots of fuss and orders being barked by the group leader. Too much stress.

We wandered further into town along a wide marble paved boulevard, lined with evenly spaced palm trees and a mixture of modern houses and older more battered looking desert buildings made from bare breeze blocks. The pavement reflected the glint of the numerous street lights. Lots of money was being spent here and with the proliferation of building sites, it seemed that Dakhla was on the move, quite literally.

A broad junction marked the centre of town, with a huge piece of abstract sculpted steel occupying a prominent spot on the town square.

Streets were lined with small shops selling the variety of goods that could be found anywhere in Morocco. There was no definable shopping area as such; every so often a clump of shops would be built into the general infrastructure and into the many plain white buildings which seemed to be a feature of the town. Also in abundance were large pavement cafes, brightly lit and dominated by loud television sets. Crowds were gathering to watch a Manchester United match. Large numbers of children played football in the streets, while their fathers settled with mint tea in rows inside and outside of cafes to excitedly watch the game which was about the begin.

Dave and I continued wandering towards the port and found ourselves in darker, emptier streets. Eventually we came across a quiet restaurant which overlooked what seemed to be part of the port area, though by this time it was too dark to see properly.

Brochettes and orange juice provided a good accompaniment to a restaurant which was colourfully decorated and clean. We were almost the only customers; it seemed that most of the usual clientele were away watching football.

The match was in full swing as we made our way back into town, with each café packed with shouting punters. A rustic cup of mint tea looked to be a hassle filled experience so we repaired to the imposing Hotel Regency Sahara in search of a beer.

The hotel dominated the main square and represented the only four star experience for several hundred miles. We settled in the lounge area with two bottles of Flag beer, ubiquitous in West Africa. We watched the comings and goings of a hotel which appeared to cater for a larger business community than we had expected in such a lonely outpost. Suited men sat around low tables, relaxing in comfortable sofas as they quietly discussed business.

A European man in his late thirties came to sit with us. He turned out to be an Irish contract fisherman who worked at the port. It amused me to hear Dave gassing away with a more pronounced Irish brogue than normal.

Our new friend lived in the hotel and seemed to manage part of the port. Dakhla boasts the largest fishing fleet in Moroccan territory and his job involved shifts of six months on and six months off. He spent his spare time in the hotel and yearned for his next break which he took either in the Canary Islands, or back in Ireland.

He had a cynical view of his local colleagues and wasn't interested in learning more about local customs and culture. To him, he had a job to do and he focussed his life around this and his next escape from the Western Sahara. He had only made the trip up the peninsular to see the country once.

He did have advice about food though.

"Never order a western dish." he said. "These characters think that everything western should be cooked like a rare steak. So you order fried chicken and it'll be burned on the outside, raw in the middle. I spend half my time in the kitchens here making sure that my food has been cooked properly."

Later, Dave mused on our chance meeting with the Irishman.

"It's a shame that so many people who come here to work don't bother taking time to find out more about the places they're at. Take this guy. He never leaves the town, doesn't bother seeing what's beyond his trip between the port and hotel and has a narrow view of the people he has to live with. A real shame."

The following day was our last in the Western Sahara. We roused early to allow time for a possibly problematic and, to us, a completely unknown border crossing into Mauritania.

A café was attached to our accommodation at the Doumes and though it was still the pre-dawn hour it was doing brisk business. A fat middle aged woman in white overalls and a white cap moved

224

purposefully about, serving coffee and breads with a stern look on her face.

The French contingent, who seemed to have spent their evening at the hotel, sat calmly at their table stuffing food into themselves in an upright, tidy and disciplined manner. Dave and I instead, slouched at our places loudly slurping coffee and eating in a more relaxed manner, dropping crumbs all over the clean white table cloth.

As the French got up to leave in military style unison, I sat back, put my feet up on an adjacent chair and lit a second cigarette. Dave poured more coffee as noisily as possible. The expedition leader gave us a sour look as he strode out after his charges. We sniggered.

We left town as the sun's disk rose above distant dunes. The low morning light cast the town into sharp relief. Under this light the scattered buildings and construction sites seemed to give a more frontier-town impression than we had felt the previous evening.

We stopped for fuel back at the main road junction at the head of the peninsular, this time filling our reserve fuel cans for the first time. The only fuel station that we were aware of was marked as G1 on my GPS and we had heard that petrol wasn't always guaranteed to be available.

We turned south, down the more minor road that led to the border. Road markings disappeared, but although this route was narrower, the surface was good and promised a day of excellent riding.

At first we cruised through a flat and featureless landscape, mostly grey sand and occasional gravel. It was cool and peaceful, with the sun to the south east slowly rising and warming us. The road ran along higher cliffs which afforded spectacular views over the sea from time to time. The morning light tumbling over the edge and casting huge shadows over the sea.

A line appeared on the GPS. The Tropic of Cancer. A good place to stop and briefly celebrate a milestone of the trip.

Also a chance to breathe in the morning air and relish the peaceful calm of the area.

As we rode, the scenery became spectacular. Mesas galore, rolling sand dunes, and rocky escarpments. But no towns and after a few miles not even the odd small village or group of buildings. There was nothing aside from the empty road to indicate humanity existed – just empty constantly changing desert landscape. This was our first taste of riding with the extra weight of fuel high up on the pillion seats, but the GS's handled the Jerry Cans as though they didn't exist.

The landscape offered much more to look at than we had seen on the previous two days. Instead of cutting along the top of cliffs, the road curved and swooped through dry river beds and areas where deep depressions sank into the land.

We stopped for a while at a place marked on the map as the Golfe de Cintre, a wide circular bay that bit into an otherwise even coastline. We climbed a small hill of rocky outcrops by the side of the road to sit at the top, where a commanding view could be enjoyed. On one side the road snaked north and south into the distance and on the other, the distant sea could be seen curving through the broad bay of brown sand.

Scattered around the spot, were the first that we saw of the billions upon billions of hard white fossilised sea shells that litter the ground in much of West Africa. They are here because much of the Sahara lay on the sea bed of millenniums past. After this, wherever we stopped the ground was covered in the things, also billions of tiny snail shells. Ancient and brittle. We later learned that there are so many of these shells that they find their way into hard-core for roads and are sometimes mixed with tar to make the poor tarmac which paves many of the roads in the region.

In millennia past, the peoples of the land created vast piles of shells. Ancient refuse perhaps. The piles are an archaeological relic which are being slowly destroyed as the shells are carted off in trucks for more modern uses.

At mid day we stopped for an hour at a lovely place where the road came almost to the edge of the ocean. A peaceful beach with golden sand and small rocks where tiny birds picked about for the odd bit of shell fish. Dave went swimming in the sea. All oddly contrasting with the image of arduous desert travel.

It wasn't the best place to lose my keys though. A brief search was fruitless and Dave asked where the spares were. A realisation dawned that they were locked in one of my panniers. Dave laughed.

"For all your planning, you didn't figure that spare keys locked into a box would be no good if you lose the key for the box!" I scowled at him – the 'twat of the day' award was clearly mine.

We tried bashing the lock off the pannier using one of Dave's tyre levers and a hammer. Hopeless – the Metal Mule lock was simply too robust for the tools we had. We loosened it, but that was all.

I sat down to clear my head of the anger I felt towards myself and to ponder what else we could utilise to force the lock. Dave decided to take another look on the beach for the keys. He soon returned holding the offending items above his head. "Just saw a glint and there they were!" He laughed.

We rode onwards, into a featureless area of white sandy hamada. There was little respite for the eyes apart from the occasional herd of camels, their turbaned attendants stood silently by, gazing at us with inscrutable eyes. The harsh sun beat down. Then in the distance, a huddle of buildings emerged from the desert floor and the broad steel canopy of a fuel station came into view.

We filled up with fuel for the final time in Moroccan territory. This was the place known to us as G1, a name given to it by desert traveller Chris Scott, who had prepared a web download of fuel station waypoints in Morocco and the Western Sahara. The station lay in the middle of absolutely nowhere and boasted little more than a small café and stinking toilets. Reports that this station didn't always have petrol were thankfully unfounded and our jerry-cans remained full.

We weren't to know it, but plans were afoot to develop the place and G1 later became an important place on the Atlantic Route – the Hotel Barbas – with full services and a modern hotel.

Blue gandourah robed nomads, with all but their eyes masked by their black head cloths, stood nearby and regarded us through hooded eyes which revealed nothing.

The road led ever southwards. Now we entered a region of wind sculptured rock, the tarmac winding between small mini-mesas topped with small piles of carefully placed rocks. For what purpose they had been left, we could not guess.

Camels became more numerous, wandering in small herds between the rocks, or lazily crossing the road ahead with an ungainly gait as we slowed to avoid them. Minefield warning signs started to appear by the side of the road.

After about forty miles from G1, which seemed to take an eternity to ride, we finally reached the Western Sahara border post at Fort Guerguarat. Our arrival was abrupt, the border post emerging ahead after we topped a rise. Marked only by a tall, slender tower of communications equipment.

Beyond the new buildings which housed police and customs, we could see that the tarmac road ended. Only a poor looking sandy piste ran ahead into the distance. Through the minefield which we knew lay beyond the border – the no man's land between Western Sahara and Mauritania.

There were several European tourists, mainly French and German, with a variety of beaten up old vans. There was also a pair of cyclists, their mounts loaded with carefully packed equipment. Cycling this desert seemed to me at the time to be either an act of utter madness or extreme bravery. Day after day under the relentless desert sky must seem all the more challenging when there are days between settlements or supplies. Perhaps the closeness to the environment which cycling allows, gives a much better and more interesting perspective of the desert. Indeed, having since read some accounts of desert cycling I have developed a deep respect for these true overland adventurers.

Exit formalities were straightforward. After exchanging pleasantries with a customs officer at the exit gate, we followed some German vans through the minefield which runs for hundreds of miles along the border between Western Sahara and Mauritania. A legacy of an old dispute between the two countries.

This was a truly appalling five-kilometre stretch of track, full of sand traps and jagged rocks. False routes seem to run in all directions, so care was needed to take the correct path. But the paths were perfectly rideable with care and with little real danger of getting stuck, or blown up, as long as you stuck to the proper track.

Curiously there were people living in the minefield, scratching a living selling parts from wrecked cars and buying and selling items from people passing through. A curious existence, living neither in one country or another.

Once in a while we rode past the twisted remains of a blown up car or 4WD, stripped of useful parts, its carcass left in place to remind travellers to keep to the tracks.

A group of huts loomed through the sandy glare ahead and after a last series of deep sand traps, we topped a small rise to park by a drunkenly leaning and desiccated wooden hut. A Mauritanian flag hung limply from a nearby rusty pole.

A soldier sat on the ground nearby washing his feet, his faded and patched uniform with bright shoulder flashes a clue to his role in this desolate spot. He motioned us over to the short queue of travellers which were stood outside the hut, each waiting in turn to enter and have their passports examined by a colleague.

When it came to be my turn, I was impressed by the cleanliness of the small interior. There was a spotless rug on the floor and bedding was stacked neatly in the corner.

Another soldier sat behind an ancient school desk, complete with ink well, writing passport details into an exercise book. His spotlessly clean Kalashnikov AK47 rifle propped against the wall behind him.

The next stop was the police 'station' a hundred yards or so down the track. This was a much more tumbledown hut, full of collapsed beds and smelling of wet dogs. A group of gandourah-clad locals sat on these, waiting to get passports stamped by an irritable cop. We were asked several impatient questions about our reasons for visiting Mauritania before entry was stamped into our passports. ten Euros was demanded for the service. It didn't seem wise to argue.

More good humoured were the customs officers who occupied (and lived in) an almost collapsed hut a little further down the track. One of them spoke excellent English. Easy natured discussion and a few minutes of patient form filling saw us legally accredited to ride in the Islamic Republic. There were mutters of approval when we produced our Carnets, though they wanted to register the bikes under a local carnet arrangement, in exchange for a few crumpled dirham notes. Amusingly, the officer used the details on our Carnets to fill in the Mauritanian version.

Brushing aside a couple of hustlers, we climbed aboard our bikes and set off along a surprisingly well tarmacked road that led away from the border post in the direction of the north/south highway. It was late and starting to get dark and we wanted to get to Nouadhibou as soon as possible.

Some kilometres later, we arrived at a junction where the main road stretched either side into the distance. We turned right, signposted Nouadhibou and immediately found ourselves on the best road we had seen since leaving Europe. Smooth and well-marked, we picked up speed in the growing gloom, wondering what lay ahead in, for us, this completely new country.

The road turned south down a peninsular, which like the Dakhla peninsular led out to sea and onto the lonely northern town of Nouadhibou. The afternoon had waned and evening gloom was growing.

Not long after, we were flagged down at an army checkpoint. There were enquiries about our purpose for being there, followed by more laborious exercise book entries. We both sat on broken chairs outside the run down army post and watched the world go by for a while. Then it was onwards through the physically and emotionally virgin territory of a new country.

Nothing much had changed in terms of terrain, but aside from the new road, we had yet to see any real infrastructure. The tumbledown border post had instantly revealed impoverishment though. Road signs were battered and some route markers were painted on rusted oil barrels.

It was dark by the time we arrived in Nouadhibou. We couldn't see much of the town, just vague shadows of low buildings, which in the absence of street lighting were eerily lit by the light of numerous small street-side fires. We passed unlit fuel stations where small groups of people stood about and set off down what we took to be the main road into town. Open doorways cast dim lights onto streets littered with debris. There were thronging crowds of people on the poorly defined sandy pavements and spilling onto the streets.

Extreme poverty was immediately apparent.

Cars slowly weaved about both on the street and pavement, following no recognisable pattern of driving standard – a very laissez-faire mix of pedestrians and people with everyone having right of way.

Nearly all the cars we saw were wrecks, only vaguely resembling the Renault 5s, 12s and Mercedes vehicles that they once were. Shot suspension, battered panels, missing windows, belching smoke. Most of them being driven around at night with no lights (the lights simply weren't there any more), which posed another hazard to deal with in our slightly culture shocked mental state.

We rode onwards, seeking something resembling a town centre and at the same time trying to avoid hitting the melee of people, cars and livestock on the dark streets. But nothing appeared to indicate that Nouadhibou contained much more than desperately poor streets and shanty town style buildings.

After a time, we seemed to have left the town behind us and we aimlessly continued down a dark road where large numbers of often unlit cars continued to make life uncomfortable for us. I was starting to feel a bit desperate. There seemed to be nowhere to stay and I felt very exposed in this entirely new, if largely unseen environment.

I stopped my bike and consulted Dave.

"What the hell do we do now?" he asked. "You've got the GPS; where are we?"

My little screen was indicating that we were still in Nouadhibou, but the lack of proper base mapping meant that the device was little more than merely indicative of the general area we were in.

"It would be helpful if we had some sort of point of reference." I said. "At the moment, it's so bloody dark that I'm not really sure what to do next. There's a couple of hotels in the guidebook, but I've seen nothing that indicates how to get to them yet"

As if on cue, a battered Renault squealed to a stop behind us, its brakes making harsh metal to metal grinding noises as it pulled up.

Ali introduced himself. Portly and smiling, he employed expansive arm movements as he spoke, his blue Mauritanian robes billowing about him and threatening to tangle his arms at any second.

"I have a campsite, come and stay!" he exclaimed in excitement.

"No thank you. Can you take us to the hotel at Cansado?" Dave replied. We had seen a reference to this place in the guidebook.

"Sure! Follow me!" Ali replied with a grand gesture of even more extreme excitement.

It turned out that we'd ridden most of the way to Cansado, a smaller settlement a few miles south of Nouadhibou. A few short minutes of further riding saw us pulling up outside the Hotel Oasian in the wake of Ali, who had driven at breakneck speed. Despite only having one headlight and showering sparks from two of his wheels whenever he braked.

No luck though. Despite its remote Saharan location, the hotel was full of UN types having a conference on immigration. This mystified me. Why here? What could attract the 'five star' brigade to place like Nouadhibou? I was to never find out.

Not deterred, Ali insisted on guiding us to a hotel that was owned by his 'brother'. Although fearing a scam, we realised that at this time of night and with our senses thrown by both an unfamiliar culture and the fatigue of a long day's ride in hot conditions, we felt we didn't have much choice other than to put our trust in the exuberant Ali.

But this time we struck gold. Ali charged back up the highway to Nouadhibou and turning away from the main road led down a broad sand lined boulevard to the Hotel Sahel. The street had proper lighting and the hotel's façade looked modern and clean.

After the uncertainty of the previous hours, just talking to the calm man on the reception desk and finding we had somewhere good to stay, allowed all the cares of the day to start washing away.

Ali seemed happy to just help out and didn't ask for cash for his services. But it soon became clear that he made his money partly from acting as an insurance agent (we later learned that half the town's population seemed to do this) and through arranging black market money transactions.

It became clear to us that black market exchange rates were much better than bank rates, so a few words with Ali and he scuttled off to shortly return with the local currency 'fixer'.

Later, over grilled fish and beers at the Hogar Canaria

Restaurant, we worked out that the local exchange rate, plus a handsome tip to Ali for all this help, had left us with more money than we'd expected for the amount we'd changed. Not a bad evening's work.

Indeed, we were more than satisfied. Arriving late in the day, in an unknown country, with little more than our noses to guide us, could have resulted in a far worse result than the comfortable, if pricey, hotel that we were in and far less cheerful fare than the excellent and huge, grilled fish and beers. This was a bonus in a country where alcohol is officially banned.

The Canaria was actually a bit unexpected. Our hotel was very clean and seemed to cater for the few wealthy business types that came to Nouadhibou. Clean but a bit soulless. We figured that there must be something else to see in the town – perhaps somewhere nice to eat. Though we hadn't seen much along the crushingly impoverished main drag that we'd ridden down.

The hotel owner pulled himself away from the internet long enough to send us on a five minute walk down some sandy and unlit back roads, up a hill and into the Canaria. We were directed out of a side door of the restaurant and around to the back of the building, where another door led into a backroom restaurant with several tables, a fridge full of fish, blaring television and a bar. All very unexpected, but another occasion to make us smile broadly at each other.

The Canaria was run by a middle aged Spaniard, who from this tucked away dining room catered mainly for the small ex-pat community in the town, who congregated regularly to eat fish and watch sport on the TV. The locals mostly used the front restaurant, where alcohol was banned and a quieter atmosphere prevailed.

We were made exuberantly welcome by our Spanish host and it was not long before we were served some of the largest, freshest and best cooked fish that I'd ever seen. All was served from a spotlessly clean kitchen where a team of white coated black African men industriously went about their evening's work.

The Canaria was indeed an excellent reward after a hard day's ride.

THE REHYDRATION TREE

The fresh sun of a new day shone over the dusty and seemingly half built small city, which although poor managed to have a business-like air about it. Lots of street trade, people busy with the daily grind of eking out an existence. Loads of scrapheap cars engaged in all kinds of trade around the town, or being nursed back to life for yet another final wheezing few weeks of smoke belching travel. One had the impression that even the most sorry looking wreck would still be slowly trundling the streets of Nouadhibou long after cars that were pouring off the production lines of Europe and Japan that very day had met their demise on Europe's oh so modern and progressive road network.

The main fish market lay across the road from the hotel, already busy in the early hour, with men and vehicles coming and going through its gates. Small market stalls were being set up adjacent to the gate.

We discovered that although impoverished, Nouadhibou was in fact an important city for Mauritania. Not just as a fishing port, but also the focal point for the export of ores.

A delay to buy insurance meant a later start than we'd planned. This was compounded by a lack of petrol in Nouadhibou. We went from filthy station to station with the same enquiry "Super?" to be met with shaken heads and downturned mouths from grubby mechanics in oil soaked overalls.

It was over an hour before we were directed to a fuel station which lay at the end of a series of sandy side roads. A long queue of wrecked and chugging cars were queuing along the road, waiting their turn at the solitary petrol pump which stood in an island of filthy discarded engine oil and piles of black and rusty engine components. Figuring that we could be waiting there for much of the morning, we risked pushing our way to the front of the line. This elicited a few harsh shouts and fierce stares. This was embarrassingly bad and arrogant behaviour, but we were determined to ensure our supply of fuel before this final station also ran out of petrol.

Dodging sharp debris, nails and bits of wire which poked out of sandy patches on the streets, we left Nouadhibou, just as the mid-morning sun began to make its temperature felt through our riding suits. A long clean run up the peninsular making a pleasant start for the long 480 kilometre stretch across the open Sahara to Mauritania's capital Nouakchott.

At that time, the new road had not yet been marked on any map. With widely varying reports about its condition, state of construction and so on, the whole route had gained mythical status in our minds. Would it be a breeze, or was the thing even finished?

We had full tanks and full jerry cans, so fuel wasn't an issue. But would it be an easy day's ride, or a hard two-day slog on the old open desert and beach route? This famous part of the Atlantic Route used to be the only sensible way to get south from Nouadhibou. It took the traveller through long sections of sand, gravel and dunes, followed by a hard ride down the beach to Nouakchott – trying to beat the tide.

The superlative quality of the road from the border had been encouraging, but traveller reports still varied about whether it had been completed or not.

We paused to photograph a curious dune formation on the coast. It looked like an upside down cone, an old minibus parked by its narrow base lending a slightly surreal air to the location.

Arriving once again at the junction where the border road snaked northwards through the sand, we paused to take a few photographs. A noise in the distance made Dave look up from his camera. There was no mistaking the sound of a train's horn and the low throb of approaching powerful diesels.

We had heard about the famous ore train and had hoped to see this leviathan of the desert, reputed to be the longest train in the world. It looked like our wish was to come true as in billowing clouds of dust and sand, the first engine of this unusual wonder of the world emerged from the east.

The train carries ore in its numerous cars between Choum in the east of the country to the port at Nouadhibou. A considerable proportion of Mauritania's GDP comes from the train. It was an incredible sight, hauled by three huge engines, a never ending line of dust belching cars strung out behind. A sluggish giant of a vehicle whose cargo of ore was topped with miscellaneous bodies, standing and waving as they were carried dustily by. The whole scene resembled something from the early days of trains in Wild West movies.

We snapped away with our cameras like excited school boys, pleased to have caught this moment before moving on. The railway track ran alongside the road for several miles.

Continuing, we discovered that the new road south was excellent. Mile after mile we headed east on impeccable black top, which cut through more of the familiar stony hamada and areas where huge mountains of rock had been piled up by diggers, for no apparent purpose. After a time, the road slowly flattened out from an area of low hillocks into a featureless flat void of yellow rock and sand.

After many miles the road turned south as it ran near a remote township. There was no one in sight as the post midday sun started to bear down upon us. The familiar afternoon glare now straight ahead of us as the desert stretched out in front.

My mind started to wander. Black tarmac was the only contrast to harsh bright yellow sand and whiter rocks. The sky became a white glare which merged into the sand. The only break to the monotony being the kilometre posts which counted down the distance to our destination in five Kilometre stages.

Counting kilometre posts is always a sure sign of boredom and lack of concentration. But something else was at work, a growing feeling of vagueness and exhaustion. A vacant sensation of slight nausea started at the fringes of my consciousness. I continued counting kilometre posts.

It got hotter and although I was aware that I was thirsty, I didn't really want a drink. I was just happy to slip into a disembodied daze of riding that vividly defined and endless blacktop.

Then I started to feel really ill and very dizzy. This brought me out of my reverie and recognising that I really did need to stop and drink; I shook myself and motioned to Dave that we needed to pull over.

But where? There was nothing around, just desert, sun and dust.

We cruised past a group of low huts, with me feeling increasingly ill, but not wanting the attention of locals which would inevitably come and gawp if we halted. Then in the distance, I spied the low branches of a small solitary acacia tree which stood by the side of the road.

Slowing and stopping unsteadily took a huge effort and I almost fell off as we came to a halt. I flung my helmet and jacket off and staggered to the shade of the tree, slumping down onto a discarded lorry tyre which had been conveniently placed underneath. Several large beetles scuttled away into the sand as I sat down.

"What's up?" enquired my companion.

"Sorry mate, I feel dreadful, seems like I'm dehydrated or summat." I started to slowly drink from one of the water bottles that I'd grabbed from the bike.

"Not surprised." was the grunted response. "You've still got the lining in your jacket. Are you mad?"

Probably. I thought as I continued to drink and also to damp down my throbbing head. The sickness was there, but not getting any worse. I realised that I just had to sit and rehydrate myself for a time before continuing. I would avoid the disaster of our first Moroccan journey. But once again, a salutary lesson in personal management.

Dave didn't say anything, but I could see that he was annoyed at my weakness and lack of attention to my personal water consumption. It must have reminded him of that miserable day in Morocco five years before. Not that he'd drunk a great deal himself. He didn't seem to need as much water as me and limited himself to the occasional sip from his water supply.

It took a long time and about three litres of slowly drunk water before I felt that I could continue. A pounding head and disorientation meant that there was no way I was prepared to go anywhere until I felt better and sharper of mind.

Dave paced about impatiently. Sometimes he played with his camera, sometimes he'd sit and pass the odd remark. For a time, he paced a wide rectangle around the tree, making tracks on his hand held GPS. We didn't talk much, but to his credit he didn't explode into a stream of criticism either.

The sun beat down relentlessly, but after a time, a cooling breeze started to eddy around my tree – the "rehydration tree" – as Dave and I later decided that it should be called.

A motorcycle roared up the road heading north, a BMW 1150GS. Loaded with gear and metal boxes, the rider wearing not much more than a loose shirt and cargo trousers. He slowed for a second and Dave waved him on. He raised his arm as his bike roared up through the gearbox and he disappeared northwards.

"I think we should have dressed like him." Dave remarked. Much lighter than these heavy suits."

I agreed.

"Though now I've actually taken the liners and all that bloody armour out of my jacket, there ain't much to these suits." I replied.

We stopped by the rehydration tree for about two and a half hours in total. Long before we left, the sun had started to become indistinct as small clouds bubbled up in the west. I still felt wobbly as we once again set off southwards, but felt that I'd had a lucky escape from my own stupidly.

Dark clouds slowly dimmed the horizon ahead and gave a welcome break from the piercing sun. Billowing higher and with clearer definition as we rode, the clouds seemed to promise an unexpected fall of rain. In my still fragile state, I did not regret the disappearance of the sun, but didn't fancy a downpour either.

Heavy drops of rain started to fall and I stopped again.

"Bloody hell!" yelled Dave "This is all we need." Seemingly underlining his annoyance at having to stop for so long under the rehydration tree.

"Is it worth putting waterproofs on?" I yelled back through the quickening westerly wind. "This lot will be on us in a second."

"Nah" replied Dave impatiently and roared off down the road ahead of me.

The onslaught of heavy rain was brief and, for me, welcome. The short sharp wetting brought refreshing coolness and a clearer head.

Forging through the sheets of rain on the glistening and slowly flooding highway, we passed a group of men on camels. Their beasts stood with heads held high enjoying the rain. Their riders sat still under their black robes and head scarves, watching the mechanical invasion of their territory riding by.

The rain slackened and clouds began to lift. To the west I could see the sun gleaming under the edge of the cloud cover. Drenched but not cold, we continued.

More miles of nothingness, though sand began to coat the stony ground more thickly and low dunes stated to appear to our left. We were nearing the Azeffal and Akchar dune areas.

We stopped to refuel, not far from where a Bedouin style tent had been set up and a roughly painted sign advertised food. We unloaded our heavy fuel cans and carefully filled the bikes as a veiled woman stood nearby watching. There was still some to spare in the cans after we'd filled up. twenty extra litres had been more than enough for the day's journey.

Dave popped open a tin of sardines and we sat on the sand munching these with some dry bread and water. A heavily overloaded lorry roared by, a wildly waving Arab perched on the roof.

There really was nothing on much this road, just the occasional hut or tent and aside from a few trucks or cars an hour, no other traffic. Earlier, we had passed a group of tents, with several 4WDs parked adjacent. On the ground had been huge 'bladders' of diesel connected to upright hand pumps. Early signs of commerce on the new road.

"A year and there'll be proper fuel stations along here I reckon." said Dave.

"Yeah, but will they be selling petrol?" I replied." It seemed that outside the towns people didn't tend to use petrol vehicles – just about everything ran on diesel.

"The scarcity of petrol in a largish town like Nouadhibou doesn't bode well for regular supplies of 'Super' in the desert." I added.

"Nah, this place will be like the M1 in a few years, you'll see." grinned Dave.

I laughed. "What McDonald's, WH Smith and tourist tat shops selling key rings with camel motifs?"

"Don't forget Little Chef." added the Irishman.

Later on, about 200k from Nouakchott, I spied something

chilling, just by the side of the road, which made me instantly accelerate away, wanting to put distance between myself and the dreadful sight.

A couple of freshly decapitated camels were lying by the side of the road, still loaded up with riding gear. Other gear was scattered about and the sand showed signs of a recent commotion. Dark patches of drying blood were splattered all over the place. It seemed to me that something very bad had happened here, maybe some kind of inter-tribal ruck The smell was terrible.

Dave had spotted the scene as well and when we stopped for a water break a while later, we discussed the implications of what we'd seen. An empty desert like this can do odd things to how one perceives things. Which sometimes magnify themselves in your mind when you're out in the sand with no safety nets. We both felt that it would not have been good to have come along when whatever had happened was still taking place. Did my enforced stop at the rehydration tree have another reason? I dismissed the thought as daft, unbelieving of such silly 'karma' or the predetermination of one's actions.

"But I bet Mutch would have been off the bike and banging away with his camera like a war photographer." grinned Dave.

High dune country was now upon us and the road rose and fell with the mighty hills of sand, occasionally taking wide curves around the base of pristine yellow dunes.

It was a relief to be riding an area where the land had definition and more interesting things to see, instead of the flat lands further north. A stop at the top of a high hump of rolling dunes allowed us to enjoy a far horizon of breath-taking marching sand, the road curving its way through the undulating scene ahead.

But now it was getting dark. Dusk drew red colours from the sand as we rode, a warm light to compensate for the moderating temperatures.

Nouakchott appeared on the edge of my GPS, still eighty kilometres away. With destination in sight, we settled down for a steady final stage of our ride as darkness finally fell around us, hiding the picturesque dunes from sight.

Then the road turned into a dual carriageway. Still empty, but a clear sign that our day's ride was almost over. I spotted a faint light up ahead moving back and forth in the gloom. Luckily we pulled up in time to see that it was a checkpoint guard waving a dim torch just ahead of an unlit steel scaffold pole barrier which had been lowered across the road.

Several soldiers and policemen manned the checkpoint and after checking our passports, one of them became quite jovial. He was keener to chat with us than let us go on our way.

Two French trucks arrived, more conversation, more forced laughter from us.

"Jaysus, are we stuck here for an all-night party?" muttered Dave under his breath. "If so, bring me a beer."

Unfortunately, beer and dancing girls were not on the agenda. We were told that the delay was due to one of the cops wanting us to wait until he shortly went off duty, so that he could guide us to his cousin's hotel. We were too tired to care about yet another hustle and knowing nothing of the Mauritanian capital were happy to follow our impromptu police escort for the last ten kilometres into Nouakchott. Our new guide was mounted on an old 175cc Honda that had no exhaust.

He led us along wide and dimly lit streets, filled by large numbers of the now familiar battered cars. He then took us west towards the sea front where the Hotel/Auberge Sabel was more than happy to rent us an apartment for the night.

I was relieved to have completed the day's ride. This had been the longest and loneliest stretch of the journey. A day filled with contrasting feelings, emotions and mild fears.

But once again, we ended the day, with food and drink on the table before us. The satisfaction of a job well done and more adventures to look forward to ahead. We relaxed and enjoyed our deep fried fish and chips and glasses of mint tea, conversing in easy tones as we watched mice scurry about the place and under the tables of the hotel's small and empty restaurant. The soothing sound of the nearby sea and a stiff cooling breeze came through a wide open window.

Later, I found that my mobile phone wouldn't allow calls, despite a good signal from the local provider. Without a word, the hotel owner, who was sitting with us and spoke perfect English, handed me his mobile to call home. I protested that the cost to him would be high, but he insisted that I make my call, indicating that it would be an affront to refuse. The surprising helpfulness and generosity of people that you meet when you travel in Arab countries is humbling and more than makes up for the low times.

*

RESPITE AT 'ZEB'

I awoke from a disturbed sleep of vivid and strange dreams, a reminder that Lariam was still working its way out of my system. The sound of my shower woke Dave, who was already packed and ready to go by the time I'd finished my ablutions.

We had coffee and then took a walk on the beach in the pre-dawn light. Breakers crashed on the shore and the silhouettes of large ocean going pirogues further down the long shoreline were an easy sight to the start of the day. Quite lovely.

Nouakchott in the light of day is an impoverished place for a capital city. It is a fairly new city which has expanded rapidly and unsustainably as desertification has driven population growth. Traffic was the usual African mêlée, but streets were well laid out and the occasional tree broke the monotony of mainly sand coloured or whitewashed buildings. Shops were busy, but the people still poor. Beggars and people dressed in rags filled the streets, mingling with the more affluent of local entrepreneurs. We passed several large government buildings, soldiers guarding entrances. One or two western hotel chains were also seen, a barrier of gate guardians keeping the locals out and the rich cocooned inside. Over the whole place lay an atmosphere of dust and diesel fumes, I felt that the air could be almost literally chewed.

Several brand new top of the range luxury cars sped about, their occupants shielded from the world by tinted window glass and air conditioning. A city of strange contrasts.

We'd spent the night in an area of town which was known to be fairly dodgy, particularly near the port. Riding towards the city centre, looking for the road south, we passed a vast area of scattered rubbish, much of it piled up into burning pyres. The stench was stomach churning, but characters were picking their way through piles of refuse looking for things to recycle. Much of it was smouldering, lending a Dante's Inferno-esque feel to the place in the low early morning light.

Supplies for the day were purchased at a small, but well stocked supermarket. We replenished supplies of sardines and tinned fruit, fresh bananas and bread. We selected our bottled water from a bewildering array of different brands.

We were both looking forward to the day's ride. Our planned route led us directly south to the Senegal River, through a final stretch of desert and back into land that would be alive with green trees and vegetation again.

We hoped to make it through the border and into Senegal and then take a day off at Zebrabar, the travellers' auberge on the coast south of St Louis. I had found out about the place from the run reports of the Plymouth to Banjul Challenge.

Our Michelin maps declared that the road south was often 'ensablee' – sand. But after the mostly straightforward riding of the day before, we relished the opportunity of a different experience.

Leaving Nouakchott, via long series of roundabouts and numerous checkpoints, we soon found the correct road and headed south on a surface which was rapidly becoming cracked and broken. Numerous pot holes appeared, though well enough spaced to allow a steady if moderate cruising speed. My luggage boxes clattered as we negotiated cracks and ruts in the highway.

Soon, the stony desert floor and tall yellow dunes gave way to the red flowing dunes of the Trarza, which in this area, adjacent to the sea, became covered by low forests of acacia as we rode south. Their branches and providing the first readily available road side shade that we had seen for days. Scattered among the acacia were small townships of corrugated iron-clad huts, with the occasional small mosque rising among them.

These signs of rural life and the gradually thickening clumps of trees were a welcome sight after days of empty desert. The warming sun and more varied and interesting sights on the road ahead made my spirits rise as I carefully picked my way along the bumpy road surface.

An hour out of town and we spied ahead a lorry that had turned over on its side. There was a small group of people standing around and children were poking about the exposed underside of the fallen truck.

We stopped out of curiosity, noting a large pile of neatly stacked tins of paint; the lorry's load. The driver and his mate were sat on a mat in the shade waiting for assistance to arrive and explained that a front wheel had fallen off while they were driving late at night. It had spilt its load of paint cans over the road and the pair had, with a little local help, stacked the tins and were hoping that someone would be along to collect the valuable load before locals started making off with it.

Dave took some pictures and then turned his attention to taking close up shots of the acacia trees. One of the group of spectators detached himself to explain to Dave how seeds were extracted from the spiky plants.

After a quick cigarette, I filled my suit with a cooling dose of water and we continued on our way.

As we rode, everything started to feel different. More black African faces than Arabic ones were gathered by dwellings or stood by the side of the road. There was more colour, more exuberance from groups of running children who yelled at us as we passed by. For some reason things felt less foreign. The desert slowly gave way to Sahel. There was still lots of red sand, but now grasses were poking up among the thickening forests of trees.

The road steadily deteriorated, becoming more and more potholed, but still good enough to keep a steady fifty mph. Occasionally large square gaps appeared in the surface, places where the locals had, we later discovered, made off with the tar to repair their roofs or put the asphalt to some other pressing use.

The township of Tiquent, about half way between the Capital and Rosso, was almost completely black African. A policeman at a checkpoint where we entered the town, sat under a tree and lazily waved us on. The road deteriorated briefly into a track of broken tar and sand, with scattered debris and running chickens.

Smoke rose from cooking fires and small stalls sold produce on the street as we picked our way between fowl, goats, children, carts and people carrying loads. For the first time we saw women balancing all manner of things on the top of their heads. Tiquent was constructed mostly from huts, with the odd mud building or shop on the main street. A fuel station with battered pumps sat in an island of spilt diesel.

The mighty Trarza dunes were now changing to wooded hummocks of land, with large areas of grass and bushes taking over from the evenly spaced acacia. Gradually the land flattened as the road descended to the Senegal River valley.

A final police checkpoint and we ran along a long straight into Rosso. We faced a decision; whether to cross into Senegal here, or take the alternative 110 kilometre piste to Diama Dam. The border crossing at the dam was advised as being less hassle than the border and ferry at Rosso.

Rosso did not inspire. A filthy place of broken buildings and patched up huts. Trashed cars littered the streets. Large numbers of people dressed in rags hawked wares on the street and groups of sullen characters stood in every doorway. Almost everyone was black African.

We pulled into a dirty fuel station to discuss what to do next. A cheerful man, in the same dilapidated clothing that everyone seemed to wear in these parts, filled our tanks from an ancient pump.

"I'd read that it was poor here, but this is something else." the Irishman said as he beckoned around him. "Look at everyone, rags, no shoes, everything's in ruins, what the heck goes on here?"

"Yup, this makes Nouadhibou look like a centre of extravagant wealth and luxury." I replied. "This doesn't auger well for the border, I bet that there's some pretty desperate scenes and agro there. Shall we go to Diama?" Dave nodded his agreement.

The border crossing between Mauritania and Senegal at Rosso is reputed to be one of the worst in Africa. There are formalities at Rosso-Mauritania followed by a short ferry crossing to Rosso-Senegal where more bureaucracy has to be faced. Stories abound of rip-offs, people having to buy their passports back, huge delays, hustlers, theft, threats, extortion and other nightmares.

By now our bikes had attracted a group of small children, who looked with awe at our modern mechanical contraptions. Occasionally a small hand would reach out and touch the bikes.

Among their number was a young girl, perhaps eight years old, with bags of oranges that she nervously proffered. I bought a bag for a few Ougiya, the local currency, which prompted a wide smile before she ran off followed by the gaggle of children who yelled excitedly at her as they ran.

Having decided to take the dirt road to Diama, which the map showed running through an interesting area of national park, our next task was to find the correct turn off into the sand and dirt. Leading, I completely missed it. Very quickly we ended up at a place where a sandy square filled with people was grouped around what we soon realised were the gates to the customs compound.

Before we could turn the bikes we were surrounded by a huge throng of jabbering faces and people all demanding our attention – offering assistance, issuing instructions. It was like arriving at the border of a banana republic which was engaged in a civil war; people grabbing the bikes, guys in uniform yelling in our faces.

I was trying to turn the bike around to get the hell out of there, when a thuggish and mottled face in police uniform yelled at us both to stop. I ignored him and continued to turn as another thug shouted "you have to listen to him, he is the police."

Dave looked the 'cop' up and down and said contemptuously.

"So if yer a real cop, where's yer gun sonny?"

"Dave, let's find the Diama piste." I called out.

The thug said; "no, no, no – Diama no good, it closed!"

"Fine" I replied, "We're tryin' it anyway." and roared off with the uniform running after me shouting "Diama OK, Diama OK!" – in a final desperate attempt to persuade me into giving him cadeau.

Dave followed toute suite. Thanks to the good offices of a genuine soldier (with a rifle), who unnoticed by me had been sitting at the correct turn off under a tree, we soon found ourselves on the sand and dirt road which led to Diama Dam.

We started out on a piste paved with a gentle mix of packed

dirt and shallow ruts, which quickly took us alongside a dyke which had been built to keep the River Senegal from flooding the Mauritanian side.

Although the surface was mainly hard packed, in many places soft sand traps lurked in wait to throw us off the bikes. We soon learned that the best place to ride was on top of the dyke, on a surface which was mostly stone and mud. Occasional ruts and sometimes patches of dreaded corrugations made life interesting.

Corrugations, or washboard road. A ridged surface created by traffic moving fast on the dirt, their wheels forcing the mud into the regular and dangerous patterns so hated by motorcycle travellers. One either rode fast, skimming the top of the ridges, with little control, or ambled very slowly, bumping and crashing. We tried both methods, neither was much fun. Fortunately, we didn't encounter these areas too often.

A few miles from Rosso and we came across a large water pumping station and a group of trees which grew by a concrete hard standing. A pleasant place to stop for lunch. One of the station workers came out to join us, silently sitting by us after a few greetings, but not a word otherwise.

The afternoon's ride took us westwards along the dyke and deeper into what we later discovered was the Diawling National Park. Flocks of exotic birds, mainly waders, estuary and other water birds abounded. We saw Pelicans, Black Storks and Flamingos. The wide lakes and reed beds which spread in all directions provided a perfect natural habitat. Smaller birds with bright plumage sat in tall trees and looked down on us whenever we stopped. Pelicans could be spied on the lakes and both black and white Egrets picked their way along the many shores, looking for food. It was magical.

The greenery was welcome and we enjoyed the route so much that we kept stopping to take photographs and shoot video film. The nearby River Senegal was hidden by high reeds, but it made its presence felt by the occasional deep inlet and small bridges took the piste across these. Once we glimpsed the superstructure of an old ferry glide by heading eastwards. On the Senegal side of the river lay the Djoudj National Bird Sanctuary, so we were clearly riding through an area of significant natural importance.

Occasional groups of reed huts marked places where people lived. We later found out that many of them were national park workers. These small communities were served by 4X4 community transport which rattled and bumped along the piste at irregular intervals. Passing them involved a showering of dust and sand.

It was late afternoon before we arrived at a junction and turned left towards the dam, which now showed itself clearly on the GPS. The track immediately deteriorated and we rattled and bashed our along a few miles of heavily corrugated road until the buildings of the Mauritanian border post came into view ahead.

We parked our bikes and dealt with the relaxed border officials and police. A small fee was payable for riding in the park, but bribes were low cost. A meal was being prepared at the police post. Seeing a young cop struggling to cut strips of goat with a blunt knife, Dave lent a hand with his own, rather sharper, multi-tool knife.

The border administration overlooked a vast lake, upon which the westering sun cast long reflections on the water. A flock of small sea birds skimmed the surface and the distant call of a curlew could be heard.

We headed across the dam, no man's land between Mauritania and Senegal. There wasn't much of a view of the river that it held back, due to the high walls of the debris strewn, but mercifully tarmacked roadway that went across the top.

On the Senegal side, the road opened into a plaza, with the usual scattering of gloomy border buildings that we had come to expect. A pole barrier blocked our path off the dam and a man in combat trousers and a tee shirt peeled himself off a chair where he sat waiting for trade.

A payment was demanded before the barrier would be opened to allow us access to the border formalities – a completely corrupt road toll. Fatigue got the better of me and when the grinning idiot, whose job it was to take baksheesh from travellers, said, in French, that the fee was ten Euro, I heard it as 100. Dave went ballistic and refused to pay.

It was late and I was tired and uncomfortable because I was in no mood to get on my high horse about corrupt border practices.

Morocco day two.
The road to Essaouira

Camel rides
at the Agadir
kasbah

Dave by one
of the Kissing
Camels. Tan Tan

Empty
beach for
100 miles
in each
direction.
Western
Sahara

Sand riding practice,
Western Sahara

The ore train
to Nouadhibou,
Mauritania

The lonely
road to the
Mauritanian
border

A visitor during
our stop at the
Rehydration Tree

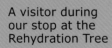

An all too common sight. On the road south from Nouakchott, Mauritania

Taking the shade on the dirt road to the Senegal border. This chap ran a water pumping station

The banana seller. Near Thies, Senegal

The crammed ferry to Banjul, The Gambia

Toasting success at the end of the outward journey. Serrekunda, The Gambia

Meeting the Riders for Health Gambia team

Dave, Barbara, author and Ian Mutch during our visit to Riders for Health

A Dakar to Dakar. En route in Senegal

The Guns of Navarone. Ille de Goree, Senegal

Barbara's boots had just melted in the heat, so thought it best to give the bike a once over

Zebrabar, Senegal. Paradise

Duplo men on the new road in Mauritania

Shipwreck in Nouadhibou,
Mauritania

Barbara. Now part
of the team heading
north. Mauritania

The road goes
ever onward.
Mauritania

Another day on
the Atlantic Route.
Western Sahara

Dave carefully guarding his GPS after my earlier mishaps

Cafe life returns as we head back into Morocco

Finally out of the Sahara. A nice moment en route to Agadir

The busy port at Essaouiea. Fish unloaded by hand basket

Inquisitive camel in the Argan forest north of Agadir

Northern Moroccan coast. Greenery again

Vollubilis again

Chefchaouen. A final night in Morocco and a celebration

My heart sank when my companion announced that he had once waited three days at the Ukrainian border because of 'official' crooks, so he'd be happy to wait here as well.

Fortunately, the misunderstanding over how much was demanded was soon sorted and although Dave was still muttering about paying, Mr Grin got his ten Euro. Dave demanded a receipt, which to his surprise was soon forthcoming.

The whole episode revealed another slight difference in our approach to travel. Dave quite rightly did not believe that we should be supporting a system where corruption at borders is both accepted and rife. He took the view that we should refuse to pay bribes and so-called fees on principle.

I felt that as an ethical stand point, this was certainly a commendable way of behaving. But would the odd high minded traveller make any difference to a system that was corrupted root and branch? Were we here to travel or waste time at borders feeling good about our principles as we grew used to setting up tent for nights of misery while border officials grinned and our available time frittered away?

No. It will take wholesale institutional change to do away with corrupt border practices, something that is beyond the means of overland travellers. All we would do by challenging the status quo would be to make our lives miserable, while border staff shrugged their shoulders and moved onto the next victim. They wouldn't care whether we were stuck there for ten minutes or ten days.

In addition, many border officials either get very low pay, or no pay at all. They often live at their posts and earn their only living from scamming those who went to and fro. Our small amount of power only lay in making sure we made noises in appropriate places once we had returned home. Although this would be unlikely to achieve much. All in all, a hopeless situation, unresolvable without a fundamental change in governing ethics and social attitudes.

For me, although I have respect and admiration for those who refuse to pay bribes, I take the view that refusal to offer anything at all is the preserve of those with lots of time to burn. I was in West Africa to travel, not sit at borders. For a short six week expedition, bribes (within reason) had to be paid if an initial protest was unlikely to expedite matters. Not the best attitude perhaps, but time pressures couldn't be ignored.

With Dave still fuming and muttering, we paid our obligatory visits to Customs and police. This was a fairly straightforward business and there were no hustlers at this quiet border crossing. The process cost around thirty Euro each, all of it in 'official' bribes, the fees presented to us as a fait accompli and receipts offered. Fortunately, Dave kept his mouth shut and I breathed a mental sigh of relief.

The cleanly uniformed officer at the Douane post was genuinely pleased that we had proper Carnets de Passage. Despite many warnings people still tried to cross into Senegal without this vital document. A morose looking German hippy with an old Mercedes van bore testament to this. He didn't have the necessary bits of paper and was in for a long night as he tried to argue for the faint possibility of a three day Laissez-Passer which is sometimes available. I didn't give much for his chances.

Neither did the customs officer who when we mentioned the hippy's hope of a Laissez-Passer to us, glanced over to the offending van and shook his head. The advice on this was specific and very clear at the time – No Carnet, no entry to Senegal.

In more recent times things changed. In 2008 for example, I rolled up to the same border to find that the Carnet was not accepted, with a Laissez-Passer issued instead. On another Senegal entry on the same trip, this time entering from Guinea-Bissau in the south, the Carnet was demanded.

Other travellers report various bureaucratic experiences and the travellers' website Horizons Unlimited is sometimes alive with debate on the issue. For me though, the Carnet is so useful for borders in general that I'd think twice before travelling extensively in Africa without one.

It was full darkness when we motored away from the border. The piste had given way to brand new smooth tarmac. Just as well because it was pitch black and there were no road markings. Mosquitoes had also got into my sleeves and bitten my arms to shreds, the result of leaving my coat on the ground when we were at the border. We were in serious malaria country, apparently the region's worst due to the dam. For once I blessed the vestiges of Lariam which were still in my system.

St Louis was only a few miles away and we passed through several villages, lit by small generators and with many people and livestock still on the streets. The outskirts of the town were vague shadows as the buildings became denser by the side of the road. From what we could see in the gloom, they seemed to be of much better quality than we'd seen for some days. Many trees lined the road, the beam of our headlights reflected from their boughs.

Traffic in St Louis was dense, but at least the cars and Mercedes buses looked something like the vehicles they had started life as. Most of them even had a full set of lights.

Again, an element of culture shock, arriving in an unknown country at night is never recommended and this was the second time that we'd had this experience. But St Louis certainly didn't feel as intimidating as the shattered streets of Nouadhibou when we'd first arrived there in darkness.

I pulled up in the forecourt of a brightly lit BP fuel station. The well-stocked shop looked like many European stations, with an array of goods, snacks and drinks in coolers. Dave waited while I tried to determine the best route to our destination for the night.

We were looking for the south road out of town and towards Zebrabar. The auberge is a campsite run by a Swiss couple, Martin and Ursula, which caters almost entirely for overland travellers in vehicles. From what I'd read on the internet, it sounded like a great place to stay and we were keen to try and get there before it was too late. All I had to guide us was a few GPS waypoints and as we pulled away again, I prayed that we would find the right route in the darkness.

The streets were busy and traffic was randomly driven. But even in the darkness we could sense hints of vibrancy that we had not yet experienced. There was more street lighting, people were standing outside bars. Music spilled out into the night air. Billboards advertised various products, including alcohol. People were better dressed.

A policeman at a sandy junction pointed us in the right direction and we left town on the Dakar road. We headed south for only two or three miles before a huge and faded sign loomed out of the darkness, indicating that we should go down a side road to reach Zebrabar.

Blackness closed around us, punched only by our headlights, as we picked our way along, following the waypoints. Then we found progress was obstructed by thorny branches across our path.

The latent fears of an unfamiliar place and nervousness enhanced by darkness came into play 'Hello' I thought, 'what's this, some kind of ambush?' Was the GPS playing up, what lay ahead? We were tired and this kind of uncertainty late at night is not good for morale.

Dave viewed the obstruction with suspicion and we idled for a second debating what to do. Then yer man spotted a route around the side of the barrier. We rode cautiously between the branches peering into the gloom with ears on alert.

But paranoia had intruded again. there was no ambush, no paramilitary characters with battered four wheel drive 'technicals' and machetes waiting to cart us off to be butchered. We were soon on our way again. The obstruction being nothing more than a marker laid to stop people driving on freshly laid tarmac.

My waypoints to Zebrabar marked where we should turn at junctions. A few miles later and we passed through a darkened village, before being directed down a bumpy piste which soon gave way to shallow soft sand. Soon after, another turn along a track and out onto a short causeway which led over a creek. We were right on the coast. Another short track and the road stopped at a dark and closed iron bar gate, with the word 'Zebrabar' welded across a zebra motif.

All was silent and pitch black. Was it even open?

I blew my horn a few times and waited. Then out of the dark a face appeared and a man scurried across and opened the gate, motioning us to ride forward.

Suddenly the world underwent one of those inversions that make overlanding so satisfying. In a moment we emerged from darkness, slight bewilderment and uncertainty into another world. Zebrabar.

Around the corner of a building, hidden from our view, Lights shone, Europeans sat at tables drinking beers, laughing and eating. It was surreal.

We climbed stiffly from our bikes and ambled exhausted over to the nearest table. One of the drinkers stood up and came to greet us, hand outstretched, an easy smile on his face which was topped by a short spiky haircut.

"I'm Martin, welcome. Would you like some dinner? Yes? Please help yourself to beer, we'll sort you out a hut when you've had a chance to relax."

In a daze we sat down as large bottles of 'Gazelle' beer appeared courtesy of an Australian chap who was sat nearby.

"Good to meet you guys." he said. A local girl appeared with placemats, knives and forks.

"Dave cracked the broadest smile I had seen for days and we both laughed loudly.

"Jaysus." he said. "Is this place for real?"

"Dunno mate, but there's beer, food and somewhere to sleep. So frankly I don't give a monkeys. Let's get pissed."

We did. Roundly and solidly – as did many of our new companions. Good food inside us, excellent conversation with fellow overland travellers and a chance to wash out the stresses and strains of the previous 2000 miles, both within and between us. When we'd finally had enough, a cool and easy night's sleep awaited in one of the shaded huts that make Zebrabar such a special place.

'Zeb' lies on the coast in the Parc National de la Langue de Barbarie, among beautiful beaches and teeming wildlife. It's a mini paradise, which I feel is slightly reminiscent of the island beach set in the movie, 'The Beach.' The place is a real oasis of joy that operates on solar power, windmills and trust. No more strongly illustrated than by the bar and food arrangements which worked on a help yourself principle, with a book to mark what you had taken alongside your name. Really good karma, a bit 'new age', but simply great.

People came from far and wide for a few days of peace and rest. There was a selection of elaborately equipped 4WDs, several motorcycles and a couple of overland trucks. Some stayed in the huts which were dotted about. Others slept in their vehicles, or had set up tents. Two Austrian cyclists had set up a tented home under a tree in a quiet corner of the many acred wooded compound.

The owners, Martin and Ursula his wife, had built themselves a very nice house which as well as being shaded by trees, was also under a vast steel awning, which covered with a bed of reeds, went over the top of the two story building. An excellent bit of design.

Shower, washing and water facilities were good and the water fresh. Hot water was provided by solar power. As was almost all the electricity in Zebrabar, with only the fridges and freezers in the kitchen powered either by truck batteries or gas. Meals were clean and wholesome, created around a basic menu. You either had dinner or you didn't. What arrived was whatever the local kitchen staff had decided to cook. It was all delicious.

Our day off was welcome. A late breakfast, followed by idling time in chairs on the small terrace outside our hut, helped recharge personal batteries. A walk up the beach, chasing the Fiddler Crabs which ambled about in large 'herds', plus taking atmospheric photographs added to the relaxing feel. I think we both felt that it would be easy to just simply stop for a while and let the world slide on by outside the gates.

Indeed, there were travellers there who had done just that. The Aussie had been there for a week after planning to stay one night. One German chap, over a month. But we had only two riding days to go before Banjul, where friends awaited. This was our incentive to move on, though we knew that riding away the following day would be tinged with regret.

We took some time in the afternoon to visit nearby St Louis where we watched the world go by at a pavement bar on the central 'island' amidst the crumbling splendour of old French colonial architecture. A relaxed town which is well worth a visit – famous for jazz and some very nice colonial style bars on the central island of the town. An area packed tight with well laid out French townhouses and public buildings. All reminding one of the time when St Louis was the capital of Afrique Occidental, the vast area of French West Africa.

It was good to leave the conservatism of Arabic culture behind for a while and enjoy the exuberance of Black Africa. Its vibrancy, colour, friendly moods, excitable culture and of course, the beautifully dressed women...

Back at Zeb, more beer, food and conversation about our plans with a very friendly and knowledgeable, but unfortunately 'been everywhere and done it all' German guy. He assured us that Banjul was an easy one day trot from Zeb, a fact that pricked Dave's interest. He also had a lot to say about different routes in the region. "That's good, that's crap, that's an easy day" and so on.

He claimed to have lived in Central and Southern Africa for some years and claimed vast knowledge about the best way to do and see things. But somehow, I didn't trust him – he was too self-assured and 'final' with his opinions. I had also come to feel that there were no absolutes when it came to African travel. Conditions change and easy journeys by 4WD could be nightmarish on a bike and vice versa.

Looking at the map, Banjul didn't look far on the small scale Michelin 741, but the border crossing, poor roads and other factors of travel needed to be taken into account. Dave urged a blast to Banjul in one hit, I argued for us to retain modest expectations. We were within our planned itinerary anyway. After some discussion, we agreed to take it as it came, despite being egged on to 'give it a go in a day' by our now fast-becoming-annoying drinking pal. With the matter settled, more Gazelle was opened and the conversation moved on.

*

THE BORDER 'SPOOK'

Tearing ourselves away from Zeb's seductive haven the following morning, we headed south once again. An early start along Senegal's respectable roads and interesting villages made for a great start to the day. The contrast from the poverty and bleakness of Mauritania was enormous. Vibrant and colourful, friendly people and lots of things to see. Each village seemed to specialise in something different. One would be full of vegetable and melon sellers, another would have streets lined with mechanics' workshops and so on.

Tall trees with dense canopies grew close to the road and people sat under them on rough benches, or waited by the side of the road for the battered, often windowless, Mercedes mini bus service. Brightly coloured vehicles with 'Alhamdoulilahi' (Praise be to God) painted on the front, with the slogan of the Muslim sect that the crew belonged to marked either on the back or front. Mostly the powerful 'Touba' Brotherhood, whose 'Marabouts' – senior figures, we later learned – called many of the political shots in the country. Sometimes we saw buses marked with the 'Lamp Fall', or 'Bay Fall' motifs – other influential Brotherhoods.

We were riding through classic picture book Africa with thatch-roofed mud huts in addition to the breeze block buildings of larger villages and townships. We saw huge Baobab trees for the first time and later in the morning disturbed a flock of vultures who were feeding on a dead cow at the side of the road. One of the huge birds flew close alongside me as I rode for a moment – a breath-taking sight.

Police checkpoints were regular and easy, the police more interested in our bikes than in us, though all were keen to ensure that we had valid insurance. They seemed satisfied with our European Green Cards. We made good progress as the sun reached its zenith and the heat of the day clamped down on human activity.

We passed by the large regional town of Thies and turned east for Kaolack at a sprawling road junction with several service stations. A place to top up petrol and buy some food and drinks from the many colourful street traders and market stalls.

The afternoon heat settled in once again – searing us, the bikes and the black tarmac ahead. We negotiated a series of low hills, where road works slowed our progress. Workers, stripped to the waist, slaved away with shovels, sweating in the burning sun.

We took some time out from the heat of the day in a village on the main road which specialised in water melons. It also doubled as a roadside truck stop. We ate bananas while sheltering from the blistering heat and watched tall, brightly dressed women operating a trade in bottled water.

Some of the bottles were frozen, so I bought one, feeling pleased with myself and waited for the ice to melt a little as we stood under the furnace-hot steel awning of a banana sellers shop.

Dave noticed the waiting truck drivers checking the seals on their water bottles – if the locals were worried about the water being clean, then clearly we should too. A quick examination of my frozen water and I decided to use the bottle to douse my clothes instead of drinking it; the seal had been cleverly tampered with. Dave smiled at me in a slightly mocking, but not unkind way.

After some time, trading our badly spoken French with the woman who sold bananas, one of the local youths came up to me with an injured and septic finger that I treated with TCP before binding it up. To my astonishment, he then demanded money as well. Unbelievable. I told him to piss off; an English phrase which, strangely, he seemed to understand but didn't seem to take offence to.

Time went by and the heat continued to build.

"It's been an hour and a half." said my companion. "It ain't getting any cooler, let's just get on with it."

I was happy to go. A bit of time off the bikes, out of the direct sunlight and soaking up local comings and goings had been good for us though. Once again we fired our bikes up and headed east.

The land flattened out into semi wooded, but dry plains covered in brown grass and low bushes. There were lots of huts dotted about, plus the occasional village and the odd cow or goat wandering about on the relatively empty highway. A pleasant and enjoyable ride, if extremely hot. But the sun was behind us, making life a bit easier.

The police in Fatick, clearly bored, took additional interest in us and wanted to see all our paperwork including our insurance papers which at that point we thought we didn't have – we hadn't yet realised that our Mauritanian insurance covered Senegal as well. We showed them our Green Cards which as we'd experienced before seemed to satisfy them. But a look at our driving licences aroused suspicion in my case, as I had numerous license categories including HGV annotated on it. The suspicion was that this documentation must be phoney.

Dave's better command of French sorted the situation out and we pressed on determined to make the last 100 kilometres or so to Kaolack before dusk. This time, we were faced with a hellishly hot wind blast from the east. This left me with a headache and a feeling of detached 'woolly' weakness, which took some hours to wear off.

We made the regional market town of Kaolack, just as dusk was fast fading onto darkness – so much for getting to Banjul in a day. The darkened streets were solid with traffic, fast and intimidating in our headlights.

We checked into a cockroach and mosquito infested guest house, which we later found out was a kind of local barracks for visiting police and soldiers. Its saving grace was wheezing air conditioning. But roaches were so numerous, that a group of local cats had taken up residence to take advantage of the ready supply of free cockroach meals, which they would eat with a satisfied crunch. After checking in we sloped off for a beer at the more expensive Hotel Paris.

Kaolack, despite being a filthy refuse strewn town, boasts the second largest covered market in Africa and an exceptional restaurant in the shape of Le Brasero Chez Anouar, run by a locally born Frenchman. He was a refugee from the era of colonial administration. He described himself as a white negro, though it was clear that he was as European as us. Excellent lamb kebabs and Gazelle beer rounded off the day nicely as huge ceiling fans stirred the hot night air – all very Bogardian.

While waiting for our food, I got a call from Barbara, who was due to arrive in Banjul the following day.

"Mutch has decided not to come tomorrow." she said "Can't really figure out why either."

"Phone Mutch." said Dave when I reported the news. "He can't not come now."

Ian wasn't at all forthcoming when I spoke to him, muttering something about magazine deadlines and other non-excuses. His airline ticket was already paid for and it would be real shame for us all if he stayed in the UK. But he wasn't prepared to change his mind and after a few minutes, I realised that I was wasting my breath.

"Well, he's a mug." retorted Dave. "What's he playing at?" He looked extremely pissed off.

Back at Roach Villas, Dave told me to hang my coat and place my boots upside down on the ground before going to bed. Advice, I promptly forgot while washing. I settled into bed with a book. Conrad's 'Heart of Darkness' – which Dave was convinced only added to my Lariam-based woes.

The following morning, he cast me 'told you so' stares as I frantically shook clouds of mossies and cockroaches out of my boots. The roaches fell to the ground with a sharp 'clack' before scuttling off into corners, or out of the door where two cats sat waiting for their crunchy breakfasts.

Blowing down the arms of my coat, Dave dislodged another cloud of lurking mosquitoes.

Banjul, our final outward destination, took most of the day. It was only about 100 kilometres away, but the road for the first forty was broken and potholed. We left Kaolack along a causeway lined with stinking and smouldering refuse, which leeched poisonous effluent into a large lake that bordered three sides of the town. Holding our breaths as much as we could, we turned south again on the final road to The Gambia border.

We bumped about and made slow progress, but the countryside was gorgeous, taking the edge off of the rough ride. We drifted by grass roofed round-huts and small plantations and took water stops under the primordial branches of behemoth sized baobabs. The air was full of birds and we spied weaver bird nests in the trees.

At one stop, we drew the attention of a troop of monkeys, who nervously stuck their heads out of the roadside grass before a group of about five emerged to sit on the road about fifty yards away and look at us with intelligent curiosity on their faces. Their companions continued to regard us from their safer position in the grass, their exposed heads betraying their presence. Tall grasses swayed in the breeze as we took in this view. Lovely.

The quiet village of Sokone, half way to the border, was a good place to take a morning café stop. A pleasant daily routine which we had missed in the Sahara. We stopped at a tidy little restaurant and bar, with posters and paintings on the walls and a cool awning looking out over the road. The women who ran the place were efficient and friendly, the coffee excellent. What more could we ask from our final leisurely day of out-bound riding?

After Sokone, a brand new road replaced the broken route we had travelled from Kaolack and we cruised on towards the border. We now passed swamps and mangrove beds, with vegetation becoming ever more tropical in flavour. A bit too dry to be completely green perhaps, but much more in the way of plants and trees than we had seen since northern Morocco.

We arrived at Karang, a dirty border town, full of engineering workshops and shabby wooden buildings. More poverty and a feeling of impoverishment than we had got used to seeing in this quiet corner of Senegal.

The Senegalese customs were straightforward on exit from the country. No 'fees', but a few cigarettes helped to speed us through the process and get our Carnets stamped.

We travelled only a few yards from the border post before arriving at the Gambian border control. A road lined with collapsed huts, desperate looking street traders and throngs of children selling bags of peanuts, or offering to clean our boots.

The immediate switch to English was welcome, but a different kind of culture shock emerged. It took a few moments to realise that I didn't need to focus on translating what was being said to me.

Gambian officials were less friendly and more thorough than we'd been used to. Passport and Carnet procedures were straightforward, but as we prepared to get kitted up and ride onwards, we were approached by a man claiming to be a plain clothes officer. He flashed an ID and asked to look in our boxes.

Dave looked sceptical.

"Let me look at your ID again." he said. The man looked taken aback. Dressed in fine flowing robes and with a cleanly cut appearance, he looked like a person who wouldn't take any nonsense.

Perhaps Dave saw his chance to kick up a fuss about what he saw as unnecessary border hassle after having to give into my acceptance of demands to pay fees at other borders. But whatever the reason, this time he stood his ground and made it clear that he thought the guy was a fake and that he intended to leave.

The mood turned instantly nasty and an argument ensued. One of the police who had dealt with our passports appeared with alarm on his face. He beckoned me over.

"Look, this could be real trouble. He is from the security police and will make a lot of trouble for you. Please persuade your friend to be quiet."

"Dave mate, he's genuine, for heaven's sake shut up, or this will get nasty. We're only about twenty miles from our final destination fer Christ's sake."

"How are we supposed to tell he's not fake if all he has is some dodgy photocopied piece of paper to identify himself?" came the reply. But recognising the situation that was emerging, Dave stood aside.

We earned ourselves a root and branch exploration of everything in the boxes, with our two-way radios and extensive medical kit subject to additional scrutiny. Eventually Dave was told to stay where he was and I was taken into a room deep inside the police station.

I was told to sit in a chair, while several more plain clothes guys came in and took up station around the room, all looking down at me in silence. The elegantly dressed cop who had held us up in the first place, came in and sat down behind a desk. He stared at me intently.

For a few moments complete silence settled. Finally and feeling desperate I said "look, we've got no drugs, no guns, nothing illegal, nothing worth hiding, what do you want from us?"

At this baring of my soul, the plain clothes 'spook' relaxed and his companions relaxed with him. The mood changed for the better and everything became quite friendly. It was explained that Dave's attitude had suggested we were hiding something and that "guns are always an issue".

The subject switched to our purpose for riding to The Gambia. The police knew about Riders for Health and some were themselves involved in local charities. We spent some time talking about healthcare work and Riders.

A small crowd of uniformed and casually dressed cops accompanied me out of the station where Dave stood waiting by his bike. This time there were friendly smiles and chatting all round. The 'secret' policeman talked for a while with Dave, who by this time had relaxed and things were smoothed over.

The ten kilometre road from the border to the ferry from Barra Terminal over the Gambia River to Banjul was a potholed and rutted disgrace. We clattered along the narrow highway, glad that there were only a few miles of the dreadful road to ride.

The ferry was worse. We had bought tickets at a way station a mile outside Barra Port and rode into a township which was run down and filthy. People were dressed in rags, broken down vehicles lay everywhere and the sickly sweet smell of sewage and old oil hung heavily in the hot afternoon air.

Crowds of hustlers hung around the port gates, waiting to scam all comers. We studiously ignored both them all and the multitudes who hawked fruit, bags of water, cheap plastic watches, tee-shirts and so on.

We resigned ourselves to a long wait in blistering sun, as the big metal gates were opened and closed innumerable times to prioritise those who'd paid the required 'fees'. Eventually I lost patience and after some debate, bribed the gate keeper with a biro and some headache tablets. The gates opened and we rode to the end of jetty, which had high walls on each side. It was an oppressive heat trap, though with fewer scam merchants preying on those who were waiting for the next ferry.

Chaos ensued when the small battered and oil stained ferry came into view. Diesels roared and thick black smoke poured from its stacks as it manoeuvred into its mooring. Foot passengers leapt ashore as soon as the gap between the boat and the jetty was narrow enough and we were pressed from behind by folk before the first dented car and wreck of a lorry had disembarked from the open vehicle deck. Eventually the unloading was completed and fighting to stay upright from the press of people, hand carts and equipment, we made our way aboard the floating cattle truck of a ferry.

Wedging the bikes into a corner, we fought our way through the rapidly growing crowd of passengers to reach the passenger deck above. Soon there was standing room only, giving us an insight into the life of a battery hen.

The ferry company operated on the principle that the ferry only left when not one more person or vehicle could be crammed on board. Smashed and battered lorries jostled for an inch of room with beaten up cars and pick-ups of various marques. Pedestrians were crammed into every available space, with many trying to sell cold drinks in plastic bags, or offering to polish shoes.

In one cramped corner a motorcyclist stood quietly by his smart and clean Yamaha 200. He turned out to be a health worker from Riders for Health and we grinned as we recognised that both our bikes and his carried the same logo, a clear sign that we had almost reached journey's end. Dave spent most of the three mile journey over the river chatting to this guy about his work for Riders.

Nearly an hour later and the wheezing, overloaded ferry deposited us in the appalling squalor and heat of Banjul, Africa's smallest and probably most impoverished capital city. We took the route out of town to the south. Passing through hectic and broken streets, filled with desperate looking street traders, semi derelict buildings and vehicles which really were beyond final redemption. A rutted and potholed road led us in the direction of Serekunda.

Once out of town, we picked up a fairly new dual carriageway. Not really knowing the way to our hotel, the Bungalow Beach, we drifted along in the afternoon heat. Some miles later, a likely-looking turn off took us down some wooded lanes to a road with several hotels, public buildings, consulates and shops.

It was a tidy looking area, with well-spaced buildings sheltering under canopies of tall broad leafed trees. This looked promising for our search, but we soon drew a blank and headed back to the main dual carriageway.

For the first time in what seemed like weeks, we came across a set of traffic lights which were on red and manned by a white uniformed traffic policeman, whose job seemed to be to ensure that drivers obeyed the lights. After asking for directions, we found the right road, which curved out onto the coast away from the main road and passed by a selection of stalls selling tourist-tat. Finally, the gates of the Bungalow Beach Hotel were before us and the ocean could be glimpsed beyond.

Parking outside reception, we switched off our engines, climbed off and stood grinning like idiots at each other.

"Bloody hell, we did it Brigadier!" exclaimed Dave. "Now where's the bar?"

*

GAMBIAN SOJOURN

We were half way down our second beers, when a message came from reception with the news that Barbara had arrived. I sprang from my seat to enjoy an emotional reunion with my wife.

"That's enough of that!" barked Mutch's voice from behind. "Too much kissing, enough already."

I wheeled around to pump Ian's arm up and down.

"You made it yer bugger, what changed your mind?" Ian looked at the ground awkwardly.

"It was me I think." said Barbara. "Ian turned up to see me off last night and I gave him his Motorcycle Outreach tee-shirt which we had ordered for the trip. He kinda looked emotional as he left.

"Then at four am, there he was banging on the door, luggage packed, ready to go – panama hat and all."

Ian smiled quietly to himself as he stood. He affected the air of a colonial traveller in his white cotton suit and a hat which wouldn't have looked out of place on an Indian tea plantation, circa 1920.

Dave was equally pleased to see Mutch and slapped him on the back with joy before ordering a round of drinks.

It was good moment as we raised our glasses and toasted the journey and our success at getting to Banjul.

"Simon would be chuffed if he could see us now." said Mutch.

I looked into my glass.

"I reckon he would, it's just a shame that he's not here to see it."

"We probably wouldn't be here either if he was still around." added Dave.

This was food for thought. Simon's death may have closed his horizons, but losing him had expanded ours.

The beer flowed and later the food came in delicious piles. Mutch, as usual, had us all in gales of laughter as we filled our bellies and continued to drink.

Later came the moment I'd looked forward to for over two weeks. Deep and dreamless sleep with Barbara by my side.

We took a day for ourselves. Wandering the beaches, avoiding the hustlers, relaxing in the sun. Three of us took a trip to the Senegambia Hotel, where Mutch had heard about trips to see Crocodiles. They were apparently organised by the improbably named 'Tony Blair', a local tour guide. Dave went exploring on his now unladen bike.

We took coffee and watched white egrets picking left over food from abandoned plates on nearby tables. The Senegambia was set in large tropical grounds which led to the beach. A stroll through the pleasant and verdant gardens took us past a place where several vultures sunned themselves on the grass adjacent to a leaking standpipe. The evil looking birds occasionally hopped over to take a drink.

That evening we walked down the beach to take our sundowner beers at a beach bar in the next bay along from our hotel. Bottles of 'JulBrew' flowed easily down our throats as the sun sank below the sea to the west and a sharp wind started to blow.

Mutch decided to 'interview' Dave and I about the trip for a magazine article he was planning. This soon descended into farce as a humorous 'take' on our various adventures was related to Ian. He gave up taking notes after Dave told him that the minefield on the Mauritanian border could be a great place to live.

Afterwards, none of us fancied taking a risky walk back along the pitch black beach; we'd all been warned that African beaches at night are not good places to be. So after a meal at a very nice place adjacent to the beach bar, we walked up to the main road and waited for a taxi at another bar. A place which was clearly a gathering place for local prostitutes.

We finished our evening back at the Bungalow Beach, listening to a local band torturing a selection of well-known songs, before retiring to bed.

Riders for Health were fantastic hosts. The morning after our relaxing beach and beer day, we were summonsed in the early morning cool to reception, where we met Ali one of the founders of Riders in the Gambia. He was waiting with a 4WD to take us to the charity's Gambia centre to meet staff and learn more about how their system of Transport Resource Management worked.

We spent a morning in deep discussions with Therese, 'Riders' Gambia Operational Director. She briefed us extensively on their system of vehicle management. We also learned that 'Riders' were managing the maintenance of the majority of healthcare vehicles in the country, in addition to the approximately 150 motorcycles which are used for primary healthcare activity. A tour of their extensive facilities revealed a highly professional operation which clearly had a lot of work on its hands.

During our visit we learned that Simon had indeed been heading there when he crashed. This raised an interesting question among the four of us. Our original plan had been for Dave and I to bury a time capsule, with some of Simon's artefacts and messages from friends, at the site of Simon's accident near Kayes in Mali. But that posed a number of problems. We had heard that the road was a rough one and under development. Was there a chance that all the disruption of a road building crew would disturb the capsule?

Another factor had been our experiences on the journey south. It seemed that wherever we stopped we hadn't been on our own for long. This had started to make us seriously question the likelihood of such a memorial staying in one place for any length of time. What prospect was there that the canister would not be churned up, or taken by one of the innumerable people who seem to pop up from behind a stone or tree whenever we'd stopped anywhere? Furthermore, if, as seemed likely, locals were to spot the efforts in progress, there was a high probability that they might dig down to explore after we'd gone.

The visit to 'Riders' had presented fresh option and after a great deal of discussion and soul searching, we agreed that it seemed safer and more appropriate to bury the capsule at the location where he was headed.

Phone calls were made to Simon's mum and family and 'Riders' themselves consulted. All were in favour of the plan.

So it was that with the four of us present plus Therese, Ali and other members of staff, we dug a deep hole by the wall at the Riders for Health HQ. In sea shell heavy soil and at a place overlooked by small banana trees.

After a brief service during which we remembered Simon's life and the profound effect he had had on us all, we buried the canister. We took it in turns to help with filling the hole, while Ian spoke a personal and moving eulogy.

The following Day, Ali took us on a field trip to one of 'Riders' regional centres. This involved crossing the Gambia River again on the dreaded Banjul to Barra ferry. A further opportunity to experience claustrophobic overcrowding of vehicles and people, while trying not to think about movies such as 'Titanic'.

We saw 'Riders' bikes in action and spoke to some of the local health workers who were gathered under a huge baobab tree with their bikes. All were keen to tell us about their day-to-day work, while a chap from the 'Riders' centre checked over their bikes as part of a pre-arranged basic maintenance check.

The trip back to Banjul in Ali's Toyota was interminable. Ali was determined not to pay a bribe to jump the ferry queue, which although was the right thing to do, resulted in a sweltering wait in the sun at Barra Terminal. Hustlers were everywhere, though aside from being concerned about pick-pockets we didn't get hassled too much. Something to do with the local registration number on our 4WD I should imagine. More disconcerting was the fascination that some seemed to view Mutch. He had an uncomfortable twenty minutes while a very small chap stood stock-still at his window looking at him with a nearly eyeball to eyeball serial killer stare.

"You wanna watch him Mutch." I said. "I reckon your great grandfather must have done something to his great grandfather." Ian muttered something incomprehensible and tried his best to look somewhere else.

Our next port of call was to see a motorcycle and sidecar combination in action. The outfit was a specially designed two wheeled ambulance called the 'Uhuru'. Getting to the village

267

where it was located meant taking a detour through the infamous 'Westfield Junction', a kind of road hub for the country near the centre of Serekunda.

Traffic jostled for position on the crowded but heavily potholed road, our Land Cruiser carefully negotiating the obstacles and other traffic. One pot hole was so huge that it almost swallowed our 4WD as Ali carefully eased it through. At one point I found myself staring up at the traffic outside our windows.

We arrived at the village to find the Uhuru parked in a large compound, but no rider. Ali made some enquiries and returned with the sad news that the elderly father of the healthcare worker who was in charge of the combination had died that afternoon. We took our leave after expressing condolences to his family, who lived in the compound.

"We take life so much for granted don't we." said Barbara as we travelled back to the hotel. "That poor family have so little that their loss must have had a more profound effect on all of them."

There was no answer to that one and we sat in silence as we cruised down the now smooth highway to the coast.

Part Four: Northward

A Dakar to Dakar

I figured that something like this was coming, after I had seen Dave spend hours poring over the Michelin map of West Africa. He'd also been deep in conversation with a Bissau-based American missionary, a fellow guest at Bungalow Beach, who knew the region well.

Dave had outlined a 'little tour' that he'd planned for himself around the Casamance area of Senegal, Guinea-Bissau, plus the interior of Mali and eastern Mauritania. Looking at the map, it seemed to me that he was planning to take in half of West Africa, with a number of the roads he'd planned to ride either non-existent, or very poor. "Well, I've been speaking to yer man the missionary and he reckons that all this is tarmac now." said Dave pointing at a huge swathe of empty map marked 'ensablee'.

I pursed my lips, thinking back to Zebrabar and the 'helpful' German chap who told us that Banjul was an easy day's ride from St Louis in Senegal – nearly two days as it turned out. I had come to treat the 'local' knowledge of overlanders with a degree of caution. Either folks operated in a different temporal zone to the rest of us, or they had breezed through difficult routes with four wheeled drives, equipped with desert tyres and enough spare fuel to keep the Afrika Corps on the move for a month.

The itinerary was clear and didn't involve Bissau or the Mali and Mauritanian interior. I didn't think that our sponsors would take kindly to changes of plan involving vastly more miles and increased possibilities for problems which would threaten their investment in us.

The plan, as we had set it out, involved straightforward stages as far as Nouakchott in Mauritania Allowing the opportunity to spend some days taking a more relaxed tour of the country that we had blasted through on a tight schedule a few days before. To actually get a feel for this part of West Africa.

However Dave was determined to give this route a go and more careful study of the map showed that although completing it involved a tough schedule of all day riding, the only real issues were the availability of fuel and a big question mark about the 100 kilometres of 'road' between Diema and Nioro in Mali.

"I'll turn back if that section turns out to be shite." said Dave "I can rejoin the main route to Rosso and then onto Nouakchott from there and arrive early to meet you." he added.

His route also took in Simon's crash site in western Mali. A place we'd originally planned to visit together. But with the burial of ashes in The Gambia and ongoing personal issues related to the Lariam I had taken, the desire to visit that place was no longer as strong within me. If the truth be known, I was making poor excuses to not go. Something I would seriously regret later and a mistake it would take a further two and a half years to rectify.

Taking my concerns further with Dave would have resulted in a destructive row, which I was keen to avoid. He was going to follow his plan no matter what I said.

I knew that I would miss Dave's company for the week that we'd be travelling separately. But I also had to acknowledge that sometimes it's good to take a break from even the most 'in tune' of travelling partners and to follow one's own agenda for a while. Dave is much hardier than myself when it comes to endless days of relentless motorcycling and I suspect that he would have got a bit restless riding the relaxed route with extended breaks that I'd planned for the early days of the return journey.

He was probably keener for a break from me than I'd realised. Our travels so far had been successful and we had a lot of travelling history together over many years. But this journey had revealed stresses, strains and annoyances that were new to our relationship. I was to blame for a lot of this.

In the face of his determination to go his own way for a while, I also began to feel that a short break from my closest friend would probably do us both a bit of good.

Another modification of plans had also materialised in the form of Barbara, who had arrived at Banjul complete with riding gear, along with a small bag of luggage. We had only been married a few weeks when Dave and I had departed and she'd been feeling quite left out of things, being more used to accompanying Dave and I on other long distance trips on her own bike.

During the planning phase, we had discussed the idea of her joining the return stage of the trip, but it didn't seem feasible or sensible at the time. However, upon arrival in Banjul she declared that having arranged work coverage and bundled the children off to her ex-husband's she was determined to come at least part of the way back with Dave and myself. As long as the bike was capable of supporting the extra weight.

A bit cautious about the whole thing, I loaded up the Dakar with all my kit and the admittedly very small number of things she'd brought with her. We filled the jerry and water cans and set off for a long test ride on Gambia's poor, sometimes absolutely dreadful roads. Barbara sat comfortably on the back.

As with everything else that the bikes had endured on the way to Gambia, the GS seemed to take the additional person and weight in its stride. There was no appreciable loss in power, or braking and the rear suspension only required minor adjustment to compensate. Handling was fine. The GS Dakar frame seemed to be designed to direct additional weight towards the normal centre of gravity, even when unevenly loaded. Although the bikes looked very rear-heavy when originally set up, neither Dave nor myself had felt this in the way the bikes handled.

If anything, the addition of Barbara's small size made the front end seem a little more stable than it had been before. Bizarre and counter-intuitive, but synonymous with the fine design and engineering that went into the bike.

I consulted Dave about Barbara joining us.

"Ah, it'll be a right laugh." he said. "yer-one is much more entertaining than you anyway. Besides, you can have that honeymoon that you missed out on while I go off and do me Mali tour; indeed, indeed."

I groaned. The pair of them had manoeuvred me into a corner. Dave got his Mali tour and Barbara got her wish to see the Sahara as well. Mind you, inside I was delighted at the turn of events which meant that I could share half the African ride with my wife.

All in all we spent four days in Banjul. The decision to bury Simon's time capsule had allowed us an extra day and given Dave some additional time to plan his 'little' excursion.

All good things have to come to an end though and it was with a heavy heart that Barbara and I packed our bike in the pre-dawn gloom on December 1st 2005. Dave was also planning to head south to Bissau later that day, leaving Mutch to catch a flight back to London the following day. We had decided to send my top-box back with Ian, in order to better balance the jerry can – a far more essential item than a few bits and pieces of personal possessions. All the luggage that Dave and I didn't feel that we would need again was also stacked in Ian's room.

"What about the excess baggage charge?" he had moaned looking at the mountain of equipment that was piled on the table of the room that he shared with Dave.

"Oh stop whingeing." said Dave; "We'll give it yer back."

"Well you'd better bloody make it back." said Mutch, clearly disappointed about missing the return trip himself.

Both of them came to see us off from the car park of the Bungalow Beach hotel. Dave bade us farewell with kind words and said he looked forward to seeing us in Nouakchott.

"I'll be pissed off if I have to get home from there without you travelling with me." he added. I could see that his sentiment was genuine.

I turned my face from the emotion of the moment and, picking a way through the potholes, I turned the GS in the direction of London, 3,500 miles away.

We planned to make it to Kaolack, Senegal that day. A feasible goal, though it would be interesting to see how we would cope two-up on the 100 kilometres or so of variable and sometimes badly holed road.

The ride to the ferry in Banjul didn't take long and this time we were loaded almost immediately. Unfortunately I followed enthusiastically waved instructions to put the bike between a car and lorry. This was against Barbara's better judgement and alternative directions to park in a small corner. This meant that I couldn't get off the bike and was trapped in position for the crossing.

A vicious wind had picked up and a choppy sea was running in the Gambia River estuary as we put to sea. Our ferry was unfortunately the slower and smaller of the two beaten up tubs which ply the river. Its shortcomings immediately manifested themselves in the fact that there was not enough engine power to get across the river against a heavy and choppy tide. The captain compensated by sailing straight out to sea, the idea being that the tide would then push us across to Barra Terminal.

So commenced a two hour crossing of the three mile river. The ferry pitched up and down in the swell, people moaned as vehicles with no handbrakes rocked about and I began to fear for our safety. The guidebook relates tales of lorries being tipped off the side of this ferry on similar occasions to avoid a sinking. There were one or two moments when we wondered if history wasn't about to repeat itself.

An hour later and it was still possible to hit Banjul port if a stone was thrown from the deck. We were still bucketing about in the tide. Then suddenly we seemed to start making progress. Half an hour later and the ferry turned away from the sea and we slowly steamed towards Barra, arriving relieved and feeling a bit dishevelled.

Leaving Gambia along the badly potholed main road, we arrived at customs in good time in case of problems. This time all was straightforward, though a Gambian official blocked the door of the police station and asked me if I wanted to give something to "your friends in the police". Resisting the urge to tell him where to get off, I presented him with a pile of low value bits of Gambian Dalasi currency. This added up to about thirty pence. I gave him a broad smile.

More worrying and tense was being pulled over by some 'customs' officers a few miles into Senegal. These characters had based themselves under the shadow of some tall trees and were dressed in bits of mismatching green uniforms. Nearby were a group of thuggish looking characters in civilian clothes who sat on a battered ex-aid agency 4WD pick-up. Clearly there to support the group of potential paramilitaries.

They had already pulled over a 'Touba' bus and were busy searching every corner, throwing things on the road and having heated arguments with the occupants. People shouted at each other, women stood quietly, trying not to offend the aggressive perpetrators of this scene.

The situation was troubling. These guys gave every indication that they were fakes. There were no IDs and no guns, but there were machetes. The whole thing felt menacing.

Fortunately, this was one of many times when Barbara's command of the French language helped to make a situation easier. Although one of the green-clad toughs insisted on taking a cursory look in the Metal Mule boxes, after some conversation we were waved on our way. Only a mile later we passed a genuine customs post and the solitary 'Douane' lazily waved us on from his chair in the shade of a tree.

We stopped for lunch and the heat of the day at the lovely clean little café in Sobokou that Dave and I had visited on the way down. Barbara insisted on lunch and in short order a shrimp baguette appeared, freshly grilled and delicious.

We spent a pleasant few hours there, during which we conversed with a French chap who ran a little guest house and campsite deep in the marshes a few miles from Sobokou. We decided to look for the turn off for his place when we set off again, it was apparently only a few miles further up the road.

Unfortunately, we missed it. Setting off in the late afternoon, the road worsened and the concentration required to avoid being thrown off in a pothole left little opportunity to check out where every side road went. Having realised that we had gone far further than we should have, we decided to press on to Kaolack before it got dark.

Crossing the huge lake full of stinking sewage and smouldering rubbish which marks the southern edge of town and riding past people's hutted homes which sat among this hellish mess, Kaolack seemed if anything more chaotic and filthy than before. So after checking into the Hotel Paris, another night in 'cockroach barracks' being an unattractive option, Barbara and I took off to enjoy the more pleasant colonial delights of Chez Anouar where food and beer was gratefully consumed.

The distant sound of a large number of men repetitively chanting some Muslim celebration far into the night, permeated our dreams. The pre-dawn call to prayer from the nearby mosque ensured that were up early an in anticipation of another blistering day.

We set off towards Dakar, clad as usual in hot weather gear. But it only took twenty kilometres to realise that we were absolutely freezing. The cooler fingers of winter were slowly finding their way into Senegal, bringing much colder nights and early mornings than we had become used to. Stopping at the police checkpoint in Fatick, we let the rising sun warm us for a while, chatting to the cops and enjoying the break. The same guy that had raised issues about my driving licence was there. Much more friendly this time.

By the time we left the temperature was shooting up towards the thirties again and we had regular stops to take photographs, guzzle water and enjoy the shade of Baobabs.

Mbour, a sprawling town en-route, was hectic and it seemed to be market day. Traffic jams stretched out of the town and negotiating these had to be undertaken with care. Children and goats ran out between the traffic, or hand carts were shoved through the jam.

We were stopped by the police for a Carnet check and Barbara spotted a small cafe tucked away by the side of the road. The place was spotlessly clean, in contrast to the dusty streets outside. The young Asian couple who owned the cafe served excellent cappuccinos from a decent coffee machine. Feeling relaxed, we planned the rest of our day.

Our destination was Dakar where we hoped to spend two nights and take a look at one of Africa's more developed cities. Besides, the idea of taking a BMW Dakar to Dakar had seemed a good one when originally planning the trip. Before we left town we paused to get a photograph of the Dakar besides a road sign pointing the way to the city. An icon in the motorcycle off-roading world.

We soon wondered if we had made a huge mistake. To get to Dakar, we left the main loop of road which is Senegal's primary network and headed down a bumpy dual carriageway to the capital itself. The junction hosted battered fuel stations and a permanent street market plagued with beggars and yelling cops.

The wide open dual carriageway soon gave way to a nightmare of traffic congestion, heat and fumes as the dual carriageway passed through a number of what can only loosely described as 'suburban' towns. Every one of these places was a bustling medley of crammed vehicles, street markets and checkpoints. An all pervading stench of unwashed bodies, burning rubbish, sewage and rotting food hung over the whole scene.

Then the nice(ish) main road simply vanished, to be replaced by gravel, pot holes and ruts – hell for any kind of motorcycle. Loose stones, bits of rubbish, broken glass and wire abounded. All competing to see what could puncture unsuspecting tyres the fastest. Any vestige of lane discipline disappeared with the tarmac and we soon found ourselves playing a strange version of two and four wheeled dodgems, with us being the target.

Fortunately, the tarmac reappeared and although undulating and potholed it felt good to be able to get ahead of the tooting lorries and homicidal taxis as we headed into Dakar itself. The tall buildings of the city rose out of the smog ahead of us at the end of a long open downhill blast into the heart of the city.

*

CORRUPTION IN PARADISE

Dakar mixes modern infrastructure development, with the grubby semi-chaos more associated with other Senegalese towns. Any panoramic photograph of the city shows a modern skyline with impressive structures. This is deceptive.

Only at street level do you get a better feel of the real Dakar. Main routes are tarmacked, with most side roads a medley of rubbish and potholes. Sewage sometimes overflowed from manhole covers. It's a busy city, having a certain vibrancy of its own. Large corporations, small business and a colourful mix of people go about their daily life – an almost extreme mix of rich and poor. Late model BMW and Mercedes cars, mingling with the familiar sight of battered Renaults, old Mercedes taxis and the ubiquitous 'Touba'-adorned minibuses

Then there's the hustlers.

Stopping outside a reasonable looking hotel on a main route filled with hooting traffic, it took about ten seconds for a youngish chap dressed in a mouldy looking pair of trousers and a shirt to latch onto us. Trying to be our guide, offering to take us to 'his cousin's' hotel and so on. The hotel we'd stopped at was full. After a minute or two trying to figure out the map, we took a risk and followed our new 'friend' to what had been billed as the best accommodation in town – if you believed what you heard.

After negotiating narrow streets crammed with a medley of people, carts, animals and cars, we arrived at 'cousin's' hotel, which was on one of the main streets in Dakar, a busy place full of shops, markets and street traders. Traffic streamed along in African dodgem style.

Many roadside stalls seemed to double as mini shanty homes and crowds of people milled about, often touting everything from wrist watches to phone cards in traditional 'spiv' format. Some wore long coats and sleeves draped with whatever they were selling. Phone card salesman were thick on the ground.

Barbara went in to check things out. I stayed with the bike, wary of the potential for theft. Hustlers immediately zoomed in on me, doing their best to flog their various wares in a much more aggressive manner than I'd encountered elsewhere. The more I said "no", the harder the sell became. Things were getting rather uncomfortable and the crowd of desperados was growing, all competing to shove cheap goods in my face.

Suddenly the minarets of the local mosques started a sonorous wailing through their worn out speakers. As if by magic, the hard sell stopped, out came the prayer mats and relative peace descended as the call for prayers was answered.

Although the street around me didn't exactly grind to a halt, the faithful made it their business to make life difficult for those who didn't have a mind to observe the mullahs. Lines of genuflecting men spread out from the pavements right across the road, bringing the traffic to a halt. These guys seemed to have no concern for their safety, with two characters practically under the wheels of a bus which had pulled up only just in time.

I didn't get much chance to enjoy the relative peace before a very tall man with long robes, beads and a Rastafarian hair-job stopped to harangue me, wild eyed, face to face in some totally unrecognisable language. His tenor sounded like a recital of some sort and I had the uncomfortable feeling that he was choosing the more provocative sayings from some fundamentalist tract to damn all non-believers to hell. I found out later that his dress and style allied him to the Bay-Fall sect of the Muslim faith.

Barbara reappeared.

"It's a shit-hole, it stinks, there's bodies everywhere. Let's get the hell out of here." Easier said than done, I thought, as she climbed aboard and I thumbed the starter button, trying to figure out how I could avoid running over one of the prone figures on the street.

We stopped a few junctions further on, far enough away to have lost the hustler who had taken us to the hotel. We consulted the map again. The guidebook recommended the nearby Hotel Oceanic. So heading along some rough and sandy side roads, we pulled up in a quiet street outside what turned out to be to be a very nice, if faded and basic old French styled hotel.

We checked in, the hotel had a nice courtyard bar and a room with high walls with original fittings. There were views over the city through full length French windows and the place 'sold' us on its antiquated charms. The only issue was the lack of secure parking for the bike, but we were assured that security was 'on post' 24 hours a day and it was safe the leave the bike outside on the street.

Across the street were a few tourist-tat stalls selling wood carvings, trinkets and so on. There were also several cages crammed full of tiny exotic birds, which chirruped in a subdued way. A sight which made me instantly sad. I resisted the temptation to buy the lot and release them.

Later that day we took a walk to see what Dakar had to offer.

The city has a bad reputation for muggings, scams and petty theft. But aside from endless hassle from street traders and hustlers we didn't feel at all threatened. The trick is probably to recognise that there could be trouble and be prepared for it, plus try not to visibly festoon oneself with cameras, maps and guidebooks. In other words, do your best not make yourself a target.

There's plenty to see in Dakar if you're into cities with a different feel – a real mix of modern and traditional African. Modern buildings jostled with old French era structures, with tin huts or rubbish strewn waste ground filling the gaps. Traffic noise, fumes and crowds of people sat alongside an exotic range of colourful street trade. Food sellers were everywhere, preparing offerings from rickety stoves on the pavements, or doing a brisk trade in cups of instant coffee. Stalls selling wood carvings, ethnic jewellery and other touristy items often also sold small birds and animals.

After taking some refreshment at a bar where the staff seemed to comprise entirely of young western-dressed women, we had a walk around Independence Square, the heart of the city. At its centre lay a well-kept small park, surrounded by administrative buildings, banks and a couple of tall buildings. Trees lined the edge of the grass and several people were asleep underneath these.

Sitting on a wall in the relative peace, we mused over how long it would take for us to get hustled.

"Twenty seconds" said Barbara. "Nah, forty." I predicted. Ten seconds later someone tried to sell us fake jewellery. We sighed and moved on.

Feeling the need to escape, we headed for the peace, quiet and spectacular views from the bar on the roof of the sixteen-storey Hotel Independence. A ride up a rickety unserviced lift gave us a few nervous moments.

We needed some CFA francs which was how we discovered that the cash point machines were guarded by the police. There must be something in the tales of muggings, I mused to myself.

According to the guidebook, one of the best value restaurants in town was the 'La Dagorne'. This was conveniently adjacent to our hotel and turned out to be an excellent place for dinner. The food was French in flavour, clean, low priced with great service and nice staff.

Relaxing after a good steak and enjoying a bottle of wine, we considered our options. Neither of us was keen to spend another day in Dakar, but we didn't want to get too far ahead of our itinerary – we still had a few days to go before our rendezvous with Dave in Nouakchott.

Our musings were interrupted by a voice from behind, with a distinctly Essex accent.

"Sorry for interrupting, but why don't you check out the Ile de Goree?" Essex man and his wife were on a package holiday and seemed happy to chat to another English couple. They both felt similarly to us about Dakar and had escaped to the small island which was just a fifteen minute ferry ride from the city. They related a tale of tranquillity and historic interest that sold us on staying in town for another day.

It was a decision that we didn't regret. We took an early morning ferry to the island, running the gauntlet of groups of street hustlers on the way to the port.

The small Ile de Goree turned out to be a wonderfully peaceful place of great beauty. No motorised vehicles are allowed in the narrow streets which seemed to be straight out of French colonial history books. Hustlers were much rarer and certainly more polite. It was pleasant just to wander through the town exploring the narrow paths and enjoying the calm ambiance.

Wandering out of the down and up towards the World War Two fortress of Le Castel at the northern edge of the island, we explored the extensive fortifications. They included two sixteen-inch guns which sank the HMS Tacoma during the Second World War (The ferry to the island goes around the site to avoid the wreck). I've heard it said that this impressive ordnance became an inspiration for the movie 'The Guns of Navarone'. Perhaps an urban myth, but having seen the guns, it's a good one.

A colourfully dressed character told us quite a bit about the history of the place. He was from the same Bay Fall sect as the chanting Rasta that had accosted me the day before. He told me that I'd probably run into one of their missionaries. The Le Castel fortifications were inhabited by the sect, with this witnessed by colourfully painted concrete gun emplacements, scattered with local art that were sold to make a small living.

Indeed, local artisans lined the tree covered avenues up the fortress. Their wares almost a free to view art gallery of vibrant colours and abstract subjects. The people we met were very friendly and quite gentle in their attitude towards us. Rasta man may have had too much sun perhaps …

Lunch was a relaxed affair of grilled fish at a small restaurant by the port. Cooked to perfection and accompanied by cool drinks. This was followed by further wanderings through narrow streets, drinking in the sights and generally unwinding.

We explored other artefacts, including a large number of Napoleonic era cannons which were lined up on the ground near the older, perhaps 18th century, fort at the northern end of the island. We wandered narrow streets of faded colonial era architecture and visited the place known locally as Maison des Esclaves – the House of Slaves.

A famous and grim doorway opens directly from the slave cells to the sea, where ships would lie waiting to transport their tragic cargos to the New World. It's one of those places which makes one sit back and think. The building has enormous spiritual significance for black Americans in particular, whose ancestors were shipped as slaves to America. This was a slave house of more minor significance than the larger affairs in countries further south, but its dungeon-like lower rooms still carried long dead ghosts of despair.

Remembering our buttock-clenching entry to Dakar, we elected to leave before first light the following morning. The noise of generators during the late night power cuts, and the stench of diesel wafting through the open windows, didn't do much for a good night's sleep. But we were still able to get on the road in good time to beat the local rush hour.

Leaving Dakar was a much more agreeable experience aside from taking an unintended detour into an area of tumbledown slums full of broken carts and running sewage. But we soon found ourselves on the dual carriageway heading out of the Cap Vert Peninsular.

Heading north towards St Louis and glad to be in open countryside again, we stopped in Thies for perhaps the nicest coffee and breakfast of the whole trip. Thies was one of the nicer places we visited in Senegal. More or less hassle free and clean quiet streets, with plenty of official-looking Government buildings.

This was to be one of the hottest days of the trip and as the temperature soared so did the discomfort of cooking inside riding gear and crash helmets. West African countries didn't seem to have helmet laws at this time, but a lid is necessary if a person is to avoid a charred and boiled head. We pressed on because it seemed daft to stop for the heat of the day when our destination, Zebrabar, was only about three hours ride from Thies.

The heat shimmered on the road ahead as we avoided badly driven 'Touba' buses and kept a weather eye on the rear-view mirror for the numerous overloaded Mercedes which were being driven like Formula One racing cars. Several rehydration stops brought a variety of people out to make small-talk, or stare in wonder at the rich western 'Two-Bobs' (us) who had entered their impoverished lives for a brief moment or two. Young boys would yell "Dakar, Dakar!" at us when they saw the model name on the GS. The Dakar Rally, which was due to start just after we arrived home, was a big national event in Senegal until threats from al-Qaeda forced the organisers to move the event.

The people of this fine country must have been gutted by the way that the French organisers of the Dakar rally later so easily caved into remote threats of terror attacks, despite how awful some of the isolated incidents were. In many cases, it has been found that sub-Saharan groups who claim to be connected to international terrorism are often local separatists, tribesmen, or criminal groups. With perhaps only a loose affiliation to al-Qaeda of the Maghreb – if affiliated at all.

One terrible attack on a French family group in Mauritania, widely reported as being the responsibility of al-Qaeda, sent the global media into frenzy. Only much later, the murders turned out to have been perpetrated by smugglers who had been disturbed during their nefarious business. But the labels have stuck.

Western commentators don't help the situation, labelling

attacks by such drug smugglers or groups with an axe to grind against local government forces, as moves by extremists to consolidate territory. They rarely, if ever, check the facts on the ground properly. This is not to take terror threats lightly – such threats do exist, but the security situation in West Africa seems to be fluid, with attacks mostly disorganised and probably not part of some great Islamist grand plan.

I have mixed feelings about the issue. On one hand I can see how the Dakar organisers felt the need to play it safe – incidents do occur. But on the other hand I do feel that with proper routing, biasing the rally towards the Atlantic coast en-route to Senegal and avoiding the deep desert areas of Mauritania and Mali, would create a manageable situation in security terms and still represent a hugely challenging event.

The organisers may have organised a viable event in South America, but the Dakar it ain't. They should show some guts and return to Africa. They would get massive support from the people and Governments of the region. Plus demonstrate to terror and other groups that they're not going to win.

After all, the often vague security concerns are not deterring many groups and individuals from taking the long route south to Senegal and Mali each year.

However, all the above said, I would urge anyone planning such a journey to avoid eastern Mauritania and northern Mali for the foreseeable future. Timbuktu became a focal point for insurrection in 2012/13 and the situation remains unstable. Even on the Atlantic Route, care is needed as raids and kidnappings do occur. Though mainly at night when no one with a brain between their ears should be on the road anyway.

Particularly pleasant when stopped was resting in the shade of the huge Baobab trees. The primordial-looking behemoths providing something to sit against, or the privacy to take a leak. It is said that the gods ripped the Baobab out of the ground and thrust it back in upside down in a fit of anger. Looking at the tree it's easy to see where this amusing legend came from. They can survive for hundreds of years and are held in awe by the locals who use their pendulous seed pods for a variety of purposes. The leaves are used to make a sauce and the flowers gathered for celebrations. The core of the tree can even be tapped for fresh water in times of drought.

Stopping later for Barbara to find somewhere to 'powder her nose', we were surprised to note that her boot soles had started to melt in the heat. The bike mounted GPS must also have been feeling the heat, because while we were pondering Barbara's now slightly gungy boots, it decided to shut itself down, its core temperature having reached seventy degrees centigrade in the direct glare of the sun.

Finally, we reached the causeway piste which led to Zebrabar and once again had the great pleasure of a Swiss welcome to that wonderful and peaceful place.

The trouble with Zebrabar is that it can kind of 'eat you up'. An odd way of describing the effect the place has perhaps, but it becomes very easy to let the world go by in timeless fashion. The day's agenda was only dictated by mealtimes, sunrise and sunset. We took one of the ethnic round huts that overlooked the estuary and enjoyed the company of fellow travellers, read books, or walked the beaches – taking amusement from annoying the huge colonies of Fiddler Crabs. Sometimes it was good to simply sit and clear my mind of thoughts and enjoy the shade from the numerous palm trees. Watching small brightly coloured and exotic birds flit about, or listen to the unfamiliar tropical calls of other larger birds.

This time there were more motorcyclists. Fellow two-wheeled travellers who were also hiding from the world for a few days. All had BMWs and were happy to laze about with us and chat over numerous large bottles of 'Gazelle' beer.

A couple of Dutch lads were also taking time out from their overland journey. They were driving an old, but well equipped Toyota Land cruiser. One of them had been north as far as the border with Western Sahara and had enjoyed several days driving desert and bad piste along the route of the ore train. He had made it to Choum and Atar, but had spent so much time digging himself out of sand that he headed straight down the main road to meet his mate who had flown into Dakar. Their plan was to re-enter Mauritania and drive up the beach to Nouakchott.

Martin, our Swiss host remarked; "Two things. Don't cross the border at Rosso and secondly, avoid the brown sand – stay on the yellow sand." He paused for a moment of reflection.

"Brown sand is usually waterlogged. Bad news".

"So that would be the end of that then?" I asked.

"No." replied Martin "But it would be lots of digging to get out. Much good work."

More beer was opened as we reflected on Martin's interpretation of 'good' work.

Martin told us about how Zebrabar came about and showed us his amazing photo albums. The auberge had been going for about ten years at that time and was founded by Martin and his wife who had both fallen in love with the location when they were travelling. Deciding to start a new life on the beautiful coastline of the nature reserve south of St Louis, they hauled two lorry containers across the Sahara with a massive truck. These became the first 'buildings' and the core of the site. They still stand to this day, serving as the kitchen and store room, with new buildings and other additions now spreading out from this metallic hub.

"So do you actually own the site?" I asked.

"Yes, no, but we're still here." said Martin. "We bought the site, or thought we had, but then we started to understand Senegalese bureaucracy. The national park authority said that we owned it, but the Government said no. In the end everyone agreed that we owned the infrastructure, but not the land. So we just fenced the land off anyway and got on with it.

"The legal status is always precarious; it's just a matter of knowing how to deal with the officials. We get by and we're not going anywhere. People know this. They also know that we create jobs here. Each year I get a tax bill. It's always huge and we think we may have to close. But I go see the tax inspector with a large crate of tea and we make a deal. We're still here."

Martin also had a lot to say about how regulations can wreck tourism and trade.

"Take the Carnet de Passage." he said. "This stupid piece of paper means that overland tourism to Senegal is made expensive and difficult. Travellers avoid the country and Senegal gets fewer vehicles on the market which are cheap enough for ordinary people to buy. The problem is that in five years all the cars will probably be wrecks like they are in Mauritania and many companies in the tourism trade will go out of business.

"I said this to the Minister for Tourism at a conference. He doesn't like me anymore."

Martin was right. Despite the pontifications of the Senegalese Government who say that the Carnet is about stopping the country from becoming a dumping ground for old European cars, the Carnet is really about corrupt 'big men' in Government thinking that they can get their hands on high taxes from imported new cars. This is completely flawed thinking because local incomes aren't going to suddenly increase any time soon. So the number of new cars sold is unlikely to increase very much, even with the increased availability of cheap cars from Asia.

Senegal is one of the beautiful jewels of Africa which, although by any African measure is stable and peaceful, the first to to democratically replace presidents without accompanying civil war, is sullied by root and branch corruption from the top to the bottom of public life. From siphoned off international aid and trade wealth at the top of Ministries and by favoured big business, to corrupt border officials, to the cops, customs officers and transport operators who demand 'cadeau' and bribes at every opportunity. Senegal is trapped in a cycle of institutionalised madness which keeps the poor very poor and those who sit behind the veneer of democratic government in positions of power.

In the 1970s and 80s, Africa's 'Big Men' dictators horrified the world by the way that they preyed upon their people, stole their country's wealth and ripped the heart out of the continent with meaningless wars and racial discrimination. Aside from a few notable exceptions, these monsters may now have gone. But the promise of new and more benign leadership will not translate into results for the African people unless root and branch reform of all levels of public administration takes place. A complete change of culture will be needed.

Yesterday's Big Men have been, mostly, replaced by legions of nameless 'little-big-men' of an entirely different breed. Powerful officials who hide behind the façade of public administration, weaving webs of corruption which are less immediately obvious to the casual observer, but still just as damaging to the prospects for a country and its people. The Heart of Darkness has been replaced by a Black Hole of poverty and injustice.

In fairness, Senegal has maintained stable Government since independence, with leaders coming and going by democratic plebiscites which have been more or less fair depending on your point of view. There has been none of the horror which was experienced by so many of Senegal's neighbours. But the depressing daily expressions of institutional corruption, so common in Africa, still lie under the surface.

In the so-called 'Developed' world, we wail about the terrible injustice of Africa. Liberal observers rend their clothes looking to entirely blame historical excesses and current UK and US foreign and domestic policy for Africa's problems. It's become fashionable for us to seek atonement on the altar of overseas aid and make national budget commitments.

Only the most callous would dismiss the terrible oppression and terror that European empires sometimes reaped upon Africa during the time of Empire. One only has to read about King Leopold and the Belgium Congo to feel slightly sick. But the end of Empire was two generations ago. In some cases, countries were handed over to home rule with highly developed public administration, social infrastructure, healthcare, transport networks and sanitation. The terror that followed in many African countries, sometimes long after independence, cannot be fully blamed on the developed world or the long gone colonial era. Neither can the corrupt systems that exist today.

That said, The West is not completely innocent. Consider the 'proxy war' in Angola and American policy which propped up the most ravenous and terrible African dictator of them all – Zaire's Mobutu Sese Seko. Consider also the reams of protectionist international trading rules that exist to this day. Designed mainly to favour the developed world. Globalisation seems only the favour the most powerful nations.

The Africa Union makes all the right noises about stamping out corruption, but the sad truth is that nothing substantial is being done. The new wave of more promising African leaders seem unable to shake off the legacy of corruption that they inherited. In the meantime countries like Senegal continue to have their heads held just above the waterline as their wealth and the possibility for growth and development is siphoned off by the new big men in powerful positions.

This is not to dismiss the importance of foreign aid projects. It would be ethically unacceptable to make today's African poor pay for the sins of their former leaders and the current corrupt governance that remains. If it wasn't for Riders for Health and other such organisations with an ethos that revolves around local empowerment, it is certain that things would be much worse for those who are most vulnerable. The work of organisations like these is absolutely essential as it fills a vital gap which has been left by decades of bad governance.

But aside from dealing with the poverty-sustaining injustice of current world trade rules, if we are to see real change in Africa, it is vital that aid which goes directly to Governments – particularly from organisations like the World Bank – is linked to measures to stamp out corruption and bad governance. With this firmly policed by more than just high words and 'agreements' at extravagantly expensive United Nations conferences.

Aid should not be conditional on requirements to replace those local systems which work with western style free market policies. Long standing local social 'norms' indicate that this approach is often un-African and in the main leads to abuses by officials. It also encourages corruption and backhanders to and from unregulated business. Plus the destruction of existing local economic systems, slave labour and environmental damage.

There is also a strong argument to suggest that aid should not go to governments at all, but instead to local businesses, communities and groups, who can make more direct and productive use of what is given. Making a difference where it really matters.

Some even argue that all aid should stop, that leaders be forced to confront their country's problems or face losing power. That countries should be finally weaned off aid dependency. The

Kenyan economist Dambisa Moyo set out a powerful argument in favour of this in her book 'Dead Aid'. But would such medicine of change result in new horrors before it took effect?

What is certain is that without a new approach, Africa will remain forever a pauper continent, reliant on hand-outs from western charities to keep its people fed and able to access healthcare. The commitment of world leaders to provide 0.7% of GDP to aid is to me wrong headed if that money simply goes to Governments. The people of developing countries need empowering, not kept in a state of aid dependency.

The following day, our two Dutch friends packed up their Land Cruiser and headed for the Mauritanian border. We wished them well, not expecting to see them again. However just as the evening dinner bell was rung, the pair appeared again looking hot and dishevelled.

"What happened?" I called out. "Beer." they said in unison giving a good impression of zombies who had had enough for the day.

Over dinner they related a sorry tale of woe. Arriving at the Diama Dam crossing into Mauritania, they left Senegal and presented themselves at Mauritanian customs. Our man who had flown into Dakar didn't have a visa for Mauritania, with this only being available at Rosso. So they both had to turn-tail and re-enter Senegal, trying to persuade each other that Rosso couldn't be that bad.

It was. Leaving and re-entering Senegal in the same hour meant that officials in Rosso were able to gleefully declare that 'there was a problem'. When this had been finally sorted out hours later (they didn't say how much had to be paid) and exit visas had been stamped, a 'problem' had been declared relating to their Toyota's Carnet. Again, the out/in stamps on the same day were the issue.

Hours later, they started to get desperate. Fantastic sums of money had been quoted and the correct official was either 'not there', 'at lunch', 'at prayers', 'five minutes away', 'ten minutes away', 'almost here' and so on. They later found out that the guy was actually sitting in the corner waiting for Dutch patience to run out and money to come his way.

Officially they had left Senegal, so the Rosso authorities had them by the balls. Both weren't budging on the financial issue. So with the last ferry about to leave for Rosso Mauritania and the prospect of a dodgy night on a relatively lawless quayside, they re-entered Senegal and high-tailed it back to Zebrabar, ninety minutes away from the dreaded border crossing.

Both were totally exhausted. It had been a burning hot day and they were completely demoralised and extremely angry at the way they'd been treated.

I listened to all this with mounting concern. I had been considering the northern route for some days and was concerned about the wisdom of tackling the 100 kilometre Diama/Rosso Piste two-up. Not because I was worried about the bike, more because of the time it would take me as an inexperienced off-road rider to traverse the route two-up, particularly with road tyres. It had taken Dave and I most of the afternoon to do it on the way down, though we had stopped a lot for photos and to muck about.

I had stupidly left the tent with Mutch to take back to London thinking we wouldn't need it and as a result we were now reliant on finding guest houses of some sort each day. I also knew that the Rosso to Nouakchott road was poor enough to make it dangerous to ride at night and the Diama route meant riding from Zebrabar to Nouakchott in one hit.

Therefore, my plan had been to brave Rosso on the way north, with this idea based on reports that it was a great deal easier than trying it north/south. But the experiences suffered by our Dutch friends did not auger well for this idea.

Another funny thing about travel is that sometimes other people's bad experience hardens one's resolve to try and overcome the difficulties encountered. So after thinking about things further and discussing the whole thing with Barbara and other travelling folk, we decided to go for it.

Martin, our Zebrabar host, thought we were mad. He shook his head and smiled laconically.

"Send me a postcard from Rosso."

Peter, one of our Dutch compatriots drew a detailed map of the

Rosso border formalities – something that proved to be invaluable later on.

That evening we heard from Dave. He'd been keeping in regular contact via text message, or through the many teleboutiques – phone shops – that are a feature of Africa. He'd spent some days in the Casamance region of Senegal. He then visited Guinea Bissau before heading into Mali. He was now in Ayoun el Atrous, Mauritania having completed 150 kilometres of tough piste and sand between Diema in Mali and Ayoun and was running ahead of time. He still had a very long desert stretch to complete, but he expected to reach Nouakchott a day earlier than planned.

We still had three days to go before meeting Dave on the revised itinerary that we'd agreed in Banjul and Nouakchott was a theoretical day's trip from Zebrabar. However, our strategy for the 'raid on Rosso' meant spending an evening in a place called Richard Toll, which would set us up nicely to 'raid' the border in the early hours. Dave's good progress meant that we now needed to leave Zebrabar the following afternoon.

After a last night of good company and the wonderful peace of the palm-fronded coast, leaving the calm of our Senegalese oasis was a wrench. But the journey had to continue. It was hard to say goodbye and several people came to see us off. Zebrabar is a real gem and we looked forward to returning.

The 150 kilometre run to Richard Toll under a blistering afternoon sun was one of the less pleasant rides of the trip. Douane officials at several checkpoints conspired to burn up time and it was very hot, with heat reflecting from the soft black tarmac under our wheels. The road took a turn for the worse once we passed the Diama Dam turn off. For a time it seemed as though the piste might have been a better option as I steered the Dakar around an obstacle course of bike sized potholes.

Richard Toll lies alongside the River Senegal in what can best be described as serious malaria country. It's the centre of Senegal's sugar industry and is dominated by a large processing plant which emits a noxious stench. The edge of town was lined with the usual shanties, but even the centre of this important commercial centre was very shabby and run down.

Arriving there at last light, it initially proved impossible to find somewhere to stay among the busy streets and markets. Stopping the bike outside the Chateau de Baron Roger, the Claude Richard designed gardens of which lend the town its name (Richard Toll means 'Richard's Garden'), we both began to wonder if we'd made a big mistake.

The run down town packed with ultra-inquisitive people, buzzing clouds of mosquitoes in the dusk light, combined with no tent and nowhere to stay, was a cocktail of circumstances that could be extremely unpleasant.

Finally, after yet another run up the main street, Barbara spotted a battered sign for the Gite d'Etape. Heading down a dirt track we found ourselves outside what we took to be an abandoned building. A man appeared from behind a low wall. "yes this is the hotel. We have rooms. I take you through."

We parked the bike and walked around the corner to be greeted by yet another of those wonderful inversions that Africa can spring upon the weary traveller. There was a serene view across well-tended lawns, a swimming pool and open-sided bar. This opened towards the best aspect of the River Senegal that we had seen so far.

After checking in, we took our regular 'sundowner' on reclining chairs by the banks of the river and watched the last of the sun disappear out of the sky. Outside this tranquil spot was another world. Here was peace and quiet.

*

ON THE BORDER

Five am. Furious packing and loading took place, while Barbara negotiated the bill for the previous night. We got away before six, stopping only to fill up with 'Super'.

A motorcycle cop on a garishly equipped 250cc bike held us up in the garage, wanting to chat about BMWs as the minutes ticked away. We finally got free and dashed up the Rosso road as quickly as the light of a fast approaching dawn would allow.

What's this? Oh no, not another checkpoint. This guy was OK though. He was regular Douane. Very friendly. He told us to; "ignore everything you see and go straight to the ferry port gates. Don't stop, don't talk to anyone – they want to take all your money." A friendly wave and we were on our way into town.

Rosso. What a dump, just like Rosso Mauritania on the other side of the river. As we entered town we passed dead trucks, piles of nameless filth and ruined or half patched up buildings. People were stirring into life from piles of blankets which were scattered all over the broken pavements and in every available doorway.

There was a huge queue of trucks which were parked bumper to bumper right out to the edge of town. We negotiated these slowly as people caught sight of us and tried to run alongside shouting "Stop! Talk to me – I can help you!"

"Not this time matey." I muttered to myself and we pushed on without slowing.

A few minutes later and we were weaving in and out of closely packed vehicles, which now occupied just about all the available road space. Now people were popping up from all directions to hassle us, but we managed to keep focused and finally arrived at the tumbledown gates of the port.

I stopped and put the GS on its stand, determined to act deaf and stay focused.

"I'll stay with the bike." said Barbara. "Today though I don't speak French". Her strategy was to act dumb and hopefully avoid the worst of the hassle.

I headed though an open wicket gate. For a moment I pondered riding the GS through – the entrance was just wide enough. But there were too many guys wanting me to do just that. Sensing a possible trap I moved on to find the customs post instead.

It was shut and the windows were dark. I banged on the door in determined fashion and after a few moments a bleary eyed man in uniform answered.

"Stamp this please." I said, thrusting the Carnet in his face.

Sleepy-eyed he looked at me, beckoned me inside, took the Carnet and slumped behind a desk.

"OK. It's early, but no problem." A nervous wait as he read the

Senegal page from top to bottom.

"Sign here and here." I indicated, "stamp here and you keep this part".

"OK." he said. "I've just been posted here, this is the first one of these that I've had to do. Boss always looks after Carnets." He motioned towards a snorting bundle of rags that only partially hid the form of an obese caricature of the African border official. Clearly the guy who creates and solves customs 'problems' in these parts.

Bang! Down went the stamp. "no; no money." he said.

I offered the guy a full packet of cigarettes – he was clearly in for some heat when the boss-man found out that he'd 'let one go'. He refused, smiled and shook my hand.

I went back through the gates to a town that was coming to life. More people were milling about and smoke from cooking fires was in the air. The next stop was the Police. Two or three guys ran alongside me as I strode purposefully towards the police station. "You need my help." they said "Police here." "Police there." "No, not police yet, change money first." Ignoring them, I entered a low building guarded by two tough looking uniformed characters with rifles. They smiled and nodded me through. Not the hustlers though, when one tried to follow me, the smile turned to a snarl and my unwanted companion was shoved into the dust by a deftly wielded rifle butt.

Now came a language barrier. The police, who sported heavy gold braid seemed friendly enough, but my French wasn't up to the questions. I was too focussed and 'wired' for my brain to slow down and translate.

A tall slim woman, with the elegant look of the Wolof people about her, was standing nearby holding a bag of bananas. Noting the look of confusion on my face she said in perfect English.

"They only want to know how many kilometres you are travelling today."

She started to translate for me. The cops wanted to see Barbara, but my new friend talked them out of insisting on this. Some moments later and with a shrug from the officer, both our passports were stamped. No cadeau needed for the Police either. I offered a few Francs to the woman. She gave me two bananas and wished us good fortune.

Senegal, some of the best people in the world – and some of the worst.

Back at the gates, Barbara was under pressure. She was surrounded by a good-sized crowd of the quietly inquisitive and aggressive hustler alike. Her tactics for dealing with the attention was to exude an outward air of calm; keep quiet, smile and shake her head. Only her eyes showed her true feelings. I squeezed her arm and went back through the wicket gate.

The gate-keeper – a portly gentleman in flowing robes – announced himself.

"I get you in: Ten Euros." he said. "No:" I replied. "5,000 francs." This was about seven or eight Euro. After a short conversation he agreed.

"But first, you see police in the compound and do your vehicle checks – then I let you in."

I head for the final building on my round of officialdom. The sun was rising in the sky and shadows were being cast by nearby trees in the sharp morning light. By now, it seemed that everyone had woken up and a queue was forming outside the police post.

One hustler was different from the rest. He'd been following me about, but not making a fuss, or giving me hassle. He'd seemed more curious about me as a person than anything else. Occasionally he had pointed in the direction of places I needed to visit. I took a risk and talked to him. He told me that he was a Gambian who had been stuck at Rosso for some time, trying to raise money to get across country to The Gambia. Maybe true, maybe not. But he was quiet and unassuming, so I asked him for some help getting me to the front of the growing queue.

He knew his stuff and only a few moments later, I was waved to the front of the queue by another guy who wore a worn out police shirt and was guarding the door. I went inside the tumbledown concrete block building and joined a small crowd of people who were stood around an office desk. This was empty apart from a tall pile of dog-eared personal documents.

The stack was being treated like a deck of cards by those

waiting. Individual documents moved up and down the pile as different hands emerged from the waiting throng to rearrange them. My own papers stayed resolutely at the bottom as I was unsure what the reaction would be to a 'Two-Bob' joining this document shuffling game. The Gambian held no such reserve and seeing that I was unsure what to do, moved my papers to the top of the pile muttering under his breath in the local tongue to those around him. Lots of muttering came back, but nothing unfriendly.

A yawning and stretching cop appeared at a person-sized hole which had been roughly bashed in the wall between two offices. With a great flourish he pulled a ledger and a pile of stamps from a locked cabinet. The muttering stopped as the policeman with great ceremony sank into a chair behind the desk. This was clearly his big moment – the most important person both in the room and for that moment at least, in the lives of those who were gathered.

He opened his ledger and laid out his stamps. The throng pressed closer around the desk and the document rearranging took on a new fervour. The 'Emperor of the Desk' ignored this quiet flurry of activity, lit a cigarette and waited for a moment.

As if on cue, money started to appear. CFA notes were waving about, some were swapped between individuals and documents moved about on the pile.

"Offer 10,000 franc." said my Gambian. I proffered ten Euro instead (6000 CFA). The addition of my European money to this strange tableau prompted more muttering. But at this point the cop took the set of documents from the top if the pile. Some CFA notes from the one of the hands went straight into his pocket as he started writing laboriously into the ledger. Document shuffling continued as the cop reached for the next set of documents. In an easy and well-practiced motion, he transferred money to his pocket with one hand while he started writing with the other.

Meanwhile, the Gambian had been muttering furiously to those around him and it seemed as though my documents were now staying somewhere near the top of the pile. More hands, more money and the order of documents changed again. The Emperor ignored this new activity and reached for the top set of papers.

Ours! My ten Euro disappeared in an easy motion.

"Profession?" barked the cop "Employee." I replied. A few moments of laborious handwriting and I was done.

The Gambian followed me as I tracked down the portly gatekeeper, who had already unlocked the gates in anticipation of my arrival. I then went out to the bike, where my wife was now looking hunted. We scattered the crowd of hustlers as the GS engine started and rode though the tiniest of gaps which the gatekeeper opened for us. The gates slammed behind to a clamour of yelling from the crowd outside. Barbara paid the Proconsul of the Gates and we parked the bike a short distance from the ferry ramp.

We'd managed to get through this part of the dreaded border crossing in under an hour. Clearly, the early start at Rosso had been a good plan, but what now? The ferry was on the other bank, about a quarter of a mile away and showing no sign of moving.

The Gambian said "It comes at nine am, I'll get you straight on". The problem was that nine am African time could be any time at all.

We settled down to wait as the morning heat started to build. I chatted to the Gambian for a while. He used to run a business in the Gambia which had failed. So he set out on foot to get to Europe. Some months later he found himself on the Moroccan side of the border at Ceuta unable to get through to the enclave and onto Spain. The Moroccans then threw him out and after some adventures; he'd made it south as far as Rosso in Senegal. Home was only a few hundred kilometres away, but he said that he couldn't afford the equivalent of thirty euro for the bus ride. I felt that there was more to his story than he was letting on, but kept quiet. He had been extremely helpful just when it was needed and was polite and calm.

Meanwhile, the crowd of hustlers which had accosted Barbara, had come through the wicket gate and were once again hanging around the bike giving us general grief. Small children were begging, elaborate stories and promises were being told and made. We did our best to ignore this and waited quietly. In the meantime small hands persistently ran their hands over our luggage, testing the bungies, trying out the locks on the Metal Mule boxes and generally trying to find a crafty 'in' to our possessions.

I wandered down to the waterfront to sit quietly and smoke a cigarette. It was really quite a nice spot. If it wasn't for the air of desperation and hassle, Rosso riverside could even be described as a lovely place. People plied trade in food, fishing boats were being prepared for the river and women, naked to the waist, washed clothes in the river.

After a time, there was a flurry of activity came from across the water. Distant shouts and the sound of a roaring, worn diesel engine. Emitting a long plume of dense black smoke from the funnel, the ferry started its slow journey over the river.

On our side, engines started up and I moved back to the bike, got it off the stand and waited for my moment to move. Ready for the inevitable stampede when the ferry docked.

The arrival of the heavily dented and rusting river ferry prompted a dodgems style jostling of vehicles large and small. Ferry workers tried to keep some order in the loading process but were largely ignored. We clearly weren't going to get called in a hurry so, seeing a gap, I rode down the jetty and onto the open decked wreck ignoring someone in dirty overalls who was gesticulating for us to stop.

Like the Barra ferry, the vessel departed only when it seemed about to sink with the excessive weight of overloaded vehicles. "Not so much roll-on, roll-off, but roll-on, roll-over" was Barbara's wry comment. The worn engine thundered and banged as we crossed to the Mauritanian side. Towards the huge crowd of waiting people on the ramp and surrounding jetties.

Once we docked, all hell broke loose. Uniforms and civilians ran up the ramp shouting and pushing. Engines roared again and the car behind us tried to push the GS off the boat. Almost losing balance on the bike, I just got it upright again when an angry individual in 'police' uniform started yelling "give me your papers, your passport, your Carnet NOW!" into my face.

I wasn't going to fall for this fake cop routine and I knew that I was entitled to be seen by officials in the proper office. So I held my ground and a shouting match ensued. This guy got angrier and angrier. Things were starting to look ugly, when Barbara said quietly "I think he may be a genuine customs guy." I looked him up and down again as he continued to shout at me. It didn't seem that we were going to get past this guy, so I handed over our papers.

He promptly vanished and we moved the GS up to a group of buildings which housed customs and immigration.

A hustler appeared holding our papers.

"You follow me." he said.

I couldn't believe it. The cop had given our papers to a hustler! "Bloody rip-off merchants" I said to Barbara. "Looks like we're in for a shite time here".

I followed our new 'guide'. Firstly the Carnet. Mauritanian customs were no problem. The guide gave him the carnet and it was quickly stamped. No cost. The officer looked at the guide and said to me, "This person is dirt. He is nothing. Get rid of him if you can."

Once out of the office I made an attempt to get our papers back. I seized the Carnet and stuffed it in my jacket, but the guide started yelling "crazy English, you know nothing of our ways, you are mad" and as if by magic three or four other 'guides' appeared to support him. Further seizures of papers were no longer an option, but I was glad that I'd recovered the Carnet.

Although this institutionalised corruption was making me seethe (it seemed that the cops work with the hustlers to extort cash from travellers, who then shared their ill-gotten gains between themselves and the police), our unwanted guide was quite efficient. Within ten minutes we had passports stamped and vehicles registered. Then I was led over to pay for the ferry and finally had to pay off the guide and a mate of his, who had apparently performed some unknown service or other.

We'd heard some horror stories about how much people had been forced to pay, but the whole deal, including the ferry ticket came to about 35 Euro.

Barbara had been continuing her sentry duties while all this was going on and was relieved to finally get on the GS when formalities had been completed. Both of us were very happy to get out through the gates and past the teeming throng of hustlers which Dave and I had almost come to grief with on the way down.

THE ORE TRAIN

We headed north, keen to put some miles between us and Rosso before stopping for a break. We had taken on the reputed worst border in Africa and survived without losing all our money. We felt pretty good about it.

The whole experience had taken four hours, including the ferry crossing. Not bad we thought. It seemed that research and timing had been the key, plus staying focussed. I hear that the border between Libya and Egypt is worse. But like everything else when travelling in Africa, I suppose the maxim is that if you want to get through, just do your best to take it all in your stride.

Once the Senegal River valley was left behind, the green countryside quickly gave way to rolling red Sahel sand, with large numbers of acacia trees growing in the arid wilderness. Buildings gave way to run down huts mostly made of corrugated iron and the busy business like air of the border was replaced with quiet stillness and isolation.

Stopping an hour later, Barbara commented on how empty, still and hopelessly poor Mauritania was compared to Senegal. For me, it felt good to be back in the Sahara region. I had been looking forward to riding these roads again. It was also nice to return to a place where people stopped their vehicles to ask if we needed assistance whenever we were taking a break. This goes on in Senegal on occasion as well, but in Mauritania, this polite and genuinely helpful enquiry happens regularly when you're on the road. But I was also regretting the passing of Black African exuberance. We were back to more conservative Arabic culture and social norms.

Although we were heading back towards the desert, it didn't seem all that hot to me. Certainly it was hardly a mild summer's day, but the high-ish ambient temperature wasn't bothering me that much. Acclimatisation, I surmised.

As we rode, the sand changed hue from red to different shades of yellow and orange and back to red again. Camels started to appear, sometimes eating the spiny acacia, sometimes standing still. We saw the occasional person when we rode through villages of corrugated iron huts. But overall it was very quiet.

The road seemed in a worse state than I remembered on the way down. At one point about half way to Nouakchott, I looked ahead and saw what looked like a huge dune covering the road. As we got closer I saw that in fact it was a 400 yard stretch of road which was completely missing – the tarmac removed since we had ridden this way a couple of weeks earlier. Carried off by local folk for use on something else, perhaps to tar roofs.

We approached Nouakchott about mid-afternoon. Acacia-filled Sahel had already disappeared to be replaced by Hamada. Huge deep-desert style dunes were now becoming more the norm. We also started seeing more traffic of the tragically battered and broken Mauritanian variety.

Approaching the outskirts of town, we passed several small groups of people with donkey carts digging chunks out of the edge of the road. The middle 'lane' of a roundabout was being dug up as a bored cop looked on quietly from a checkpoint at the side of the road.

We headed straight for the centre of the city. I had no desire to show Barbara the Dante-esque desolation of the area of town near the beach and we were both becoming concerned about how we were going to find Dave in the Mauritanian capital.

Our man from Ireland had sent me a text message with two possible hotel addresses to try. These were in the guidebook, but the map that we had of Nouakchott didn't seem to bear much resemblance to the city that we were navigating. We turned off the fairly good quality dual carriageway which traversed the city. Then down a broken street, littered in rubbish and smashed glass, looking for someone who could give directions.

By the entrance to a very clean shop in what was a pretty rough looking area, sat a man in a blue robe. He was washing his feet in a dirty bowl. Keen to help, he was quite happy to guide us to the two hotels if we were OK to follow him in his Mercedes.

After a five minute wait he appeared behind the wheel of a sagging wreck which was once a Mercedes. It had no rear window or lights. Stopping by us, he motioned over to a group of about six youths who had been hanging around nearby, trying not to look too interested in us. They all piled into the Mercedes and we set off, en-convoy, back the way we had come.

Before long we were passing Government compounds and much better quality buildings. Even one or two monuments. Nouakchott was only built in 1960 and draws much of its influence from desert culture. It was planned with wide streets and space around public buildings. Now surrounded by shanty townships, it has four times the planned 200,000 population. All the time the desert continues to encroach on the city.

We followed the Mercedes for about two miles and were just starting to wonder where the heck we were being taken – and wondering if it wouldn't be wise to lose the car – when parked by the kerb on the other side of the road was a GS Dakar. Dave sat astride peering at a map. An incredible stroke of luck to meet him like this!

We stopped and waved. The Mercedes continued onwards without us. Dave rode over beaming from ear to ear, his face burning bright red from the desert sun. Both his bike and Rallye 2 suit were plastered with red mud, dirt and oil.

"In all the cities, in all of the world, how did you come to end up in mine?" he said to general laughter and merriment.

In truth, it was a lucky break. Nouakchott is quite a big city and both his map and ours weren't much use. We set off to where we thought one of the hotels was located and after winding through some very nice streets, lined with large well-kept houses, we stopped outside what looked like a Sheik's palace. Barbara went in to checked the price and emerged from the reception laughing. We moved on. Hotel number two was OK, but the security was hopeless. It was a busy street and I was somewhat put off by a swollen dead dog which was lying on the pavement outside the door.

Third choice was the Auberge Nomades. A travellers hostel and campsite right in the heart of the city. There was secure parking in a high walled and gated yard, room for camping, plus several dark cell-like rooms with low beds and little else. Very basic, but just the job for a night stop. We checked in.

It was great to see the mad Irishman again. He'd had a terrific ride and although not having the chance to soak up the feel of Mali, had covered considerable mileage through the Sahel and Desert. Casamance and Guinea Bissau also sounded like a great experience and he had much to tell.

He had tried to get through the Casamance towards the east in an attempt to avoid going through The Gambia. But the roads had been so bad, he had been forced to ride north, through the central area of The Gambia and back to Kaolack. The road east from there had been good and passing into Mali, he spent time at the place where Simon had died, carving a memorial to him in a Baobab tree which stood nearby.

Although our change in plan had meant an interesting unplanned adventure for Barbara and myself, I was now deeply regretting not keeping my original promise to also visit the site where our friend had died. The time alone with Barbara had been precious and much needed, but I realised that I still had unfinished business in West Africa.

Dave told us that a brand new road now ran from the Senegal border to Kayes in Mali, so it was now even more difficult to figure out what had happened to Simon. A photograph taken by the police at the time of the accident had shown Simon's bike balanced upside down on a dirt track and Dave had managed to locate the site from the position of trees in the picture. Considering the area overall, Dave was now of the view that Simon may have been riding too fast on corrugations and had lost control of the bike when he encountered ruts which had been made by trucks turning off down a side road.

Dave had continued east into Mali, encouraged by the new road. But on reaching Diema, he had found that the road north to Ayoun in Mauritania had not yet been built – as we had suspected back in Banjul. But having been told that the gap in the tarmac was only about 100 kilometres wide, he had pressed on – a full day's riding on indistinct piste, soft sand and open Sahel.

The final stretch to Nouakchott had been an 800 kilometre stretch of good tarmac which he had done in two extremely hot stages.

His GS bore testament to his ride, plastered with earthy souvenirs of his trip. The main cost had been to his tyres. The tread was wearing quite near to the minimum markers on my bike, on Dave's, they were beyond that and heading for 'rizla' status. But there was hopefully enough tread to get home on the reasonable roads that we knew lay ahead.

A British truck full of English folk en route to South Africa was also parked at the auberge. About fifteen of them were crammed into a heavily modified sixteen-ton lorry. All had diverse backgrounds and had signed up for the trip after answering an advert. It was nice to chat to them, particularly to an older Cornish couple. But the three of us felt that this kind of travelling could be a recipe for disaster.

The choice of travelling companions can make or break a journey and is something which should not be taken lightly. Horror stories abound and even for regular travelling partners such as Dave and I, there can be, and are, tensions. We wondered if this crew weren't going to face personal problems ahead – they seemed simply too diverse in character and attitude.

Searching for beer, we took a walk through the Capital's busy streets to the Novotel. Guards at the gates to the hotel grounds ensured that only the rich and favoured were allowed in. Once inside, the contrast between the world of wealth and the realities of everyday life in Mauritania were laid out in stark fashion. The Novotel was in an enclosed and pampered world of its own. This was also reflected in the prices. Small tins of Heineken worked out at about £3.50 each. Meanwhile outside on the street, large sections of the populations grubbed a living on the streets, or in the desert, on perhaps a dollar or two a day if they were lucky.

With this thought leaving a nasty taste in our mouths, we left to look for more reasonably priced food. We ate in a nice pizzeria a few blocks away, where at least we knew that the Mauritanian Ouguiya that we were spending would go back into local pockets.

The next day a pre-dawn start set us on the long Sahara road to Nouadhibou. We discovered that we couldn't get coffee anywhere until after eight am. So forced to visit the Novotel again, we found ourselves spectacularly ripped off for just three cups of coffee. This set Dave off.

"Bloody big corporations, feeding off developing world countries that they sit in like parasites. Charging the earth to keep locals out and taking profits out of the countries that they infest, instead of putting it back to help these countries stand on their own two feet."

"Well they do create jobs, need local suppliers and encourage business to operate." I ventured, knowing what was coming next and content to hear it.

"Yeah, slave labour wages for a handful of local people and a 'developed world' fantasy for executives from parasitic multinationals to hide in." retorted Dave. "Oh and where do you think this overpriced Lavazza coffee came from? – Not bloody Nouadhibou I'm sure."

Sharing Dave's ire, we nonetheless emptied our wallets to pay the bill and headed for the metaphorical 'hills' of sand which awaited us.

We knew that the day's journey to Nouadhibou necessitated extra fuel. I had been concerned at the effect on the bike of the weight of a full jerry-can in addition to Barbara. Once again though, the GS stoically took the additional high-up weight in its stride and we headed purposefully out of Nouakchott for the last time. We rode into the deep desert as the sun rose in the east.

It felt good to be once again riding with Dave and frequent photo and water stops allowed plenty of opportunities for the regular banter which we had enjoyed on the way down. This time joined by Barbara, who was careful not to take sides. It helped the long day pass more easily.

All too soon, the picturesque long marches of dunes gave way to flat sand and gravel desert. This stretch was easily the most featureless of the whole trip, with an uninspiring view stretching from skyline to skyline. But the colours were very different to the journey down. This was partly due to a change in the direction that the light was coming from and partly because a layer of thin cloud created a different 'feel'.

The cloud was to remain with us all day and although it kept the direct heat of the sun away from us, it didn't stop intense waves of solar radiation from breaking through. By the end of the day, Barbara and I were both as red-faced as Dave had been when we met him the previous day. It also helped that as the sun passed its zenith, we were no longer troubled by its glare coming from straight ahead. It made the whole trip north very much more comfortable.

This time we exploited photo opportunities more often. Having a good photographer in the form of Barbara with us, meant some decent pictures could be taken for sponsors. There were also opportunities to mess about in the sand, fall off, get stuck and laugh out loud. But we never strayed far enough from the road to necessitate a back-breaking effort to escape the deep and very soft sand.

On the way down, there had been nothing about the condition of this long stretch of road to excite particular comment. But as the road ran out straight ahead northward on the return journey, we found that sand was increasingly encroaching on the road. It was one of those things which helped to keep the senses sharp. But after negotiating a couple of small, but road-width 'berms' later that day, it seemed apparent that unless regular sand clearance was timetabled, the 'new road' would eventually disappear like a mirage on some sections.

A South African chap had commented on this when we were on the border between the Western Sahara and Mauritania on the journey down "They may have a great road, but the Mauris don't have any decent sand clearance kit like the Moroccans do. Plus they can't seem to stop the locals from digging the bloody tarmac up to use on roofs and boats." Part of his views had proven correct, but we had seen some tired looking sand clearance equipment as we had travelled. Unfortunately no real regime had yet been established for keeping the new road clear, with this evidenced by quite extensive desert encroachment since we had been that way before. However, later journeys revealed that the Mauritanians had indeed taken steps to keep the road open and in fair shape.

We took a break at the rehydration tree, about two thirds of the way north to Nouadhibou. A group of figures emerged from one of a series of tin shacks which stood some way back from the road. Coming over, they offered us a large bowl of what turned out to be camel's milk. I'd never tried it before and was surprised to find that it's slightly lumpy, sweet taste was replaced with a very refreshing feeling in the mouth once swallowed. One of the group recognised Dave and I from before and a pleasant time was spent breaching the language barrier and taking photographs.

At length, the terrain started to change to large areas of broken rock and the road started to turn westwards; the beginning of the final stage of the day's journey.

Although we still had plenty of fuel due to the spare capacity of our cans, we stopped at a fuel station out of curiosity regarding the availability of petrol. Three fuel pumps were there; two diesel, one petrol. One of the diesel pumps leaned drunkenly on its mounts and the rubble forecourt was soaked in spilt fuel.

It seemed that an entire family emerged from a concrete shack to greet us. Lots of smiles all around, accompanied by comments in excited Arabic. Downturned mouths at the mention of 'essence' confirmed the continuing Saharan petrol drought.

"But!" exclaimed an excitable male member of the extended family; "you give me your motorcycle and I will give you my son!" A baby was thrust in my face.

Being suddenly eyeball to eyeball with a small snivelling child with a snotty nose took me by surprise. Dave and Barbara smirked until it became clear that the guy was deadly serious about striking a deal. Making apologies we escaped to lots of shouting and waving from the exuberant family.

The road joined up with the route of the Ore Train.

"Bloody shame you probably won't get to see the Ore Train." I yelled back at Barbara. "One of the modern wonders of the world you know."

"Oh yeah?" she yelled back "So what's that then?" Pointing ahead I made out a long line of low rail cars and a huge cloud of dust billowing over the road.

"Blimey, that's a stroke of luck." I yelled. "Thought this thing only ran two or three times a day."

We caught up with and overhauled the very slow moving

leviathan, the very length of it meaning that we didn't get to the front for a good ten kilometres. We stopped a kilometre or two further on and Dave ran across the 200 yards or so of scrubby sand and rocks which separated rail from road, with his camera at the ready.

The train was slowing down with an ear piercing and seemingly never ending scream of hundreds of brakes. Ore dust was pouring out of each car, caught by the wind, billowing towards us and filling our eyes with grit. The train's passing seemed never ending – an impressive sight.

Finally the last car trundled by and Dave wandered back.

"There's more than 150 ore cars you know."

Then with a thunder of huge diesels an empty train came the other way, building speed as it came.

"Thought this thing only ran occasionally?" said Barbara. "Indeed, indeed. Looks like yer luck's in." replied the Irishman.

More pictures and we pressed on, overhauling the first train again. Harsh daylight was giving way to softer late afternoon tints and we were glad a few kilometres later to see the first of the two checkpoints which marked the approach to Nouadhibou.

While waiting for the obligatory, but laborious long-hand recording of our passport details, the first train hammered by again. This time right by the road. Impressive, huge, dusty and loud. The driver waving from his cab, the dust blackened hitchhikers in each car joining in. It was a memorable sight.

"So that's the third time I've seen it." said Barbara; impressed but trying not to show it. "Bloody men and big machines…"

"Well this one doesn't count, we've seen it already…" said Dave. A fierce stare from my wife halted this line of conversation.

So finally, Nouadhibou and a return to the strange world of shanty style, wrecked, or half-finished buildings. The now familiar worn out and dented cars weaving slowly in and out of the roads and pavements, sharing space with a great mass of pedestrians, donkey carts, hand carts and half dead trucks.

Remembering the anxious hunt for fuel on the way down, we filled up the bikes before looking for accommodation. This time, the second garage we saw had petrol – we'd arrived on a good day.

I thought about getting shot of the fuel cans and discussed this with Dave. But with no guarantee that G1, the isolated first and last fuel station in the Western Sahara, would have petrol, we felt it best to play it safe and ensure that we had at least one full can.

That evening we stayed in another campsite-cum-auberge, which had great, if very basic rooms. It was another of those places which is favoured by overland travellers and the walls of the communal lounge were covered in post cards and posters from all over the world.

We introduced Barbara to the impressively large fish and cans of beer at Restaurant Canaria and later, we tumbled into our beds for one of the best night's sleep of the trip.

Another early start and our last day in Mauritania. A deep fog had settled overnight and the roads were wet, creating a nice slippery mess of wet diesel and finely ground dust. Dave wanted to see the ship wrecks which were known to clutter the coast at Nouadhibou in large numbers. Although I spent the rest of the day wondering if we would complete this 'stage' of the journey, it was worth taking the time out to see the haunting maritime remains.

There were dozens of ships on the beaches outside Nouadhibou. Some were abandoned wrecks, others insurance 'jobs' which had been sailed straight up the beach and left to rot. Most were ocean going deep water trawlers, others quite large freighters dating from the early to mid-20th century.

Riding carefully down the damp coast road in a fog which the sun was doing its best to dispel, the ships started to emerge ghost-like from the eerie early morning mist. We stopped to take some pictures and walked down the beach marvelling at all the wrecked and rusting tonnage which lay with a certain air of grand dignity at their final resting places.

It's a shame that the global demand for metals, mainly from China, has now seen most of these evocative hulks cut up for scrap. Another visual wonder of the world now vanished.

After coffee in the Hotel Ossian, overlooking a bay which seemed alive with closely packed fish, the water looking like a vast live fish soup, we continued our journey north. The Ore Train clattered slowly by again.

"That's the fourth time." said Barbara wearily. "So we're lucky if we see it heh?" I stayed silent.

*

THE ROAD OF BLOOD

Leaving Nouadhibou behind, we took the highway towards the border. After negotiating a few berms of sand which lay across the road, we arrived at the scattered border posts which marked our exit from Mauritania.

In stark contrast to Rosso, there was only a short wait and formalities were speedily completed. We headed into the minefield and no-man's land. No demands for payment and no hustlers. Much more straightforward than on the way down.

Dave, who while in Banjul had jokingly expressed the view to Mutch that minefields were great places to live, proposed that we stopped for lunch in the middle of the muddle of broken tracks and rock which make up the path to the border with the Western Sahara.

"Grand spot indeed." the Irishman remarked in a moment of eccentricity, as we munched on a meal of pastries, figs and biscuits which we'd brought with us from Nouadhibou. The backdrop of the blown up and rusting remains of what was once a car added to the general oddness of our repast.

The weird thing was that it was actually quite nice to sit in the sun of a cooler day than we were expecting. Safe in the knowledge that no one was going to pop up from behind a rock and try and sell us something.

"Hey, you wanna sell some stuff, or buy anything?" The three of us spun around in unison. Unbelievable. There stood a broadly grinning Arab with broken teeth who had crept up from goodness knows where. Was there no end to African persistence?

He told us that he scratched a living buying and selling car parts and exchanging money from a compound of wrecked vehicles just the other side of a small dune. We quizzed him about the minefield.

"Oh, none just here." he said "But walk a minute away from the track and bang!" He made an expansive theatrical gesture. "No one has blown up recently, but it does happen."

He wandered off.

"See, minefields really are grand places to live." said Dave. Barbara battered him on the head with an empty water bottle.

Moroccan formalities were similarly straightforward, though Barbara's lack of visa for any downward journey through Morocco created some interest. A policeman said "Oh, we don't do visas here – you'll have to go back and get one from the consul in Nouadhibou."

Faces dropped all round. "Hah, I got you there!" laughed the comedian copper.

"Hah, bloody hah." I retorted. The cop continued to find the whole joke so amusing that he smeared the entry stamp in my passport and had to annotate Barbara's Moroccan ID number in her passport, having made a complete mess of the stamp as he giggled.

A truck load of Brits showed up travelling south. Passengers were huddled on benches in a flat-bed lorry with clear plastic sheeting rigged up to protect them from the elements – an extremely rough and uncomfortable way to travel.

A few words and we knew straightaway that we really didn't want to talk to them longer than we had to. Goodness knows why, but the idea of sharing time with our fellow countrymen seemed an alien concept. Easy to understand from the Irishman's point of view perhaps, but both Barbara and I felt the same. Odd really, they were friendly people, who seemed understandably a little dismayed at our slightly offhand manner. Our odd attitude to meeting these good folk troubled me for some time afterwards. I never could figure out why we had been so defensive towards them.

Northwards we rode, through ever changing desert terrain. It was almost as though someone had decided to give all the less interesting flat sand to north western Mauritania and the beautiful wild and rocky outcrops of desert to the Western Sahara. It was good to be back, riding past impressive dunes and wind-blown rock.

G1 did have petrol and we pressed on to the beach where Dave took a swim and I'd lost my keys on the way down. He'd already decided that he wanted to camp there that night, while we pushed on 200 kilometres further to Dakhla. Remembering the lovely spot on the way down it seemed like a good choice.

"Great place, this beach." I yelled to Barbara as we rode.

"Strange idea of a 'great' place." said Barbara after we'd arrived a few kilometres later. In the different light of a cooler day, what seemed a wonderful beach some weeks before was in fact a grubby rubbish strewn strand of dumped rubble and grubby-looking sand. The sea and rocks were still nice though.

"Fine company I'm in." retorted my beloved. "This character here" she motioned to Dave "thinks that minefields are great places to live and my husband thinks that rubbish dumps make great beaches. I give up."

"Remind me never to book a package holiday with you guys – we'd end up in Beirut." She added.

"What's wrong with Beirut?" Dave shot back. "Grand beaches and they're not always at war." Barbara laughed helplessly.

"Well I'm staying here anyway." He added. "It's possibly the last chance for some camping and I'm gonna take it. Besides all this rubbish seems to have been washed up, not dumped."

I couldn't figure out why the place seemed so different this time. A grand coastline still, but yes, a great deal of rubbish. The angle of the sun can make a great deal of difference to how a place looks and feels.

We topped up the tank of my GS from Dave's still full jerry can before Barbara and I resumed the journey up the road.

It was approaching late afternoon and the westering sun cast strange light and shadows across the desert. Sand which seemed golden on the way down now appeared grey, then orange. Long shadows from small mesas created optical illusions on the road ahead. There was almost no traffic, just the occasional locally owned Land Rover or European registered vehicle passing us heading south along the snaking road.

We stopped for a while near the Golfe de Cintre and I climbed a mesa to look at the sun sinking towards the ocean a mile or so away. Barbara found dozens of nice examples of the ubiquitous semi fossilised snail shells and carefully packed some of them into her spare clothes. It was warm and peaceful and nice just to be able to spend a little time together on our own.

But the light was starting to fade and we still had 100 kilometres to ride before reaching Dakhla. Pressing on we started to pass the beginnings of habitation, biking past closed fuel stations and small villages. In the distance the sky grew pale and then grey. Odd, as the sun was still up. Then like a smothering blanket, a dense cloud of fog descended around us.

Knocking our speed back to about 35mph, we crept forward through the cool dim gloom. The desert that we could still see took on a cold haunting aspect and the GS's mirrors and my visor fogged up. It was a strange world to ride in and not unpleasant, just a very odd experience. We didn't have far to go now and I was happy to just relax and creep forward, feeling our way along the road.

Then suddenly the fog lifted and ahead of us was the 'outer marker' police checkpoint at the head of the forty kilometre peninsular which Dakhla occupies. A welcome, but brief respite and the fog clamped down again as we travelled the last few kilometres into town. This time it was much heavier and relief at seeing the street lights of Dakhla emerge ghost-like ahead was tangible.

After another night at Hotel Doumes, followed by a leisurely breakfast and we lazily rode to the police checkpoint by the main north/south road. We rode slowly, enjoying the spectacular views of wide seascapes and marching dunes, fully expecting Dave to be late.

"I've been here for over half an hour." he complained. "We've a lot of miles to ride today you know."

Apologies proffered and our two bikes headed northwards once again.

The ride was once again straightforward. The desert had flattened out and mile after lonely mile droned under our wheels. Being much more on what passed for the beaten track in these parts, the road once again had decent markings and traffic was heavier. The majority of this was fish trucks going to and from Dakhla and the huge markets in the north.

Sometimes we'd pass lorries parked on the side of the road, with the driver draining melted ice and fish blood onto the verge.

The stench was overpowering and we held our breath whenever we passed a nasty looking half dried strip of rotting blood on the side of the road. It was something we'd not noticed on the way down.

This discarded blood found its way onto the highway and slick smelly patches were commonplace. Atlantic Route? We re-christened it the 'Road of Blood' – as these fetid spillages and the slippery combination of blood and diesel on the road were commonplace all the way from Dakhla to Tan-Tan.

We stopped whenever there was something interesting to look at and we explored several dried river beds and ancient land-slips. At some point during the day, Dave decided to bury his jerry-can, no longer having a use for it. We waypointed it in my GPS. But when Barbara and I returned three years later, it was gone.

On several occasions we passed the small townships that had captured my attention on the way down. Places which were in as-new condition – new buildings, new roads and other infrastructure – but no people. We decided to explore, riding into the centre of one of these odd places.

Each one consisted of brand new housing, administrative buildings, a mosque, shops and markets. All carefully laid out and ready to use. But every building was boarded up. There were even children's play areas, with swings moving lazily in the breeze.

These places were irregularly spaced along the road and in the middle of nowhere. All very odd. "I reckon that the Government built these places to encourage Moroccans from up north to come and live in the Western Sahara." said Dave. "Think about this. You're wanting to manipulate a referendum to ensure that the country stays under Moroccan control. What better than to dish out free homes, free land and say that people who move here don't have to pay tax."

There was logic in Dave's argument, particularly as Moroccan efforts to keep control of the Western Sahara are well documented.

Later that day we found ourselves stuck at a police checkpoint outside Boujdour. The car ahead of us, a packed taxi, had been stopped and the cops were not too happy with the driver's credentials. A shouting match in Arabic had ensued with the taxi driver employing a creative range of arm waving and foot stamping. What seemed like dozens of his customers extricated themselves from the depths of his weathered Mercedes and stood around in an unconcerned manner.

The police kept their cool, but weren't letting the man go. Sensing that things would work themselves out in African time, we parked the bikes and took our ease on a wall while the spectacle unfolded before us.

The whole thing was certainly engaging for the casual observer, but bit by bit the police were losing their patience as the traffic behind built into a small queue. We were generating visions of arrests and irate cops wanting to give us a thorough going-over as well, when one of them extracted himself from the argument and motioned us to continue along the road.

Not quite beating the falling sun, we made it to Laayoune just after dark. Traffic had become quite heavy as we neared Western Sahara's capital and we were all tired. So the sight of Hotel Stink was welcome. Less welcome was finding that it was full of UN types. So after cruising up and down the main streets of town, which when lit by streetlights, could have been any provincial city in Europe, we settled on the reasonably priced Hotel Jodesa. The bikes were parked out of the way in a disused shop next door.

Pizza seemed like a plan, so we settled on a place which looked likely near the hotel. The food was good and beer was obtained by the owner taking an order and sending one of his lackeys out to buy some from a local source.

The original itinerary had called for us to ride all the way from Laayoune to Agadir the following day. But after riding the long and exhausting distance between these two towns in one hit when travelling down to West Africa, we decided to break the journey in Tan-Tan. This allowed more time to keep my promise to Dave to see the small town of Tarfaya and the monument to Antoine de San Exupery, the aviation pioneer.

On the way we crossed the unannounced border into Morocco itself, finally leaving the deep desert lands behind us and returning to a country which lies on Europe's doorstep.

A few miles further on a break was taken at the edge of a vast hole in the ground which spread into the distance to the east. The edge a dramatic escarpment rather like the location in the movie 'Ice Cold In Alex'. Where the heroes descend in their overlanding wartime ambulance into a huge desert Depression, in their bid to escape the Afrika Corps. The place could have come straight from the film.

Not feeling too much like John Mills, Anthony Quayle and Silvia Syms, we moved onto Tarfaya. This was a tumbledown town of great character. It sat near Cap Juby along some side roads where sand encroached to create wide berms which we negotiated with care.

There was a magnificent promenade and clean beach which looked out to a ruined fortified house from the Napoleonic era. The ruin sat in the surf about 100 yards from the shoreline. The Exupery monument was nearby and proved to be a large rusting model of a biplane. Some local lads came over to practice their English and we gained the impression of Tarfaya as a fairly relaxed town, the most southerly in Morocco.

Leaving town via the sand covered roads, the long haul continued northwards.

For some reason, the day's ride became much less enjoyable. We found that we were stopping more often and generally feeling less positive about the ride, a mood which seemed to have infected all three of us. I figured that we all needed a rest. A lot had happened since Zebrabar and Dave hadn't had a day off since Banjul. I suppose we were all starting to look forward to a change of scene, though there was still a day of Sahara riding to go.

The scenery didn't vary much, though we did see the last of the big desert dunes. In one or two places, these had started to extend across the road.

The wind changed direction and a hot blast came out of the east. Unwelcome, as we had been relishing our escape from the oppressive heat further south.

Late in the afternoon, the Road of Blood passed very near the sea for the last time on the northward route through the Sahara. Seeing a winding track which led to the shore, we rode down some rocky paths to the beach and took a break.

The small cove was near Tan-Tan Plage and was another desert fishing spot. Although remote and beautiful, the beach and surrounding rocky ground were scattered with small fishermen's huts, with the occasional moped propped outside these.

Dave and I parked the bikes strategically so that we could take some photographs. Barbara found an old dog's skull, which Dave taped to his front mudguard in a moment of amusement.

Riding confidently up the steep track to the road, I stopped at the top, realising that it had only taken a few moments to ride the long rocky piste from the beach to the road; and this two-up. The nervous rider who had fallen off after riding about ten yards off road into sand a few weeks earlier had been replaced with someone far more confident in both his bike and his own abilities. It was a good feeling and made me realise that I would miss riding in this region.

The short journey inland to Tan-Tan went via some vast and steep ridges in the land. We overtook several lorries, which were grinding along in first gear, to reach the top of a ridge. Ahead was a spectacular view of Tan-Tan and the hilly countryside around. The flat bleakness of the desert was finally behind us.

Coasting into town, we pulled up at The Hotel Sable D'or and checked in. An enquiry about the possibility of beer at reception drew a blank.

"But." said our female hostess "My son knows someone who may know how to buy beer. You go with him."

Leaving Barbara at the hotel, we walked towards the centre of town with a Moorish looking chap who didn't have much to say for himself, apart from the occasional, "follow me." or "Down here." Tan-Tan was a real gem of a place, with well laid out streets and an extensive market. Shops sold just about everything imaginable and a wonderful vibrancy pervaded the atmosphere.

"We see ourselves as Saharans here, not Moroccans." said our guide. "In Tan-Tan we have our own way of doing things."

They certainly did when it came to getting something alcoholic to drink. Our man flagged down a mate of his in a Mercedes with cracked windows. We all jumped in and roared off for a bewildering tour of town at high speed. Dave kept his hand held GPS on and figured out that when the car stopped ten minutes later, we were only about a hundred yards from where we had first been picked up. There was no charge for this strange ride. What followed was a circuitous tour by foot which took us eventually to a narrow dimly lit alley where our guide asked us to wait.

As he walked further on, a figure extracted himself from a doorway and a hushed conversation took place.

Our man returned and said "Give me 300 dirham. I can get eleven beers."

Taking our grubby notes, he disappeared, with what must have been the look-out into the doorway. He reappeared after about five minutes with a black carrier bag.

"I have beer, we must go. Right now."

No mad car ride this time, just a long walk through the interesting and diverting market and back to the hotel. A can of beer for our guide for his troubles was all that he would accept. We went up to our room, bursting through the door laughing at the experience of 'scoring' beer and relating the amusing experience to a bemused Barbara.

The following morning was our last in the Sahara. Passing regretfully under Tan-Tan's Kissing Camels, we headed for the distant hills of the Anti-Atlas. Riding through the dramatic and ever-rising scenery of the northern edge of the Sahara. We stopped briefly just before Guelmim, on the actual edge of the desert to take a few photos and to bid our farewell to the most amazing of motorcycling experiences.

Climbing aboard the bikes, we waved to a couple who came roaring by. They were heading south on a heavily overloaded 1970s Triumph Bonneville. Hats off to life's truly intrepid motorcycle explorers, I thought. As a Meriden Bonneville owner myself, I wished them the very best of luck.

After Bouizakarne, the Anti Atlas road rose via switch backs to about 3,000 feet and passed through the wonderfully rocky landscape we had enjoyed on the way down. The landscape was mottled with smallholdings, their boundaries marked by numerous dry-stone walls, which wound their way among the hills and valleys. Stopping at the summit, we drank in the landscape to the north. It fell away below us to a distant view of semi cultivated brown and gold coloured hills and valleys.

Descending, we passed through the same smoke filled truck-stop towns that we had seen on the outward journey. The whole Moroccan 'feel' had returned to the ride and I was glad to be back.

We slowly wound our way through hairpins, locked behind lorries which tried to use the entire road on blind corners. Stopping occasionally where the dramatic views allowed a photo opportunity.

Soon we were travelling out onto the plain near the city of Tiznit. We stopped for a break and some fuel.

"I reckon that this road here could be grand." said Dave pointing to the map. He was suggesting taking one of the Michelin 'green routes' from Tiznit to Agadir, via the mountain town of Tafraoute.

Barbara and I also peered at the map.

"Yup, looks like a good trip OK." I said "But I reckon that we'd need to thrash along it if we're to make Agadir tonight."

"Indeed, Indeed." said Dave "Think I'll give it a go anyway. Wanna come along?"

Barbara shrugged her shoulders in a non-committal fashion.

"Nah, perhaps not this time." I said after thinking for a second. "I reckon that we'll head to Agadir, make an early stop, get us all a room and chill out for a bit."

"No probs." Frenchie replied cheerfully. "Get me a beer in and I'll see you later!" He started his engine and roared up the road in a cloud of dust.

We rode the final 100 kilometres, breaking the journey with coffee at a pavement bar which also doubled as a truck stop for several heavy duty Renault pick-ups. These were identically branded by a local business. Eventually, we negotiated Agadir's rush hour traffic to find the hotel that we had used before. Texting the details to Dave, we retired to the comfortable sofas of the bar to watch the world go by.

"They have a dreadful karaoke act and pub singer here." I said to Barbara. "So awful, it's almost laughable."

As if on cue a now familiar form, the lean Moroccan who had assailed our senses last time, appeared at reception. Hauling PA equipment and a synthesiser keyboard. A few minutes later and he was set up for the evening, running through his selection of canned music, a few bars at a time. At a volume which was enough to send even cockroaches scuttling to the corners.

I winced. "Time to find somewhere to eat I think. Dave will just have to text us when he arrives."

We wandered out of the hotel and had a nice stroll along the sea front before settling down at a beach front restaurant for a nice meal of fish, washed down with some excellent local wine. It got dark and as time ticked by, we wondered how Dave was getting on, trying not to feel too concerned about him and his ambitious diversion.

The problem is that things like this prey on the mind and by 9.30pm, I was becoming quite alarmed about his whereabouts. It was not just dark, but also quite cool – in the mountains it was probably brass-monkeys. Then my phone beeped. 'Checked in' said the message. I sighed with relief and settled back to demolish our bottle of wine.

We met Dave back at the hotel. He was grinning and working bottles of Flag into himself as fast as he could.

"What a bloody ride!" he exclaimed. "It was grand for the first half of the route, but then it got dark. Trucks all over the road, cars swervin' about, feckin' dangerous so it was. Then it got bloody cold and there I was inching along at about two mph on this really bad road when the police pulled me up to see if I was OK.

"Mind you, here now." He finished and raised his glass.

"Was it worth it?" said Barbara.

"Indeed, indeed, grand views of the mountains. Took loads of pictures. Got a bit spooked after dark though"

"Have you eaten?" I asked.

"Yup, a pizza at that English-themed place next door." he replied while waving to get the attention of the bar staff.

FISH, PUNCTURES AND ROMANS

Agadir lay near the end of the long and lonely Atlantic Route. Although there was still many miles of great motorcycling to do, we felt a great sense of achievement from having made it across the Sahara and back to the 'beaten track' of Morocco. A sense of sadness as well. But we were looking forward to working our way up a country which had already proved itself to be more interesting and enjoyable than it had done during our previous journey in 2000.

The following day we planned to ride only as far as Essaouira and then take a day off. Before leaving, it seemed only fair that Barbara had a chance to see the fantastic view from the old Kasbah. So after filling up with fuel, we headed up the winding road to the top of the splendid overlook of the surrounding area.

We were joined by a fellow overlander on his BMW R1200GS that we had met in the fuel station. He blatted in and out of the traffic as we followed in a more measured fashion. This guy seemed to know some of the locals and it turned out that he spent a great deal of his time in Morocco, only heading back to Europe when he had to every few months.

"Life's better here." he said.

Two months before I would have thought such a sentiment to be completely bonkers. But having had the opportunity to spend a more extended time in North and West Africa I was much more sympathetic to such a view.

Life is undeniably tough in Africa. It can be dirty, on rare occasions dangerous and hygiene is always an issue. The 'African time' that officials operate on can be mind-numbingly tedious. Corruption is endemic, people and communities are impoverished.

But in the Muslim cultures we visited – so often viewed as oppressive by our media and politicians – the sense of community really shone through. People were friendly and helpful just about everywhere we went. Aside from the numerous police checkpoints, it felt like there was true freedom of the roads for the traveller and a lack of commercialism.

I also appreciated absence of any form of Western political

correctness and the kind of puritanical nimbyism and peevish commentary about small lifestyle choices that increasingly pervades life in England. It made me wonder about the kind of intrusive and judgemental society that was emerging in Northern Europe. The certainties of the Cold War replaced by the ever widening hunt for the 'enemy within' in social terms.

But this was a travellers 'rose-tinted specs' view of things. We were operating on a different 'level' to those who live in Morocco, A Westerner refreshed by the lack of speed cameras, off-roading bans, or a restaurant smoking ban, is not exposed to cultural laws and norms in the same way a local person is. These can be far more individually oppressive than a ban on firing up the evil weed in a European bar.

Try being a woman in much of Africa for example – or holding public views that are contrary to prevailing social and religious attitudes. Perspective needs to be maintained when enjoying what to us seems to be a freer life outside our increasingly homogenised and politically correct Europe – when in reality, life for many is much less free.

We sat for some time looking at the spectacular view from the Kasbah walls as the sun rose higher and a pleasant warmth set in. The huge port was largely empty and only faint noises came from the town below.

We bade goodbye to our friend on the BMW and set off along the coast road northwards. Passing again through small the small coastal communities which catered for the European surfing trade. We stopped a few times along the coast to admire the huge surf and the skill displayed by refugees from northern European winter weather – where the surf is good, but the water frigid.

Taking a coffee break in the small town of Tamanar, we were joined by yet another BMW GS rider. This time the bike was a lot older – an original R80 G/S. The rider was a member of a party which was swapping travelling time between a truck and various bikes they had brought with them. Their intention was to work their way to Dakar, following some of the route of the forthcoming Dakar Rally.

Before we departed, I noticed that the dog's skull had disappeared from Dave's mudguard.

"Ah, yes, I took it off last night." said Dave. "It was dark, cold and, well, things started to seem a bit weird on the road out of the mountains." He turned away and put his helmet on.

So I wasn't the only one who got nervous from time to time.

"You want to watch out for your reputation as Iron-Man Dave." I said. "Mutch would be most disappointed." The Irishman smiled.

Leaving the coast behind us, the road wound its way through rolling stony hills full of Argan trees. Local people hopefully waved jars of Argan oil from makeshift stalls by the side of the road. We only stopped once though and that was to stroke some camels and chat to the herder, who was also looking after a party of goats. One camel was genuinely friendly, the other one seemed more interested in chewing on Dave's Rallye suit.

Arriving in Essaouira later that day, we checked into the Hotel Tafraoute, which was on the seafront. There was an excellent panorama of the long beach and the bay beyond. The rocky outcrops of a small island could also be seen. Dave had stayed there with Anna in 2000. It was good to relax in the knowledge that there was no riding the following day.

Dave had enthused about the Chez Sam restaurant on several occasions, having had a memorable fish dinner there on his last visit. The restaurant is right inside the small port, with great views of the coastline. The port itself was showing no signs of winding down for the evening and many of the traditionally built trawlers were getting ready to put to sea. Others, packed with hard working crews, were chugging into the harbour to moor among crowds of people who were waiting to open holds and offload the catches. The crews made ready for sea again while the boats were emptied of cargo.

This was traditional sardine fishing. Using methods which have long since been replaced elsewhere by factory fishing, which involves huge ships and extensive mechanisation. When the three of us had been in Nouadhibou, overlooking the 'fish soup' bay at Cansado, Dave had told us about an Irish registered factory ship. A vast behemoth which trawled the oceans, hoovering up fish for western market consumption. A pariah which was barred from many ports, it had been implicated in fishing stock depletion, particularly off the West African coast.

The fleet was operating quite close to shore. The need for a fast turnaround using the antiquated and highly labour intensive methods meant a hubbub of activity such that I hadn't seen since I was a small boy staying with my family in Cornwall.

Our restaurant table afforded a view of all that was going on in the port. The place had a theme which was a cross between an old ship and a traditional pub, rather like many found in the English countryside. A fire roared in one corner. A barrier against the now much cooler evenings. Light Jazz music played quietly from stereo speakers and the walls were lined with photos covering a variety of subjects, many music based.

"You don't get much fresher fish than this." said Dave as steaming platefuls of local produce were served up. Washed down by even better Moroccan wine than we had tasted so far. Small trawlers chugged in and out past the windows and the whole thing was very atmospheric.

"I have this mental picture of some guy on a boat slinging our fish straight into a waiting pan as he chugs by." added Barbara.

We simply didn't have it in us to do much the following day. Barbara and I hung around the hotel and Dave spent much of his time reading a book. It soon became apparent that we were all subconsciously looking for a reason to take a further day off in the lovely town.

Hanging around at the hotel wasn't a bad way to spend time. The place itself was quite well laid out and decorated in a pleasant if nondescript way. There were good facilities and an excellent coffee bar next door. The view out to sea was superb and we regularly saw trawlers sail by, closely followed by clouds of seagulls. Barbara sunned herself on the beach and we both went for a long walk later in the day. A relaxed evening in the hotel bar set us up nicely for a good night's sleep.

The following morning we had a light breakfast and discussed what to do. The notion of pressing on to Rabat that day, our next scheduled stop, did not raise feelings of enthusiasm. But this raised an immediate problem with ferry and flight bookings. An extra day at Essaouira meant missing the ferry from Bilbao and subsequently, Dave's flight to Poland from London. Our actions that day were dependent on resolving these travel issues.

Barbara hit the phone and found that changing the ferry booking was unexpectedly easy. Though missing the new booking, meant a long ride through a frozen France, given that this was P&O's last sailing of the year. The flight was another matter and it took several calls before a new booking could be arranged.

Feeling satisfied with ourselves, we took a gentle stroll to explore the town. We loitered around the port, taking pictures of the boats and the hubbub of activity. After this we wandered the old town and Kasbah, enjoying the Portuguese fortifications and market wares. Lunch was at a rather expensive pavement fish bar, though the location adjacent to the port was perfect. We enjoyed meals that we picked out ourselves from a stall at the front. A great display of variety and colour from the various species of fat fish which were offered.

Barbara's live Cray Fish made an escape bid from the tray after they had been selected, but before long they were cooked. Served along with our other meals of bass and bream – washed down with clean water.

That evening we ate in the Hotel Villa Maroc. Barbara had found the place in the guidebook and we had visited it and booked dinner during the afternoon, while Dave had been exploring the less tourism orientated parts of town. The meal had to be paid and the menu chosen long enough in advance to allow enough time for the hotel to purchase the food. It was all rather exclusive.

The Villa Maroc itself was a converted medieval town-mansion, or Riad, with small courtyards open to the sky. A small anonymous front door opened into a Tardis-like building of numerous passages, communal areas and small rooms, all making for a labyrinthine hotel. The place dripped with traditional Moroccan style and antique furniture.

We ate in a private suite with beautiful décor and a roaring fire. It was one of those places which engendered total relaxation assisted by pleasant conversation and good food. Highly recommended and less than £10 each for a five star experience. After several bottles of excellent Moroccan wine, we quietly chatted until Barbara fell asleep on the huge cushions and my eyes started to droop.

"Aw, let's stay here tonight." Barbara protested as I shook her into a semblance of wakefulness. Staying felt like an attractive suggestion as we stepped out into the cool night air.

Dave got us out of bed earlier than usual the following morning.

"It's cracking weather and I want to travel!" he declared. We loaded the bikes and with a great deal of regret set off once again.

Instead of the grind of the long main road to Marrakech and then onto Rabat, we chose instead to ride the coast road via Safi and El-Jadida. We joined the road out of town via an unplanned diversion into less salubrious quarters of town. In one place we had to turn back to avoid riding through a vast lake of discarded engine oil which filled the street.

The more detailed map of Morocco makes a mistake here, showing the road going directly north from the centre of town. In fact one needs to travel east before joining the road north.

Very quickly, sand and rock gave way to green grass and scrub. The road wound its way along a dramatic coastline with tumbling cliffs and long beaches. The rolling hills covered in welcome green pasture after weeks of desert sand and glare. Dry stone walls divided the hillsides and long, low stone buildings became the norm. The area felt like Dartmoor.

Several photo opportunities afforded themselves and it was nice to have the excuse to stop and warm up. The weather was clear and sunny, but cooler weather had finally arrived and warm liners had gone back in our suits.

We stopped in Safi for coffee, after passing through an unpleasant industrial complex on the edge of town. There was a huge chemical works, disgorging millions of gallons of effluent straight into the sea. An unpleasant scar on a beautiful landscape.

We didn't see much of the town itself, only the main road through. But the greater prosperity of the area was obvious, both in the condition of the buildings and the large number of new cars on the streets.

Between Safi and El-Jadida, the land gave way to intensive agricultural small holdings. We passed pick-up after pick-up loaded with carefully packed vegetables of every kind imaginable.

El-Jadida is a resort which caters for holidaying Moroccans. Wide boulevards passed through avenues of tall white buildings. We took lunch in a roadside café. The brochettes and Coke were welcome enough, but not the extortionate bill or, for me, the loose bowels that were to later follow.

The road north from town was immediately of excellent quality. The wide smooth tarmac was a contrast to weeks of rougher road and tracks. The only problem was that any idea of road sense among the local drivers seemed to vanish and we found ourselves competing with Roman style driving aggression and high speed overtaking. The number of rusting car wrecks on the side of the road increased and we found ourselves alternating between riding cautiously to avoid possible near misses and riding much faster to avoid being cut up by overtaking lunatics.

A few miles of this tiring riding and we entered a busy town which was full of trucks and long queues of traffic. Police were diverting traffic down a rough side road which added to the chaos. Then after only about two kilometres, the road suddenly improved once again and took us out onto a modern motorway slip road.

After a month of the most varied riding conditions we had ever encountered, we found ourselves back on the Moroccan motorway network. Gaining speed on the smooth six-lane blacktop which slashed through the countryside ahead.

An hour later and we were pushing through rush-hour Rabat, negotiating the busy streets and major routes of the capital city. So European and such a contrast from weeks past. There was no particular joy in returning to what we in the UK are conditioned to consider normality. I thought wistfully of the quieter roads and picturesque locations further south.

Finding a hotel that was reasonably priced and comfortable didn't take long, but as we waited for Barbara to check us in, Dave's front tyre promptly went flat.

"Not having the best few days are we?" I said. Dave groaned and said nothing. Of all the places to get a puncture, this had to be one of the best though. The hotel allowed us to use their underground garage so, in warmth and light, we took our time replacing the inner tube in Dave's front wheel.

The Ultraseal 'Smurfs Blood' we had filled the tubes with before setting out weeks before, had done a partial job in that a disastrous blow out had been avoided on Rabat's busy roads. There was a small rip in the inner tube, but air only came out slowly, partially blocked by the Ultraseal compound. Less pleasant was cleaning the mess of dripping sealant out of the wheel and tyre. But on balance, I do feel that the blue gunge had saved Dave from a more dramatic incident.

Barbara retired to our room for a bath, so Dave and I sank a few beers in the hotel's secluded bar. As with so many Moroccan city hotels, several prostitutes hung around, waiting their chance to catch the eye of the many suited businessmen who came in for a drink.

Barbara joined us looking clean, but slightly bothered.

"I was in the bath and couldn't shake off the feeling that someone was in our room." she said. "But the door was locked, so it was all rather odd. It was a really strong feeling."

A pizzeria provided dinner. A clean western place where service was slow and choice was limited. We were too tired to look further afield for a meal, so this place had to do. My pizza arrived long after the other two had started to eat theirs. The waiter knocked a full glass of Coke into my food. Not the best evening of the journey.

I woke up the following morning feeling like death warmed up. Vivid and alarming dreams had stalked my sleep. Barbara reported the same strange experience.

"Perhaps it was the cheese at the pizzeria." remarked Barbara, who otherwise felt OK. I, on the other hand, felt as sick as a dog.

Bleary eyed and ill, I picked at my breakfast as the day's plan was discussed.

Rescheduling the ferry meant that we had actually gained an extra day. The original plan had been to ride straight to Ceuta and then onto Gibraltar the following day. But Dave now suggested visiting the Roman ruins at Volubilis near Meknes.

We had both been there in 2000 and the road north from there made for a great ride.

I wasn't enthusiastic. I had been looking forward to the chance of seeing Gibraltar again and favoured a straight run north.

My bad night also felt like a sign that we had dawdled enough and should focus on getting back to Spain early, allowing time to rest for a day in Gibraltar before dropping Barbara in Malaga for her flight home.

Barbara had the deciding vote and opted to see Volubilis.

"When am I next going to get the chance to see the place?" she asked. "Seems silly not to go." This of course was the common sense decision. I popped an Imodium.

We left Rabat along the modern motorway to Meknes, partly retracing our year 2000 steps. A good, if bland, road, livened up by the occasional pedestrian or goat crossing the highway. Plus the occasional hand held speed camera of the Gendarmerie Royale. There was little of the colourful motorway 'life' that we'd experienced years before.

The terrain quickly changed from flat lowlands covered in forests of cork to vast rolling brown hills, rising towards the Middle Atlas in the distance. The motorways swept through deep valleys and over huge steep hummocks. It was incredibly picturesque and I felt better for being on the road again.

We passed swiftly through Meknes, wincing at the incongruous sight of a McDonald's drive-thru near the gates of the famous old Kasbah. We headed north on a single track road towards Moulay-Idriss.

Once out of Meknes, the road traversed more rolling green countryside, through vast fields of olives. The harvest was in full swing and we saw huge piles of olives outside several smallholdings, being sorted and made ready for market.

It was good to see Moulay-Idriss again, five years after Dave and I had last visited and a chance to wash away the memory of the row I'd had with Anna on that trip. The spiritual city lying on a steep escarpment of hills, the white buildings and steep passages curved around the folds of the hills. The huge mosque and market a focal point.

The white pillared market square proved to be a good place to stop for coffee. It was a busy day and the bustle of people and stallholders bellowing through hand held bull-horns in competition with each other, added to a very pleasant melee. Interruptions were offered by regular wailing from the numerous minarets.

Dave explored the narrow streets while Barbara and I took in the street scene with our coffees. The three of us later looked around the main square and marvelled at the huge crowds of people going in and out of the medieval gates to the medina.

Volubilis was only five minutes ride from the town and we spent a few hours wandering the dramatic ruins. For Barbara, this was a first visit and she was determined to make the most of it. Dave was also enthusiastic to see the place again.

I could see that we had no hope of making Gibraltar that day and felt irrational impatience with our lack of progress. The feeling spoiling my return to this fantastic set of ruins.

Since we had last visited, a lot of building work had been done to develop tourist infrastructure within the site. Diggers moved around adjacent to the site and buildings were springing up.

I had mixed views about this. Back in 2000, the site was quiet and empty, with only a basic guidebook to dull or enliven the imagination that such a place evokes. Our visit this time saw us running a small gauntlet of 'guides', building work and a modern 'interpretation' of history in the detailed and glossy literature that was on offer.

I can see the value of developing educational resources at Volubilis, but all too often this means a 'themed experience' and reduced accessibility to the sites themselves. One only has to see how Newgrange in Ireland has changed over the last twenty years to understand this. I prefer my historical experiences to be delivered in a straight manner, not 'interpreted'. This all too often involves a kind of revisionism which is tainted by inappropriately modern PC attitudes to the past, plus related ideologies.

Additionally, the huge building works that were taking place seemed to be badly prioritised when the need to preserve the wonderful mosaics, which were exposed to the elements was clear.

I was convinced that they'd faded somewhat since we saw them in 2000. Dave felt that I was imagining things as the mosaics were so ancient. But we didn't know when they were first exposed to the elements – this may only have been in recent years. Some kind of protection was needed from the worst effects of exposure to sun and rain.

Leaving the ancient site, we rode along more minor roads which allowed great views and the chance to experience the quieter backwaters of northern Morocco for the final time. The road was full of ruts and in many places the right hand edge simply fell away due to badly laid foundations, but it was still a very enjoyable ride.

As the afternoon wore on, we held a discussion about staying at a campsite near the town of Ouazzane, another of our stops on the 2000 trip. But this time I argued strongly to press on as I was keen to minimise the journey across to Europe the next day. Barbara supported me, but I could tell that Dave had been keen to stop.

Ahead of us rose the mighty Rif Mountains, famous for Berbers and drugs. As the road started to climb through some of the most spectacular scenery of the entire trip, the temperature plummeted, but in a way which seemed to creep up on us. It was only when we stopped for a short break that I realised that I was absolutely freezing.

Dave's enthusiasm had returned.

"These views are great in this light." he said, as I struggled into warmer clothing. He wandered off to take some pictures and we stood for while enjoying the cool light of the low sun.

The encroaching darkness meant that we settled on Chefchaouen for our last night in Africa. To get there, we left the spectacular views of the mountain highway and headed higher on a more minor, but very busy road. This took us across a tall crest and as the land beyond opened out, we saw the breath-taking view of the small white city spread out before us; a haunting view in the last sunlight of the day. The towering mountains beyond adding a dramatic backdrop to the ancient city.

We checked into the Hotel Rif. Basic but clean and with an incongruous picture of a ruined Cornish engine house on the stairwell. The owner spoke good English and directed us to a restaurant which apparently served beer. Our walk there took us through the ancient medina and narrow alleys crowded with small stalls and shops set into the old stone walls, selling pretty much anything that you could think of. Barbara bought a small bottle of Argan oil and Dave stocked up with spices.

The narrow passages opened into the main square, which surrounded the old Kasbah and mosque. The square was lined with several restaurants and the low light against a backdrop of medieval buildings and tall trees projected an almost Christmas-like air in a light mist of a cool winter's evening.

The recommended restaurant proved to be a tall building with traditional Berber-modelled rooms, painted turquoise-blue at several levels. A rooftop area had spectacularly atmospheric views over the town. Braving the cold, this was where we ate, enjoying tagines, brochettes and fruit juice, the promised beer failing to materialise.

A tall cedar tree had been draped with lights, further lending a festive feel to the view, filled as it was with medieval buildings.

"Stuff London for Christmas." said Barbara. "I reckon this place has a more authentic feel – and, bizarrely, it's Muslim!"

We took a final walk around the market, stopping to buy a few souvenirs before retiring to the Hotel Parador for a nightcap of Casablanca beer in its discrete bar. Then back to our accommodation for a well earned kip.

*

OFFAL AND WINE

Our final day in Morocco started with a terrific ride through challenging Rif Mountain twisties on the road towards Tetouan. We hoped to make the ferry at Ceuta before lunchtime, though much depended on how long it took to get out of Moroccan jurisdiction at the border crossing in Ceuta.

We only stopped briefly for photographs and coffee and were soon bypassing Tetouan, which sprawled its grubby suburbs in all directions from the city centre.

Soon we were on the multi-roundabout dual carriageway of the road to Ceuta. Diving in and out of moderate traffic, we found ourselves part of a group of mixed large touring bikes with Spanish number plates.

The ocean ran alongside the road and the promontory of Ceuta was standing out in the distance. We continued to follow the Spaniards as they entered the customs compound at Sebta/Ceuta and past the long line of traffic waiting to get through.

The usual mêlée of hustlers were ready for us, but we resolutely followed the Spanish riders who ignored the gesticulating crew of robed Moroccans and eased themselves up to the border gates. The guard waved the first bike through and the others followed without stopping. As did we, unconcerned for now that we'd not stopped for Morocco exit stamps in our passports. Ah well, I'd be happy to argue about that when we returned.

Yes; we knew that we would indeed be back.

Spanish border controls took no interest in us and it seemed like seconds later we were spat out into the noise and confusion of the little enclave of Ceuta itself and back in EU territory.

We lunched in Ceuta. A strange experience and very Spanish. Packed with families on a Sunday outing. It was warm on the coast and the sun shone. Overweight people abounded, a sight that we'd not seen for many weeks – even among the richer communities of Africa. This sparked an inconclusive debate about European dietary habits.

Anticipation marked the ferry journey from Algeciras to Ceuta weeks before, sadness and reflection the return trip. So many things experienced, seen and felt. Much to think about as well. We sat on the stern of the fast ferry looking at the Rif disappear into the distance, lost in our own thoughts.

But we still had Europe to cross. Arriving at Algeciras in the late afternoon light, we headed straight for Gibraltar, aiming to find a hotel before it got too dark.

After jumping a huge queue of traffic to negotiate the border, we crossed the airfield into the town, marvelling again at English road signs. Dave checked into a youth hostel while Barbara and I settled on the more luxurious Hotel Bristol. This was to be our last night together before Barbara flew home from Malaga and although the place was quite expensive, it did seem on balance to offer the comfortable night's stay that we both desired before parting for a few days.

After an evening of English beer and food, amused at the oddities of Sterling currency in cashpoint machines and lager louts in bars, we set our minds to the relentless miles which awaited us on Spanish winter motorways.

Day one of the Spanish section saw us press on with a grim determination to get as far as we could in one hit. We left Gibraltar at first light, hammering up the autoroute towards Malaga.

Seeing Barbara going through the departure gate at the airport was a wrench and not just for me. The three of us had made a great team in Africa and Dave also knew that he'd miss her bright company and sense of humour on the cold grinding miles ahead in Spain. We looked forward to seeing her again in four days.

Riding away from the airport, my bike felt light and the empty space behind me was alien. I felt a well of sadness and a desire to get the hell on with the ride, put miles under my wheels and get home as fast as possible.

Reduced daylight hours and growing cold didn't stop us from putting hours at a time in on the saddle. Only stopping when our fuel tanks were dry. Trying to maintain a steady seventy mph, while Jack Frost slowly crept into our riding gear. We climbed the hills towards Granada, as the temperature fell with the altitude and headed north to Juan. The motorway negotiated snow covered mountain peaks. Ever northward we rode, measuring stops by the number of times we needed fuel.

We were soon clad in every stitch we had and I was grateful for my heated jacket. This was a piece of kit that for weeks had seemed an entirely useless addition to my baggage, but which now came into its own. The heated grips were also welcome for the first time.

But by five pm we'd had enough. As dusk settled and a freezing mist rose, we checked into a very nice roadhouse just south of Madrid for some welcome hot food, wine and shut-eye.

Frost blanketed everything as we departed the following

morning. The lonely motorway stretched north and we settled down to eat miles.

The confluence of motorways in and around Madrid was frantic with traffic and like a plonker, I took a wrong turn, dumping us both in the city centre. Riding aimlessly through busy streets, I peered at my GPS trying to find a way out. Dave casting me the odd jaded look when we waited at traffic lights.

Half an hour later we were free, but behind on time as we headed up the motorway towards Burgos. Climbing ever higher through the frost, clouds and into the Sierra De Guadarrama.

The 3,000 ft high pass at Puerto De Somosierra was bitterly cold. But it also marked a weather front and we broke through to brilliant sunshine the other side. The weather stayed bright until beyond Burgos, we found ourselves in freezing fog again. This slowed our rate of progress as Dave became concerned about his almost treadless tyres on the slippery surface.

But soon we were traversing the southern edge of the western Pyrenees and started the long descent to Bilbao.

We were looking for a roadside hotel which meant we would have only a short ride to the port the following day. But aside from seeing one many miles up in the mountains – further away than we wanted to ride the following morning – it seemed that our luck had finally ran out.

Finally, reaching the east west motorway that runs along the northern coast, we passed the turn off to Bilbao and rode a few miles through an industrial area looking for somewhere to stop. Then high on a hill by the motorway, we saw the sign we had been hoping for.

Our final night in mainland Europe saw us safely ensconced in a nice little hotel about fifteen kilometres from the ferry port. A mood of celebration overtook us and after a few beers in the hotel's small bar, we wandered down the road to another bar, a place which was like the front room of someone's home. Good beer flowed before we set off looking for food.

A restaurant was nearby, but the fare was purely local Basque and the menu incomprehensible. We took a risk and ordered what turned out to be pigs trotters in a thick tasty sauce.

We did our best, but neither of us could face finishing the

plates full of greasy fat and jelly like flesh, so we tried again with the menu. This time large chunks of oxtail, gravy and potatoes arrived. Much better.

Two bottles of wine washed down our meals. Conversation flowed and we found much to make us laugh, the stresses and strains of the six week journey now behind us.

Several nightcaps were drunk in a night club over the road. Not so much a night club, but a good quality brothel, where girls plied their trade from a comfortable bar. No one seemed to mind that we were only there for the drink and we were left alone to tour the range of beers which were available behind the bar.

Groaning from monumental hangovers, we arrived at the port at lunchtime the following day and waited for the delayed ferry. Another English biker was also waiting, his shattered bike propped against a wall. He'd tail-ended a lorry on the motorway after coming down off the mountain passes.

He was philosophical about the whole thing and we killed time talking biking matters with him as we waited for the ferry.

The Pride of Bilbao had suffered an engine failure on the way south from England. But we were assured that there would be no problem making Portsmouth, though we would now arrive six hours late.

When we finally boarded, late that afternoon, it seemed that we were finally leaving our journey behind and the real everyday world of our regular lives once again beckoned.

The crossing was uneventful, though an irritating deep swell was running in the Bay of Biscay. Both of us were very tired and not looking forward to journey's end. After all we had seen and done, it seemed more than a little odd to have to readjust to Christmas in northern Europe.

Hordes of drunken, booze-cruising Brits didn't do much for our general mood either. Fat, scantily clad girls staggered about, acres of flesh on view, bulging from over-tight clothing. One or two were violently sick in corners. Yobbish binge-drinking twenty-something men bellowed drunkenly and aggressively at each other, vying to see who could down the largest quantity of cheap lager. The entire tacky tableau dismayed us. We retired to our cabin feeling fairly disgusted with our own kind.

The following afternoon, while relaxing on our bunks, watching the English Channel drift by, we discussed how we had felt about travelling together.

"Let's be honest, we pissed each other off this time didn't we." I ventured.

Dave nodded. "Yes, but not fatally so. It didn't seem wise to moan too much about things did it?"

I agreed. "Perhaps sometimes it's best to deal with a problem by not dealing with it – if you know what I mean."

"Yup, not all the time, but perhaps for us it was the best thing to do."

"How do you feel about what we've done together?" I asked.

Dave started to smile. Slowly at first, then a broader smile.

"Ground breaking mate. A classic."

This wasn't an 'air-clearing' conversation, just an acknowledgement that we both had faced issues with each other and learned from them.

Would we travel together again? Yes. What we had learned about each other was experience which would only strengthen further travelling partnerships, not weaken them.

Had my overall feelings about Dave changed? No. Being regarded as a friend by David is and always will be a remarkable privilege as far as I'm concerned. We've come a long way together since that damp day in Luxembourg all those years ago and I reckon that we'll go much further together in the future.

In a similar way that he had seen us off from Beckenham, Steve Manning was waiting behind the lens of his video camera on the ferry ramp, making us feel welcome and marking the official end of the journey. He accompanied us on the final stretch to London.

The trip in the dark along motorways seemed alien after our experiences. The vast heart of increasing social confusion, which is Britain's capital lay ahead.

As we arrived in Beckenham and turned the final corners to my home, we knew that our journey had reached its end.

It was two am, but a welcoming committee of Barbara and Mutch were there to greet us, help us unload the bikes and break open a bottle of champagne for a cheerful toast to our collective achievement. Everyone was laughing and smiling, the mood was fantastic as we downed glasses of bubbly in our dark and frozen garden.

So we did it. All the planning worked, the support from our sponsors, in particular BMW and Metal Mule, had made it happen.

There are so many thoughts and impressions which arise from the journey. But we were both pleased that we had achieved the aims of the trip and paid tribute to Simon. We were extremely grateful to everyone who had helped to make it happen.

We learned much from our time with Riders for Health which made us realise the importance of the work that Simon had started on Indonesia. Work which follows broadly in the footsteps of Riders for Health successful and effective healthcare logistics programme.

Dave and I can't avoid the imagery that arises from what some read as the completion of Simon's Millennium ride. This is not a comfortable association for me as some may view this as impertinence. I am sure that Simon would have had many more adventures and made much more impact on the people that he met. But it seems highly likely that we took pretty much the same African route north that he would have taken.

Our trip was inspired by Simon's Millennium Ride and a personal commitment to continue his work through Motorcycle Outreach from both Dave and myself. Our Bikes carried the Millennium Ride logo in addition to Motorcycle Outreach and Riders for Health. I hope that our own achievement, as small as it is, helped to keep the spirit of Simon's ride alive. I also hope that what we did highlighted the extremely important work of Riders for Health in Africa and the equally important work that is being done in Indonesia – and now also in Tanzania – via Motorcycle Outreach.

It's been a long journey since that cold day in Swindon when I first met Simon. A journey of personal discovery and inspiration. A path of life which has been partly steered by what Simon and I did together, or had shared beliefs in. He may be gone now, but his spirit still feels near. I'm glad that Dave and I played a small part in his own life's path.

Dave had to leave early on December 23rd for his flight back to Poland and later that morning I found a note that he'd written wishing us all a merry Christmas, adding 'we finished the Millennium ride'.

I hope that Simon is pleased.

THE END

Epilogue: Ambidedi, Mali,

February 2008

The exhaust of our battered BMW R1200GS popped and grumbled as I slowed down. The boxer engine making the mildest of complaints as it was forced to ingest the low octane 'pool' quality 'essence' that it'd been fed at the hand-cranked fuel pump back at the Senegalese border settlement of Diboli.

The heat pressed down us with a fiery intensity that sent temperatures soaring into the mid-forties. The huge bulbous trees of the dense Baobab forest appeared to be wilting under the weight of the dry Sahel heat.

It had been an epic three week ride down to Mali. Hotter than in 2005 and there had been fierce sand storms in the Mauritanian Sahara that had tested our endurance as the sand rose around us and the road ahead disappeared. The GS had been sandblasted to bare metal in many places along one side. We were both red faced and desiccated.

But our bike, again provided by BMW GB, had shrugged such challenges off, despite being overloaded for our research expedition to Guinea-Bissau and the edge of Equatorial Africa. This was a journey that we were undertaking on behalf of GlobeBusters Motorcycle Expeditions and would repeat only a few months later, but this time with twelve other bikes.

I stopped under the shade of one of the mighty behemoths. We were adjacent to a junction which led from the smooth tarmac of the new road, along a rough unmade piste and into the bush. A road sign pointed along it to Daramane and Sobokou. Dave's waypoint was clear in the centre of our GPS screen.

We alighted from the GS and stood quietly for a while before I walked over to the bare patch of ground by the junction where it had happened.

I looked up and down the road and tried to think what it must have been like that day in March 2005 when Simon came this way and was forced to release his spirit. The emotion of the moment became too much and I bowed my head.

A little later, Barbara and I paced about for a while. Getting a feel for the place, speculating a little about what had occurred here in 2005.

The tarmac road wasn't here then, though we knew where Simon had his accident, having seen the police reports.

A lorry driver had seen Simon overtake him at high speed only a few minutes before the crash. Poor old Si, trying to make up lost time as always. I remembered one of his last messages to me, saying that he needed to get across the Sahara before April to make an event in Gibraltar that month.

I took some comfort from the fact that he'd achieved his ambition to ride around the world on two wheels – Ambidedi is geographically west of his home town in Devon.

We found the tree where Dave had carved his message, the rough text now weathered and grown-in to become part of the Baobab. I carved my own message of remembrance. Others who knew Simon were to do the same in the future, as they passed by this place and 'Simon's Tree' has become a place of pilgrimage for some.

We sat down and broke out some food and drink. It was a peaceful spot and there was very little traffic. There was little sound from birds, most of whom were probably sheltering from the heat of the day. The inquisitive baboons that Dave had reported were also hidden away.

After a time, we found new heart and started chatting cheerfully again, enjoying the rest after a hard morning's riding.

But Kayes, our next destination, deeper into Mali, called and with regret we rode away from this peaceful place.

I had finally kept my promise.

End Piece: by Ian Mutch

To describe Simon Milward without resorting to familiar clichés about what a great guy he was and how he was always happy and how he loved life and lived it to the full, and let nothing get him down, is hard. It's more than hard, it's impossible, because in his case those clichés all fit. They fit so well in fact that they might have been designed for him.

It takes a certain kind of crazy optimist to abandon their home life and move to a country where they have no roots and don't speak the language. To do this in order to represent the interests of a group of people who on the whole don't want their interests represented, in the face of a giant and largely undemocratic bureaucracy, reflects a level of positive thinking that might be classed as a mental disorder and Simon was a bit barmy – thank God.

That he achieved what he did for FEMA against such odds is a testament to his supreme obstinacy. He wasn't the slickest talker or the best organised and disciplined of people and he cut an unusual figure amidst the corridors of Brussels in his biker gear with his permanently wind-blown appearance. Even when seated at a table with his paperwork he had that kind of vigorous disheveled look that made you think he was still moving.

It would be hard to imagine a greater contrast than that which he made with the usual manicured lobbyists who populate the EU chambers with their surgically prepared presentations. The fact that he was as successful as he was, hinged to a great extent on the obvious sincerity and overpowering enthusiasm that bubbled out of him. In dealing with Simon, the politicians knew at once that they were dealing with someone who lived and breathed the life he was defending, not some polished mercenary for big business with a well-rehearsed script.

It was that same cheerful gung ho quality that carried him around the world through so many desperate and dangerous places. The steel mud flap he used to deflect bandit's bullets in Colombia was a metaphor for the hilarious optimism that coloured his every effort.

On his trip Simon must have curbed his appetite for speed to have got as far as he did. Back in Europe there was no doubt that he was an enthusiastic rider who explored the potential of engines to the despair of anyone stupid enough to lend him a bike. Importers came to look philosophically on their investment in Simon as a rigorous extension of their R&D programmes.

You might think that the hardships and challenges of a world trip by motorcycle would focus all effort on self-preservation but Simon's first thoughts seemed to be for the underprivileged and desperate of this world with whom his journey brought him into direct contact. His writings suggest that the journey's humanitarian focus was what really sustained his obsessive commitment to what became a life mission. He even sold his house during the course of his travels to fund the trip which grew from a planned eighteen month sabbatical into an unending odyssey of discovery and altruistic effort on behalf of others.

Despite the impression that his spectacular, not to say, completely out of order partying appetite might have conveyed, Simon was a deeply spiritual man. The first hand contact with so many of the wonders of creation during his voyage probably played some role in expanding that feature of his life but there was no solemn austerity about the way his faith manifested itself. He was staunchly Christian and though I think he was sympathetic to other religions that recognised a single God, the notion of embracing any that might have challenged his appetite for Belgian beer would have been a definite nonstarter.

To Simon, his faith was more about the do's than the do nots and it provided him with a cause for unlimited celebration in which he wanted everyone to share.

I shan't say 'rest in peace' as resting is the last thing Simon was ever interested in and I don't imagine he's changed on that score, so we'll just say Ride Free Simon – forever.

FIN

Acknowledgements

Aside from my companions in this tale, there are many who deserve my thanks and respect. If I forget some, then you know who you are and can be assured of my respect and friendship.

Tony Jakeman and Adrian Roderick, formerly of BMW Motorrad deserve special thanks for making our 2005 journey possible, plus later African, European and North American expeditions. The same to Darren Hodgson and Duncan Bell at Vines Motorrad, who gave us huge support in 2005 and since then. Paul Goulding of Metal Mule for his unwavering support both in 2005 and continuing friendship after. Scottoiler saved us a fortune in chains and Interide Communications kept us connected and Dan Sager from 'Fab Biker' took care of our public relations en-route.

Kevin and Julia Sanders of GlobeBusters gave us bags of helpful advice prior to our journey and made it possible for Barbara and I to design, research and lead both the 2008 GlobeBusters West Africa expedition and the 2011 GlobeBusters Trans Canada expedition.

Sam Manicom persuaded me to develop this book after reading an early draft. He also helped me shape the format of the work and has always been there when I've needed advice on all sorts of things personal and professional.

Much appreciation to Nich Brown for being the main editor of the manuscript and for being such a great friend over the last quarter century. Thanks also to him and Paddy Tyson for taking a leap of faith by publishing this work. I feel honoured to be alongside the other superb writers who are supported by Shuvvy Press. Also, thanks to Heather Allen for editing the Morocco 2000 section of this tale.

The Motor Cycle Industry Association deserve many thanks for putting up with my various leaves of absence to pursue motorcycle travel, in particular Tom Waterer, Geoff Sherley and Steve Kenward.

I'm grateful to Charley Boorman for both his support when

we were publicising the 2005 trip and for his continuing interest in Simon Milward's round the world trip. Nick Sanders gets my thanks for his encouragement and various bits of advice in 2005 and since.

A big acknowledgment goes to Horizons Unlimited and the many people from the motorcycle overlanding community who support Motorcycle Outreach and in many cases have become close personal friends – a truly great community in the motorcycle world.

Respect to Ian Mutch for his support during my Motorcycle Action Group years and also during our journey to West Africa. I hope the excess luggage bill wasn't too high!

Deepest thanks to Simon Milward's family, in particular Jane, Mark, Paul and John T, who have done so much to bring Simon's Motorcycle Outreach vision to life, support our journey and have given unfailing support and friendship since then.

To David French for many years of companionship on the road during different journeys and for being a brother to me as we both continue to travel along life's various paths. Dave also reviewed and partly edited this book.

To my wife Barbara Alam. She never met Simon, but believed in what he did, made much of what happened in this book possible and is my life partner and best mate in all things. She's also a top overland motorcycle traveller in her own right. She also helped edit this book.

Finally, to Simon Milward. Some people have a profound effect on the path of one's life. Meeting Simon and all that we did, both together and apart, completely changed mine. I miss him.

Motorcycle Outreach

Motorcycle Outreach is a registered charity which works to introduce effective healthcare delivery in remote areas of the developing world. They instigate complete vehicle management and don't just buy and present motorcycles that medical staff can use.

www.motorcycleoutreach.org